펼쳐 보면 느껴집니다

단 한 줄도 배움의 공백이 생기지 않도록
문장 한 줄마다 20년이 넘는
해커스의 영어교육 노하우를 담았음을

덮고 나면 확신합니다

수많은 선생님의 목소리와
정확한 출제 데이터 분석으로 꽉 찬
교재 한 권이면 충분함을

해커스북 중·고등
HackersBook.com

WHY HACKERS GRAMMAR SMART?

Completely master English grammar

누구나 쉽게
이해할 수 있는

간결한 문법 설명

실생활에서 그대로
사용할 수 있는

유용한 표현과 예문

Smart Check → Practice →
Writing Exercise →
Chapter Test로 이어지는

단계별 문제 풀이

HACKERS Grammar Smart Starter

HACKERS Grammar Smart Level 1

HACKERS Grammar Smart Level 2

HACKERS Grammar Smart Level 3

Effectively prepare for middle school English exams

학교 시험 기출경향을
완벽 반영한 문제로

서술형 포함 내신 완벽 대비

풍부한 문제의 Workbook과
다양한 부가 학습 자료로

학습효과 Up Up!

Hackers Grammar Smart 시리즈를 검토해주신 선생님들

경기
강무정 광교EIE고려대학교어학원
강민정 김진성의 열정어학원
김민성 빨리강해지는학원
윤혜영 이루다영어수학학원
이창석 정현영어학원
이창헌 더블원영어학원
정필두 시흥배곧 정상어학원
조은혜 이든영수학원
최희정 SJ클쌤영어
탁은영 EiE고려대학교어학원 태전퍼스트캠퍼스
한지수 위드유어학원
홍영숙 솔로몬학원
황정민 한수위학원

부산
배미경 삼정아카데미학원
이미영 수영학원

서울
신봉철 강북세일학원
양세희 양세희수능영어학원
이현아 이은재어학원
채가희 대성세그루학원
최세아 씨앤씨학원

인천
송인택 변화와도전학원

해커스 어학연구소 자문위원단 3기

강원
박정선 잉글리쉬클럽
최현주 최샘영어

경기
강민정 김진성열정어학원
강상훈 평촌RTS학원
강지인 강지인영어학원
곽은영 나디아잉글리쉬어학원
권계미 A&T+ 영어
김미아 김쌤영어학원
김설화 업라이트잉글리쉬
김성재 스윗스터디학원
김세훈 모두의학원
김수아 더스터디(The STUDY)
김영아 백송고등학교
김유경 벨트어학원
김유경 포시즌스어학원
김유동 이스턴영어학원
김지숙 위디벨럽학원
김지현 이지프레임영어학원
김해빈 해빛영어학원
김현지 지앤비영어학원
박가영 한민고등학교
박영서 스윗스터디학원
박은별 더킹영수학원
박재홍 록키어학원
성승민 SDH어학원 불당캠퍼스
신소연 Ashley English
오귀연 루나영어학원
유신애 에듀포커스학원
윤소정 ILP이화어학원
이동진 이룸학원
이상미 버밍엄영어교습소
이연경 명품M비욘드수학영어학원
이은수 광주세종학원
이지혜 리케이온
이진희 이엠원영수학원
이충기 영어나무
이효명 갈매리드앤톡영어독서학원
임한글 Apsun앞선영어학원
장광명 엠케이영어학원
전상호 평촌이지어학원
전성훈 훈선생영어학원
정선영 코어플러스영어학원
정준 고양외국어고등학교
조연아 카이트학원
채기림 고려대학교EIE영어학원
최지영 다른영어학원
최한나 석사영수전문
최희정 SJ클쌤영어학원
현지환 모두의학원
홍태경 공감국어영어전문학원

경남
강다훤 더(the)오르다영어학원
라승희 아이작잉글리쉬
박주언 유니크학원
배송현 두잇영어교습소
안윤서 어썸영어학원
임진희 어썸영어학원

경북
권현민 삼성영어석적우방교실
김으뜸 EIE영어학원 옥계캠퍼스
배세왕 비케이영수전문고등관학원
유영선 아이비티어학원

광주
김유희 김유희영어학원
서희연 SDL영어수학학원
송수일 아이리드영어학원
오진우 SLT어학원수학원
정영철 정영철영어전문학원
최경옥 봉선중학교

대구
권익재 제이슨영어
김명일 독학인학원
김보곤 베스트영어
김연정 달서고등학교
김혜란 김혜란영어학원
문애주 프렌즈입시학원
박정근 공부의힘pnk학원
박희숙 열공열강영어수학학원
신동기 신통외국어학원
위영선 위영선영어학원
윤창원 공터영어학원 상인센터
이승현 학문당입시학원
이주현 이주현영어학원
이헌욱 이헌욱영어학원
장준현 장쌤독해종결영어학원
주현아 민샘영어학원
최윤정 최강영어학원

대전
곽선영 위드유학원
김지운 더포스둔산학원
박미현 라시움영어대동학원
박세리 EM101학원

부산
김건희 레지나잉글리쉬 영어학원
김미나 위드중고등영어학원
박수진 정모클영어국어학원
박수진 지니잉글리쉬
박인숙 리더스영어전문학원
옥지윤 더센텀영어학원
윤진희 위니드영어전문교습소
이종혁 진수학원
정혜인 엠티엔영어학원
조정래 알파카의영어농장
주태양 솔라영어학원

서울
Erica Sull 하버드브레인영어학원
Jung Nick 이은재어학원
강고은 케이앤학원
강신아 교우학원
공현미 이은재어학원
권영진 경동고등학교
김나영 프라임클래스영어학원
김달수 대일외국어고등학교
김대니 채움학원
김문영 창문여자고등학교
김상백 강북세일학원
김연희 이은재어학원
김정은 강북뉴스터디학원
김혜경 대동세무고등학교
남혜원 함영원입시전문학원
노시은 케이앤학원
박선정 강북세일학원
박수진 이은재어학원
박지수 이플러스영수학원
서승희 함영원입시전문학원
신지웅 강북세일학원
양세희 양세희수능영어학원
우정용 제임스영어앤드학원
이박원 이박원어학원
이승혜 스텔라영어
이정욱 이은재어학원
이지연 중계케이트영어학원
임예찬 학습컨설턴트
장지희 고려대학교사범대학부속고등학교
정미라 미라정영어학원
조민규 조민규영어
채가희 대성세그루영수학원
허민 이은재어학원

울산
김기태 그라티아어학원
이민주 로이아카데미
홍영민 더이안영어전문학원

인천
강재민 스터디위드제이쌤
고현순 정상학원
권효진 Genie's English
김솔 전문과외
김정아 밀턴영어학원
서상천 최정서학원
이윤주 트리플원
최예영 영웅아카데미

전남
강희진 강희진영어학원
김두환 해남맨체스터영수학원
송승연 송승연영수학원
윤세광 비상구영어학원

전북
김길자 맨투맨학원
김미영 링크영어학원
김효성 연세입시학원
노빈나 노빈나영어전문학원
라성남 하포드어학원
박재훈 위니드수학지앤비영어학원
박향숙 STA영어전문학원
서종원 서종원영어학원
이상훈 나는학원
장지원 링컨더글라스학원
지근영 한솔영어수학학원
최성령 연세입시학원
최혜영 이든영어수학학원

제주
김랑 KLS어학원
박자은 KLS어학원

충남
김예지 더배움프라임영수학원
김철홍 청경학원
노태겸 최상위학원

충북
라은경 이화윤스영어교습소
신유정 비타민영어클리닉학원

HACKERS GRAMMAR SMART

LEVEL 2

Contents

Preview

명쾌한 설명과 실용적인 문장으로 Smart하게 학습

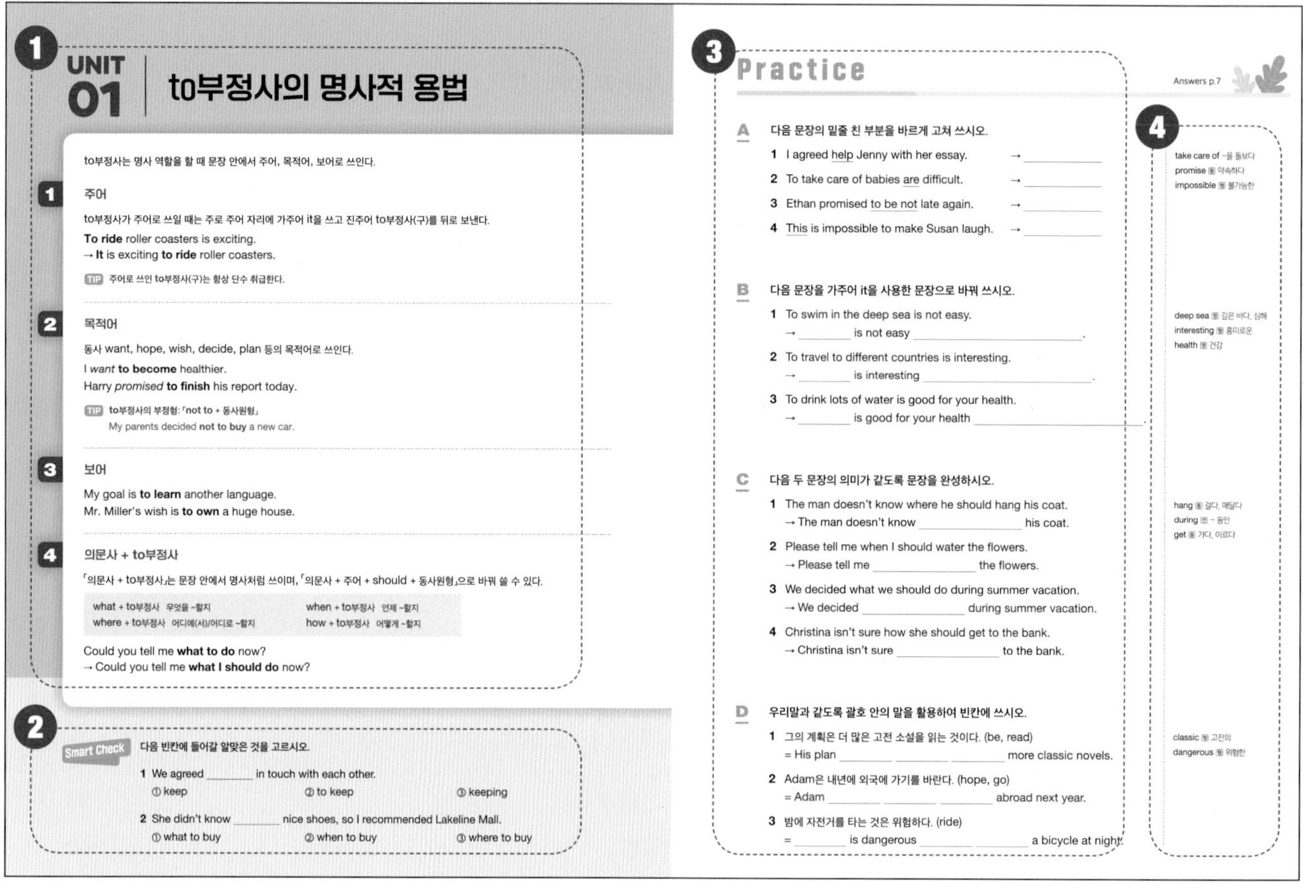

1

UNIT 01 to부정사의 명사적 용법

to부정사는 명사 역할을 할 때 문장 안에서 주어, 목적어, 보어로 쓰인다.

1 주어

to부정사가 주어로 쓰일 때는 주로 주어 자리에 가주어 it을 쓰고 진주어 to부정사(구)를 뒤로 보낸다.

To ride roller coasters is exciting.
→ **It** is exciting **to ride** roller coasters.

TIP 주어로 쓰인 to부정사(구)는 항상 단수 취급한다.

2 목적어

동사 want, hope, wish, decide, plan 등의 목적어로 쓰인다.

I *want* **to become** healthier.
Harry *promised* **to finish** his report today.

TIP to부정사의 부정형: 「not to + 동사원형」
My parents decided **not to buy** a new car.

3 보어

My goal is **to learn** another language.
Mr. Miller's wish is **to own** a huge house.

4 의문사 + to부정사

「의문사 + to부정사」는 문장 안에서 명사처럼 쓰이며, 「의문사 + 주어 + should + 동사원형」으로 바꿔 쓸 수 있다.

what + to부정사 무엇을 ~할지	when + to부정사 언제 ~할지
where + to부정사 어디에(서)/어디로 ~할지	how + to부정사 어떻게 ~할지

Could you tell me **what to do** now?
→ Could you tell me **what I should do** now?

2

Smart Check 다음 빈칸에 들어갈 알맞은 것을 고르시오.

1 We agreed ________ in touch with each other.
① keep ② to keep ③ keeping

2 She didn't know ________ nice shoes, so I recommended Lakeline Mall.
① what to buy ② when to buy ③ where to buy

3

Practice

Answers p.7

A 다음 문장의 밑줄 친 부분을 바르게 고쳐 쓰시오.

1 I agreed help Jenny with her essay. → ________
2 To take care of babies are difficult. → ________
3 Ethan promised to be not late again. → ________
4 This is impossible to make Susan laugh. → ________

B 다음 문장을 가주어 it을 사용한 문장으로 바꿔 쓰시오.

1 To swim in the deep sea is not easy.
→ ________ is not easy ________.
2 To travel to different countries is interesting.
→ ________ is interesting ________.
3 To drink lots of water is good for your health.
→ ________ is good for your health ________.

C 다음 두 문장의 의미가 같도록 문장을 완성하시오.

1 The man doesn't know where he should hang his coat.
→ The man doesn't know ________ his coat.
2 Please tell me when I should water the flowers.
→ Please tell me ________ the flowers.
3 We decided what we should do during summer vacation.
→ We decided ________ during summer vacation.
4 Christina isn't sure how she should get to the bank.
→ Christina isn't sure ________ to the bank.

D 우리말과 같도록 괄호 안의 말을 활용하여 빈칸에 쓰시오.

1 그의 계획은 더 많은 고전 소설을 읽는 것이다. (be, read)
= His plan ________ ________ ________ more classic novels.
2 Adam은 내년에 외국에 가기를 바란다. (hope, go)
= Adam ________ ________ ________ abroad next year.
3 밤에 자전거를 타는 것은 위험하다. (ride)
= ________ is dangerous ________ ________ a bicycle at night.

4

take care of ~을 돌보다
promise 동 약속하다
impossible 형 불가능한

deep sea 명 깊은 바다, 심해
interesting 형 흥미로운
health 명 건강

hang 동 걸다, 매달다
during 전 ~ 동안
get 동 가다, 이르다

classic 형 고전의
dangerous 형 위험한

각 레벨에 딱 맞는

Essential Grammar Units

❶ Grammar Lesson

해당 레벨에서 익혀야 할 문법 개념을 명쾌한 설명과 실용적인 예문을 통해 정확하게 이해할 수 있습니다. TIP을 통해 내신 시험에서 출제되는 심화 문법까지 학습하여 고난도 문제에도 대비할 수 있습니다.

❷ Smart Check

간단한 문제를 통해 위에서 배운 문법 개념을 잘 이해했는지 바로바로 확인할 수 있습니다.

❸ Practice

다양한 유형의 풍부한 연습문제를 통해 문법 개념을 자연스럽게 이해할 수 있습니다.

❹ Vocabulary

연습문제에 쓰인 주요 어휘를 추가로 학습하여 어휘력까지 높일 수 있습니다.

*어휘 정리에 사용된 약호

명 명사 동 동사 형 형용사 부 부사 전 전치사 접 접속사

기초부터 실전까지 Perfect하게 완성

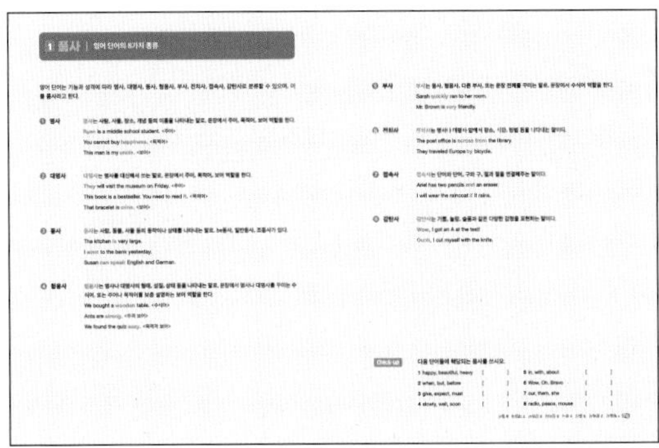

기초를 탄탄히 다지는
기초 문법

중학영문법을 이해하기 위해 꼭 알아야 하는 기초 문법이 정리되어 있어, 문법 실력이 부족한 학생들도 기초를 탄탄히 다지고 본학습을 시작할 수 있습니다.

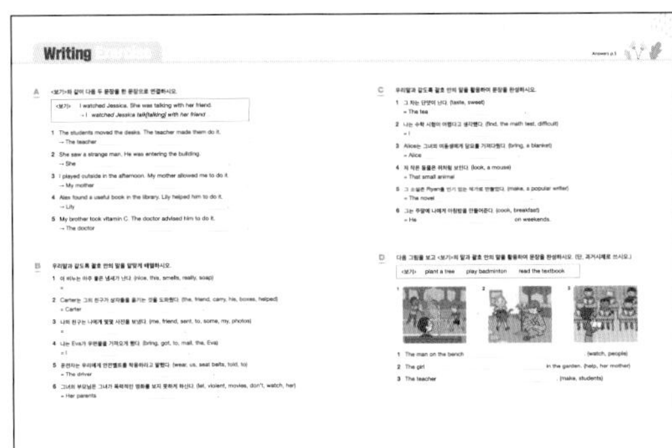

쓰기 활동으로 문법을 체득하는
Writing Exercise

다양한 유형의 서술형 문제를 풀어보며 쓰기 연습을 충분히 할 수 있습니다. 이를 통해 서술형을 강조하는 최근 내신 평가 트렌드에 대비할 수 있습니다.

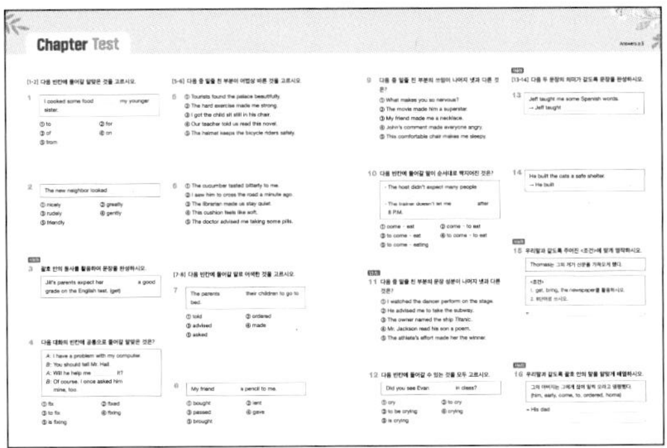

문제 풀이로 학습 내용을 확실히 점검하는
Chapter Test

전국 내신 기출문제 출제 유형을 기반으로 한 다양한 문제를 풀어보며 실제 시험에 대비할 수 있습니다. 서술형 주관식 문제 및 고난도 문제로 학습한 문법 개념에 대한 이해도를 점검할 수 있습니다.

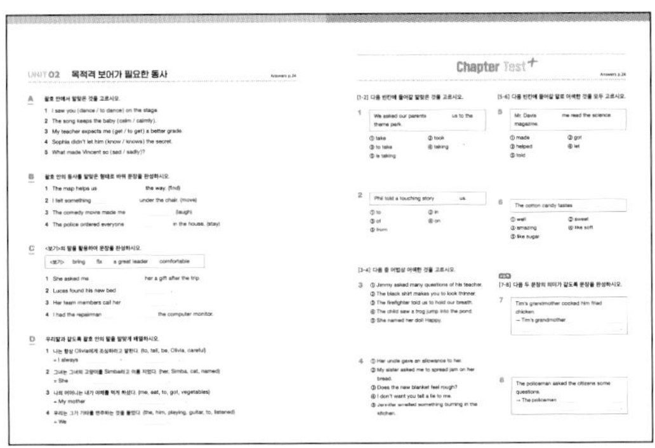

학습 효과를 더욱 높이는
Workbook

각 UNIT별, Chapter별로 풍부한 양의 추가 문제를 풀면서 본교재에서 익힌 문법 개념을 확실히 복습하고 부족한 부분은 보완할 수 있습니다.

기초 문법

영어 문법, 그 기초부터 알고 들어가자!

1 품사 | 영어 단어의 8가지 종류

영어 단어는 기능과 성격에 따라 **명사, 대명사, 동사, 형용사, 부사, 전치사, 접속사, 감탄사**로 분류할 수 있으며, 이를 **품사**라고 한다.

❶ 명사

명사는 **사람, 사물, 장소, 개념 등의 이름을 나타내는 말**로, 문장에서 **주어, 목적어, 보어 역할**을 한다.

Ryan is a middle school student. <주어>

You cannot buy **happiness**. <목적어>

This man is my **uncle**. <보어>

❷ 대명사

대명사는 **명사를 대신해서 쓰는 말**로, 문장에서 **주어, 목적어, 보어 역할**을 한다.

They will visit the museum on Friday. <주어>

This book is a bestseller. You need to read **it**. <목적어>

That bracelet is **mine**. <보어>

❸ 동사

동사는 **사람, 동물, 사물 등의 동작이나 상태를 나타내는 말**로, **be동사, 일반동사, 조동사**가 있다.

The kitchen **is** very large.

I **went** to the bank yesterday.

Susan **can speak** English and German.

❹ 형용사

형용사는 **명사나 대명사의 형태, 성질, 상태 등을 나타내는 말**로, 문장에서 명사나 대명사를 꾸미는 **수식어**, 또는 주어나 목적어를 보충 설명하는 **보어 역할**을 한다.

We bought a **wooden** table. <수식어>

Ants are **strong**. <주격 보어>

We found the quiz **easy**. <목적격 보어>

❺ 부사

부사는 **동사, 형용사, 다른 부사, 또는 문장 전체를 꾸미는 말**로, 문장에서 **수식어 역할**을 한다.

Sarah **quickly** ran to her room.

Mr. Brown is **very** friendly.

❻ 전치사

전치사는 **명사나 대명사 앞에서 장소, 시간, 방법 등을 나타내는 말**이다.

The post office is **across from** the library.

They traveled Europe **by** bicycle.

❼ 접속사

접속사는 **단어와 단어, 구와 구, 절과 절을 연결해주는 말**이다.

Ariel has two pencils **and** an eraser.

I will wear the raincoat **if** it rains.

❽ 감탄사

감탄사는 **기쁨, 놀람, 슬픔과 같은 다양한 감정을 표현하는 말**이다.

Wow, I got an A at the test!

Ouch, I cut myself with the knife.

Check-up **다음 단어들에 해당되는 품사를 쓰시오.**

1 happy, beautiful, heavy [ ]

2 when, but, before [ ]

3 give, expect, must [ ]

4 slowly, well, soon [ ]

5 in, with, about [ ]

6 Wow, Oh, Bravo [ ]

7 our, them, she [ ]

8 radio, peace, mouse [ ]

정답 **1** 형용사 **2** 접속사 **3** 동사 **4** 부사 **5** 전치사 **6** 감탄사 **7** 대명사 **8** 명사

2 문장의 성분 | 영어 문장을 만드는 재료

영어 문장을 만드는 여러 가지 재료로 **주어, 동사, 목적어, 보어, 수식어**가 있으며, 이를 **문장의 성분**이라고 한다.

❶ 주어

주어는 **동작이나 상태의 주체가 되는 말**로, '누가, 무엇이'에 해당한다.

Jacob answered the phone.

The soup is boiling in the pot.

❷ 동사

동사는 **주어의 동작이나 상태를 나타내는 말**로, '~하다, ~이다'에 해당한다.

The baby **cried** last night.

The teacher **is** angry.

❸ 목적어

목적어는 **동작의 대상이 되는 말**로, '~을/를, ~에게'에 해당한다.

Hannah bought **a flower**.

The chef cooked **us the delicious pasta**.

❹ 보어

보어는 **주어나 목적어를 보충 설명하는 말**이다.

The castle looks **old**. <주격 보어>

The news made Ms. Barnes **sad**. <목적격 보어>

❺ 수식어

수식어는 문장에 반드시 필요하지는 않지만 다양한 위치에서 **여러 가지 의미를 더해주는 말**이다.

That **brown** jacket is Jonathan's.

He parked the car **in front of the building**.

Check-up 다음 밑줄 친 부분의 문장 성분을 쓰시오.

1 Mary called you yesterday. [ ]

2 I made the room clean. [ ]

3 Jackson jogs at night. [ ]

4 We invited Andy to our home. [ ]

5 They climbed the mountain. [ ]

6 Greg can play the drum. [ ]

정답 1 주어 2 보어 3 수식어 4 수식어 5 동사 6 목적어

3 구와 절 | 말 덩어리

두 개 이상의 단어가 모여 하나의 의미를 나타내는 말 덩어리를 **구**나 **절**이라고 하며, **구**는 「주어 + 동사」를 포함하지 않고 **절**은 「주어 + 동사」를 포함한다. 구와 절은 문장에서 **명사, 형용사, 부사 역할**을 할 수 있다.

❶ 명사 역할

명사 역할을 하는 명사구와 명사절은 문장 안에서 명사처럼 **주어, 목적어, 보어로 쓰인다.**

명사구 **The new computer** arrived yesterday. <주어>

명사절 The truth is **that Michael lied to his friends.** <보어>

❷ 형용사 역할

형용사 역할을 하는 형용사구와 형용사절은 형용사처럼 **명사나 대명사를 꾸민다.**

형용사구 The milk **in the bottle** tastes bad.

형용사절 This is the necklace **which Rachel gave me.**

❸ 부사 역할

부사 역할을 하는 부사구와 부사절은 부사처럼 **동사, 형용사, 다른 부사, 또는 문장 전체를 꾸민다.**

부사구 We saw Mr. Anderson **at the park.**

부사절 Brad took a taxi **because he was late.**

Check-up 다음 문장의 밑줄 친 부분이 해당하는 것을 고르시오.

1 Jason wanted to go camping. (명사구 / 명사절)

2 The police officer on the street stopped the red car. (명사구 / 명사절)

3 They found the watch which James lost last year. (형용사구 / 형용사절)

4 You should wash your hands when you come home. (부사구 / 부사절)

5 Fred exercised hard at the gym. (명사구 / 부사구)

6 I know that you bought a laptop. (명사절 / 형용사절)

7 The books on the shelf are interesting novels. (형용사구 / 부사구)

8 Candice fell asleep while she was writing in her diary. (형용사절 / 부사절)

정답 1 명사구 2 명사구 3 형용사절 4 부사절 5 부사구 6 명사절 7 형용사구 8 부사절

Chapter 01

시제

시제는 동사의 형태를 바꿔 행동이나 사건이 발생한 시점을 표현하는 것이다.

UNIT 01 | 현재/과거/미래/진행시제

1 현재시제

현재의 사실이나 상태, 현재의 습관이나 반복되는 일, 일반적·과학적 사실을 나타낸다.

James **likes** all of his classmates.
I **ride** a bicycle to school every day.

2 과거시제

과거의 동작이나 상태, 역사적 사실을 나타내며 yesterday, last night, two hours ago, in 1990 등의 과거를 나타내는 표현과 주로 함께 쓴다.

Nina **received** a letter from Jackson *yesterday*.

3 미래시제

❶ 「will + 동사원형」은 앞으로 일어날 일이나 주어의 의지, 말하는 시점에 결정한 일을 나타낼 때 쓴다.

She **will be** a high school student next year.
I'm very thirsty. I **will drink** some water.

❷ 「be going to + 동사원형」은 앞으로 일어날 일이나 이미 예정된 계획을 나타낼 때 쓴다.

It **is going to snow** in the afternoon.
We **are going to visit** the museum next weekend.

TIP
- 공식적인 일정과 같이 이미 확정된 미래의 일을 나타낼 때 현재시제를 쓸 수 있다.
  The concert **begins** at 7:30.
- 예정된 가까운 미래의 일을 나타낼 때 현재진행시제를 쓸 수 있다.
  Brandon **is coming** to Seoul soon.

4 진행시제

❶ 현재진행시제는 지금 진행되고 있는 동작을 나타내며, 「am/is/are + V-ing」의 형태이다.

My sister **is feeding** the puppy.

❷ 과거진행시제는 과거의 특정 시점에 진행되고 있던 동작을 나타내며, 「was/were + V-ing」의 형태이다.

The kids **were smiling** when I saw them.

TIP 소유(**have** 등), 감각(**smell, taste** 등), 감정(**like, hate** 등), 인식(**know, think** 등) 등의 상태를 나타내는 동사는 진행형으로 쓸 수 없다.
I (~~am having~~, **have**) long hair.

Smart Check 다음 빈칸에 들어갈 알맞은 것을 고르시오.

1 The package ________ tomorrow.
① arrived ② will arrive ③ was arriving

Practice

Answers p.2

A 괄호 안에서 알맞은 것을 고르시오.

1 I (visit / visited) the dentist every month these days.

2 The student (studies / studied) for the exam last night.

3 Jeremy (left / is leaving) for France next week.

4 He (knows / is knowing) American history very well.

5 We (took / are going to take) a trip to Busan next Thursday.

6 Sandra (is watching / was watching) TV when I came home.

dentist 명 치과
leave 동 떠나다
take a trip 여행을 가다

B 괄호 안의 동사를 알맞은 형태로 바꿔 빈칸에 쓰시오.

1 It ________ ________ cold and rainy tomorrow. (be)

2 The baseball match ________ two hours ago. (begin)

3 Josh ________ banana muffins every morning nowadays. (bake)

4 My sister ________ ________ the guitar right now. (practice)

match 명 경기, 시합
nowadays 부 요즘에는
practice 동 연습하다

C <보기>의 동사를 활용하여 빈칸에 알맞은 말을 쓰시오.

<보기>	listen	need	publish	finish

1 We ________ oxygen to breathe.

2 I ________ ________ the science project soon.

3 Colin ________ ________ to K-pop now.

4 J. K. Rowling ________ *Harry Potter* in 1997.

publish 동 출판하다
oxygen 명 산소
breathe 동 숨을 쉬다

D 우리말과 같도록 괄호 안의 말을 활용하여 빈칸에 쓰시오.

1 Davis씨는 뜨거운 음료를 좋아한다. (like, hot drinks)
= Mr. Davis ________ ________ ________.

2 그 소녀는 어제 만화책을 빌렸다. (borrow, comic books)
= The girl ________ ________ ________ yesterday.

3 그들은 그때 보드게임을 하고 있었다. (play, board games)
= They ________ ________ ________ ________ at that time.

4 나는 극장에서 나의 친구들을 만날 예정이다. (meet, my friends)
= I ________ ________ ________ ________ ________ ________ at the theater.

drink 명 음료
borrow 동 빌리다
theater 명 극장, 영화관

UNIT 02 현재완료시제

1 현재완료시제

과거에 일어난 일이 현재까지 영향을 미칠 때 쓰며, 「have/has + p.p.」의 형태이다.

I **have lived** here since 2010. (= I started to live here in 2010. I still live here.)

❶ 완료(~했다): 과거에 일어난 일이 현재에 완료되었음을 나타내며, just, already, yet, lately 등과 주로 함께 쓴다.

She **has** *just* **arrived** at the airport.
The class meeting **hasn't started** *yet*.

❷ 경험(~해본 적이 있다): 과거부터 현재까지의 경험을 나타내며, once, ~ times, ever, never, before 등과 주로 함께 쓴다.

Have you *ever* **seen** a camel?

❸ 계속(~해왔다, ~했다): 과거부터 현재까지 계속되는 일을 나타내며, for, since 등과 주로 함께 쓴다.

Joshua **has studied** Korean *for* a month.
Joshua **has studied** Korean *since* last month.

TIP **for**(~ 동안)는 일이 지속된 기간과 함께 쓰고, **since**(~ 이후로)는 일이 시작된 시점과 함께 쓴다.

❹ 결과(~했다 (지금은 ~이다)): 과거에 일어난 일의 결과가 현재까지 영향을 미치고 있음을 나타낸다.

My best friend **has left** our neighborhood. (지금은 동네에 없음)

TIP **have been to**는 경험을 나타내고, **have gone to**는 결과를 나타낸다.
He **has been to** China. <경험: ~에 가본 적이 있다>
He **has gone to** China. <결과: ~에 갔다 (지금은 여기에 없다)>

2 현재완료시제 vs. 과거시제

현재완료시제	과거시제
과거 → 현재	과거 → 현재
과거에 일어난 일이 현재까지 영향을 미칠 때 쓴다. He **has lost** his backpack. (현재까지 배낭이 없음)	현재와 상관없는 과거의 일을 나타낼 때 쓴다. He **lost** his backpack. (현재 배낭이 있는지 알 수 없음)

TIP 현재완료시제는 특정한 과거 시점을 나타내는 표현(yesterday, last, ago, when 등)과 함께 쓸 수 없다.
I (~~have seen~~, **saw**) Katie at the mall *yesterday*.

Smart Check 다음 빈칸에 들어갈 알맞은 것을 고르시오.

1 Linda and I ________ already met each other.
① are ② has ③ have

2 We ________ an interesting movie last night.
① watched ② have watched ③ are watching

Practice

Answers p.2

A 괄호 안에서 알맞은 것을 고르시오.

1 I (was / have been) to that museum before.
2 Molly (had / has had) a cup of hot chocolate an hour ago.
3 His family (lives / has lived) in Seoul for five years.
4 She (didn't / hasn't) seen him in the school library lately.
5 Edward has used this wallet (for / since) 2012.

lately 뷔 최근에
wallet 명 지갑

B 다음 문장의 밑줄 친 부분을 바르게 고쳐 쓰시오.

1 I <u>have practiced</u> basketball yesterday. → ____________
2 It <u>rained</u> since last night. → ____________
3 Thomas <u>stays</u> at this hotel three times before. → ____________
4 <u>Have you gone</u> camping last week? → ____________

stay 동 묵다, 머물다

C 현재완료시제를 이용하여 다음 두 문장을 한 문장으로 연결하시오.

1 The ship left the harbor. It isn't here now.
→ The ship ____________ the harbor.
2 They knew each other a long time ago. They still know each other.
→ They ____________ each other for a long time.
3 Ms. Hall began to work here last year. She still works here.
→ Ms. Hall ____________ here since last year.
4 I lost my passport. I can't find it now.
→ I ____________ my passport.

harbor 명 항구
still 뷔 여전히, 아직도
passport 명 여권

D 우리말과 같도록 괄호 안의 말을 활용하여 빈칸에 쓰시오.

1 나는 지난여름 이래로 Vernon을 좋아해왔다. (like)
= I ________ ________ ________ since last summer.
2 Ethan은 점심을 이미 먹었다. (already, eat, lunch)
= Ethan ________ ________ ________ ________.
3 그들은 그들의 고향에 가버렸다. (go, hometown)
= They ________ ________ ________ ________ ________.
4 우리 팀은 금메달을 네 번 땄다. (win, the gold medal)
= Our team ________ ________ ________ ________ ________ four times.

hometown 명 고향
win 동 따다, 이기다

Writing Exercise

A <보기>의 동사를 활용하여 대화를 완성하시오.

<보기>	drink	be	have	make	taste	run

1 *A*: I ________________ to Australia once.
B: Wow! Did you go to the Opera House?

2 *A*: Why didn't Mark come to school?
B: Because he ________________ a bad cold yesterday.

3 *A*: Your skin looks very healthy.
B: I ________________ four bottles of water every day.

4 *A*: How is your soup?
B: I like it. It ________________ like a pumpkin.

5 *A*: Did you exercise last night?
B: Yes. I ________________ three kilometers around the lake.

6 *A*: Let's go on a picnic next weekend.
B: Great! I ________________ some sandwiches.

B 우리말과 같도록 괄호 안의 말을 알맞게 배열하시오.

1 우리는 주말마다 해변에 간다. (beach, go, we, the, to)
= ________________________________ every weekend.

2 Mark는 전에 스쿠버 다이빙을 배운 적이 있다. (learned, scuba diving, has, Mark)
= ________________________________ before.

3 나는 다음 주에 나의 조부모님을 방문할 것이다. (going, to, my, am, grandparents, visit, I)
= ________________________________ next week.

4 코알라는 하루에 보통 20시간을 잔다. (a, 20 hours, usually, sleeps, koala)
= ________________________________ a day.

5 넬슨 만델라는 1993년에 노벨 평화상을 수상했다. (won, the, Nelson Mandela, Nobel Peace Prize)
= ________________________________ in 1993.

6 그는 그의 친구들을 기다리는 동안 벤치에 앉아 있었다. (bench, sitting, he, the, on, was)
= ________________________________ while he waited for his friends.

7 Susan은 일곱 살 때부터 시를 썼다. (written, poems, has, Susan)
= ________________________________ since she was seven.

Answers p.2

C 우리말과 같도록 괄호 안의 말을 활용하여 문장을 완성하시오.

1 베를린은 독일의 수도이다. (be, the capital of Germany)
= Berlin ______________________.

2 나는 그 책을 여러 번 읽어봤다. (read, the book)
= I ______________________ several times.

3 태풍이 남쪽으로 움직이고 있다. (move, south)
= The typhoon ______________________.

4 우리는 이웃들을 위해 저녁 식사를 준비할 것이다. (prepare, dinner)
= We ______________________ for the neighbors.

5 Nancy는 그때 샤워를 하고 있었다. (take, a shower)
= Nancy ______________________ at that time.

6 그녀는 어제 크리스마스 선물을 샀다. (buy, Christmas presents)
= She ______________________ yesterday.

7 Evan은 지금 그의 고양이와 시간을 보내고 있다. (spend, time)
= Evan ______________________ with his cat now.

D 다음은 Kyle의 일정표이다. 표를 보고 괄호 안의 말을 활용하여 문장을 완성하시오.

MON	TUE	WED Today	THU

1 Kyle ______________________ on Monday. (cut his hair)

2 Kyle ______________________ yesterday. (water the plants)

3 Kyle ______________________ right now. (go to the post office)

4 Kyle ______________________ tomorrow. (clean the room)

Chapter Test

[1-2] 다음 빈칸에 들어갈 알맞은 것을 고르시오.

1

Andy ________ with me last night.

① study ② studies
③ studied ④ has studied
⑤ will study

2

I ________ to Europe once.

① travel ② travels
③ traveling ④ am traveling
⑤ have traveled

서술형

[3-4] 다음 문장의 밑줄 친 부분을 바르게 고쳐 쓰시오.

3

Jimmy and I have played the card games yesterday.

→ ____________________

4

Paula was jogging along the Han River tomorrow morning.

→ ____________________

5 다음 빈칸에 들어갈 말이 순서대로 짝지어진 것은?

• I ________ my friend's house next week. • Oliver ________ this book before.

① visited - has read
② will visit - has read
③ will visit - will read
④ have visited - read
⑤ have visited - has read

[6-7] 다음 중 어법상 어색한 것을 고르시오.

6 ① She loves cute and small animals.
② Benny learned Chinese last year.
③ My dad drinks coffee every morning.
④ We have gone to the movies yesterday.
⑤ The festival will begin next month.

7 ① Sam is doing the dishes when I called him.
② I have felt tired since last night.
③ Karen knows the answer to the question.
④ The girls are going to the café now.
⑤ He moved to Singapore in 2010.

8 다음 우리말을 알맞게 영작한 것은?

그들은 2년 전에 신기술을 개발했다.

① They develop new technology two years ago.
② They are developing new technology two years ago.
③ They developed new technology two years ago.
④ They will develop new technology two years ago.
⑤ They developing new technology two years ago.

서술형

[9-10] 괄호 안의 동사를 활용하여 문장을 완성하시오.

9

My grandparents and I ______________ together for ten years. (live)

10

A horse ______________ four legs and a tail. (have)

[11-12] 다음 대화의 빈칸에 들어갈 알맞은 것을 고르시오.

11

A: Why didn't you answer the phone last night?
B: Sorry. I ________ asleep earlier than usual.

① fall
② fell
③ will fall
④ fallen
⑤ am going to fall

12

A: The weather is getting worse!
B: I know. The forecast says it ________ tomorrow.

① rain
② was raining
③ rained
④ have rained
⑤ will rain

13 다음 중 밑줄 친 부분이 어법상 바른 것은?

① I have a headache an hour ago.
② Tim tries Thai food before.
③ The pasta is tasting delicious.
④ Ms. Miller will open her bakery soon.
⑤ He is going to film this movie last year.

서술형

[14-15] 다음 두 문장을 한 문장으로 연결하시오.

14

Amanda left South Korea. She isn't here now.
→ Amanda ______________ South Korea.

15

The songs were popular in the 1990s. They are still popular.
→ The songs ______________________ the 1990s.

고난도

16 다음 중 어법상 바른 것의 개수는?

ⓐ He hasn't heard the rumor yet.
ⓑ I was preparing dinner when the doorbell rang.
ⓒ Laura has bought new sneakers last week.
ⓓ The plane to Bangkok leaves at 9 P.M.
ⓔ Susie looked for her socks right now.

① 1개
② 2개
③ 3개
④ 4개
⑤ 5개

[17-18] 주어진 문장의 밑줄 친 부분과 용법이 같은 것을 고르시오.

17

I have watched the documentary twice.

① Have you ever seen a spaceship?
② He has broken the vase on the table.
③ They have been a couple for five years.
④ He has already finished the assignment.
⑤ My father has gone to China for a business trip.

18

Mia has played the flute for ten months.

① I have forgotten his name.
② Tina has never visited Jejudo.
③ Belle has planted some trees recently.
④ The writer has just released her new book.
⑤ We have worked on this report since last month.

서술형

[19-20] 우리말과 같도록 괄호 안의 말을 활용하여 문장을 완성하시오.

19

Cindy는 지난주부터 아팠다. (be, sick)

= Cindy ________________ since last week.

20

그는 오늘 밤에 역사 공부를 할 것이다. (study, history)

= He ________________ tonight.

서술형 고난도

21 다음 대화의 밑줄 친 ⓐ~ⓔ 중 어법상 어색한 것을 찾아 기호를 쓰고 바르게 고쳐 쓰시오.

A: Richard, ⓐdid you take notes in our science class? I ⓑhave forgotten to bring my pen yesterday.
B: Here, take my notes. I ⓒhave already reviewed them. You ⓓwill need them for the pop quiz next week.
A: Thank you! Do you want to go to the library with me now?
B: I ⓔam having an appointment with the dentist.

(1) ______ → ____________
(2) ______ → ____________

22 다음 글의 빈칸에 들어갈 말이 순서대로 짝지어진 것은?

John and I have known each other ______ a long time. We have been friends ______ 2014, and we both think we are best friends.

① for - in ② in - for ③ in - since
④ since - for ⑤ for - since

서술형

[23-24] 우리말과 같도록 괄호 안의 말을 알맞게 배열하시오.

23

Jenny는 오늘 오후에 요가 수업을 들을 예정이다. (to, going, yoga lesson, is, a, take)

= Jenny ________________ this afternoon.

24

나의 여동생은 이미 그 레스토랑에 도착했다. (arrived, restaurant, at, already, the, has)

= My sister ________________.

Chapter

02

조동사

조동사는 be동사나 일반동사와 함께 쓰여 여러 가지 의미를 더하는 말이다.

UNIT 01 | can, may, will

조동사는 주어의 인칭이나 수에 따라 형태가 변하지 않으며, 「조동사 + 동사원형」의 형태로 쓴다.

1 can

❶ 능력·가능(~할 수 있다)을 나타낸다. 이때 be able to로 바꿔 쓸 수 있으며, 과거형은 could를 쓴다.

Harry **can** swim in the ocean. = Harry **is able to** swim in the ocean.
I **couldn't** finish my history report. = I **wasn't able to** finish my history report.

❷ 허가(~해도 된다)나 요청(~해주겠니?)을 나타내며, could를 쓰면 더 정중한 표현이 된다.

You **can** use this copy machine.
You **cannot** bring a pet into the hotel.
Can[**Could**] you pass me the sugar?

TIP **could와 can't는 추측을 나타낼 수도 있다.**
The rumor **could** be true. <약한 추측>
That boy **can't** be Thomas. He is too short. <강한 부정의 추측>

2 may

❶ 약한 추측(~일지도 모른다)을 나타내며, might는 더 불확실한 추측을 나타낸다.

It **may**[**might**] rain in the afternoon.

❷ 허가(~해도 된다)

You **may** enter the room.
May I ask you a question?

3 will

❶ 미래(~할 것이다)를 나타내며, 이때 be going to로 바꿔 쓸 수 있다.

We **will** travel to Europe next year. = We **are going to** travel to Europe next year.

❷ 의지(~하겠다)

These cupcakes look delicious. I **will** buy some.

❸ 요청(~해주겠니?)을 나타내며, would를 쓰면 더 정중한 표현이 된다.

Will[**Would**] you hold the door?

Smart Check 다음 빈칸에 들어갈 알맞은 것을 고르시오.

1 Cindy is ________ run faster than her older sister.
① can ② able to ③ will

2 ________ you make me a sandwich?
① Would ② May ③ Are

Practice

Answers p.3

A 괄호 안에서 알맞은 것을 고르시오.

1 Mr. Allen will (open / opens) a café next month.
2 (Can / Will) I have some juice, please?
3 You (may / will) borrow my camera. Here it is.
4 (May / Would) you open this bottle for me?

borrow 동 빌리다
bottle 명 병

B 다음 두 문장의 의미가 같도록 빈칸에 알맞은 말을 쓰시오.

1 Ashley is able to repair the radio.
→ Ashley ________ repair the radio.

2 Is it OK if I use your pencil?
→ ________ I use your pencil?

3 It is going to be sunny all day tomorrow.
→ It ________ be sunny all day tomorrow.

4 She wasn't able to focus on the test.
→ She ________ focus on the test.

repair 동 수리하다
all day 하루 종일
focus 동 집중하다

C <보기>의 말을 한 번씩만 활용하여 문장을 완성하시오.

<보기>	be able to	can't	may	will

1 That girl ________ be Amber. She has gone abroad.
2 Joshua ________ write in English when he was five.
3 The room is too dark. I ________ turn on the lights now.
4 You look cold. You ________ wear my coat if you want.

abroad 부 해외로
turn on 켜다

D 우리말과 같도록 조동사와 괄호 안의 동사를 활용하여 빈칸에 쓰시오.

1 Jamie는 바이올린을 잘 연주할 수 있다. (play)
= Jamie ________ ________ the violin well.

2 나는 햄버거를 주문하겠다. (order)
= I ________ ________ a hamburger.

3 방문객들은 이 엘리베이터를 사용해도 된다. (use)
= Visitors ________ ________ this elevator.

4 Chloe는 공원에서 조깅을 할 것이다. (jog)
= Chloe ________ ________ ________ ________ in the park.

order 동 주문하다
visitor 명 방문객

UNIT 02 must, have to, should

1 must

❶ 의무(~해야 한다)

We **must** be quiet in the hallway.

You **must not** cross the street at a red light.

→ must not은 강한 금지(~하면 안 된다)를 나타낸다.

❷ 강한 추측(~임에 틀림없다)

Jimmy **must** be very tired.

My brother **must** be at the gym.

TIP 강한 추측을 나타내는 **must**의 부정은 **can't**(~일 리가 없다)를 쓴다.
My brother **can't** be at the gym.

2 have to

'~해야 한다'라는 의미로, must와 바꿔 쓸 수 있다. 이때 과거형은 had to를 쓰고, 미래형은 will have to를 쓴다.

He **has to**[**must**] go to the dentist.
Lisa **had to** skip breakfast this morning.
The guests **will have to** wait for 15 minutes.
You **don't have to** go shopping with me.

→ don't have to는 불필요(~할 필요가 없다)를 나타내며, don't need to나 need not으로 바꿔 쓸 수 있다.

3 should

충고·의무(~해야 한다)를 나타낸다.

You **should** be polite to others.
We **shouldn't** use cell phones in class.

Smart Check 다음 빈칸에 들어갈 알맞은 것을 모두 고르시오.

1 You ________ give me directions. I already know how to get there.
① don't have to ② need not ③ should

2 Kylie couldn't sleep well last night. She ________ be sleepy.
① must ② can't ③ don't need to

3 The audience ________ not record videos during the concert.
① has to ② should ③ must

Practice

Answers p.3

A 괄호 안에서 알맞은 것을 고르시오.

1 You (must not / don't must) waste water.

2 I'm alone at home, so I have (feed / to feed) the cats.

3 It is getting dark. Mia (had to / will have to) leave soon.

4 He (can't / doesn't have to) take an umbrella since the rain stopped.

5 You made Amy angry. You (should / should not) apologize to her.

alone 형 혼자
feed 동 먹이를 주다
since 접 ~하기 때문에
apologize 동 사과하다

B 다음 문장의 밑줄 친 부분을 바르게 고쳐 쓰시오.

1 Friends must <u>to respect</u> one another. → ________________

2 Emily <u>doesn't has to</u> bring her lunch today. → ________________

3 People should <u>drink not</u> too much soda. → ________________

4 I <u>have to</u> do the dishes an hour ago. → ________________

respect 동 존중하다, 존경하다
one another 서로

C 다음 두 문장의 의미가 같도록 <보기>의 말을 활용하여 문장을 완성하시오.

<보기>	must	have to	don't have to

1 I'm sure she is really upset.
→ She ________________ really upset.

2 You need not buy me an expensive gift.
→ You ________________ me an expensive gift.

3 The students must wear uniforms in school.
→ The students ________________ uniforms in school.

upset 형 속상한, 화가 난
expensive 형 비싼

D 우리말과 같도록 괄호 안의 말을 활용하여 빈칸에 쓰시오.

1 Clara는 오늘 그녀의 숙제를 끝내야 한다. (finish)
= Clara ________ ________ her homework today.

2 Miller씨는 어제 그의 차를 고쳐야 했다. (fix)
= Mr. Miller ________ ________ ________ his car yesterday.

3 놀이터에 있는 저 아이들은 행복한 것이 틀림없다. (be)
= Those children in the playground ________ ________ happy.

4 우리는 일요일에는 학교에 갈 필요가 없다. (go)
= We ________ ________ ________ ________ to school on Sundays.

fix 동 수리하다

Chapter 02 조동사 Hackers Grammar Smart Level 2

UNIT 03 | would like to, had better, used to

1 would like to + 동사원형

would like to는 '~하고 싶다'라는 의미이다.

I **would**[I'**d**] **like to** buy new shoes.

Would you **like to** watch a horror movie?

2 had better + 동사원형

had better는 '~하는 것이 낫다'라는 의미로, 충고나 권고를 할 때 쓴다.

You **had**[You'**d**] **better** take a break.

We'**d better not** be late for the club meeting.

↳ had better의 부정형은 had better not이다.

3 used to + 동사원형

❶ 과거의 반복적인 습관(~하곤 했다)을 나타내며, 이때 used to를 would로 바꿔 쓸 수 있다.

Samuel **used to**[**would**] play computer games after school.

Mr. Johnson **used to**[**would**] exercise every day.

❷ 과거의 상태(전에는 ~이었다)를 나타내며, 이때 used to는 would로 바꿔 쓸 수 없다.

My friend **used to** be shorter than me.

There **used to** be a library next to the school.

TIP 「**be used to + V-ing**」는 '~하는 데 익숙하다'라는 의미이다.

My dad **is used to driving** at night.

Smart Check 다음 빈칸에 들어갈 알맞은 것을 고르시오.

1 Nina and I ________ eat some dessert.

① would like ② would like to ③ had like to

2 You ________ buy this shirt. It's too expensive.

① had better ② hadn't better ③ had better not

3 He ________ be a famous actor in the 1990s.

① used to ② use to ③ would

Practice

Answers p.3

A 괄호 안에서 알맞은 것을 고르시오.

1 I would like (go / to go) hiking on the weekend.
2 You (have better / had better) eat more vegetables.
3 There (used to / would) be a large statue in the park.
4 He used to (visit / visiting) his grandparents every month.

statue 명 조각상
grandparents 명 조부모

B 다음 대화의 빈칸에 would like to, had better, used to 중 알맞은 것을 쓰시오.

1 *A*: I have a really bad headache.
B: You ________ go to the hospital.

2 *A*: Aren't you hungry?
B: Yes. I ________ have some pizza.

3 *A*: How do you know so much about baseball?
B: My father ________ be a baseball player in the past.

headache 명 두통
past 명 과거

C 다음 두 문장의 의미가 같도록 <보기>의 말을 활용하여 문장을 완성하시오.

<보기>	would like to	had better	used to

1 I think you should not believe the rumor.
→ You ________ the rumor.

2 Matilda took piano lessons, but she doesn't anymore.
→ Matilda ________ piano lessons.

3 I want to make new friends at school.
→ I ________ new friends at school.

rumor 명 소문
make friends 친구를 사귀다

D 우리말과 같도록 괄호 안의 말을 활용하여 빈칸에 쓰시오.

1 너는 지금 낮잠을 자고 싶니? (take)
= ______ ______ ______ ______ ______ a nap now?

2 우리는 카메라에 있는 배터리를 교환하는 것이 좋겠다. (change)
= ______ ______ ______ ______ the battery in the camera.

3 Ella는 어린이였을 때 수줍음을 많이 타곤 했다. (be)
= ______ ______ ______ ______ shy when she was a child.

4 그녀는 버스를 기다리는 데 익숙하다. (wait)
= ______ ______ ______ ______ ______ for the bus.

take a nap 낮잠을 자다

Writing Exercise

A <보기>의 말과 괄호 안의 동사를 활용하여 대화를 완성하시오. (단, <보기>의 말은 한 번씩만 쓰시오.)

<보기>	can	should	would like to

1 *A*: What do you want to do during summer vacation?
B: I ________________ a new language. (learn)

2 *A*: ________ you ________ me the list? (send)
B: Sure. I'll send it by e-mail.

3 *A*: I saw a strange person in school.
B: You ________________ your teacher about this. (tell)

<보기>	will	must	had better

4 *A*: When is your sister going to arrive here?
B: She ________________ at 5 o'clock. (arrive)

5 *A*: Our classroom is so hot.
B: You ________________ on the air conditioner. (turn)

6 *A*: I'm going to play soccer with Eric tonight.
B: He ________________ excited. He really likes sports. (be)

B 우리말과 같도록 괄호 안의 말을 알맞게 배열하시오.

1 그 소설은 실화일 리가 없다. (be, a, story, can't, true)
= The novel ________________________.

2 너는 환불을 받기 위해 영수증을 가져와야 한다. (bring, a, must, receipt)
= You ________________________ to get a refund.

3 전에는 강 위에 다리가 있었다. (be, to, a, used, bridge)
= There ________________________ over the river.

4 Brian은 약간의 휴식을 취하는 것이 좋겠다. (some, better, rest, had, get)
= Brian ________________________.

5 나는 열심히 공부했기 때문에 시험에 합격할 수 있었다. (the, able, exam, was, to, pass)
= I ________________________ because I studied hard.

6 그들은 도시에서 사는 데 익숙하다. (to, used, city, are, living, the, in)
= They ________________________.

C 우리말과 같도록 <보기>의 말과 괄호 안의 동사를 활용하여 문장을 완성하시오.

<보기>	can	must	have to	would like to	used to

1 제가 당신의 신분증을 봐도 될까요? (see)
= ______________________ your ID card?

2 그들의 집은 매우 비싼 것이 틀림없다. (be)
= ______________________ very expensive.

3 우리는 저녁 식사를 하기 위해 나가곤 했다. (go)
= ______________________ out for dinner.

4 그 소년은 오후 10시 전에 집으로 돌아와야 했다. (come)
= ______________________ back home before 10 P.M.

5 Helen은 서울에서 그녀가 가장 좋아하는 가수를 만날 수 있었다. (meet)
= ______________________ her favorite singer in Seoul.

6 나는 너에게 무언가를 물어보고 싶다. (ask)
= ______________________ you something.

7 그는 안경을 쓸 필요가 없다. (wear)
= ______________________ glasses.

D 다음 표지판을 보고 <보기>와 괄호 안의 말을 활용하여 문장을 완성하시오. (단, <보기>의 말은 한 번씩만 쓰시오.)

<보기>	can	must	have to

1 

2 

3 

1 You ______________________. (enter)

2 You ______________________. (cross the street)

3 You ______________________. (drive slowly)

Chapter Test

[1-2] 다음 빈칸에 들어갈 알맞은 것을 고르시오.

1

I ________ live with my grandparents in the past, but I don't anymore.

① can ② must
③ used to ④ don't have to
⑤ had better

2

You ________ talk loudly in the library. People are studying here.

① must ② would
③ had better ④ may
⑤ should not

[3-4] 주어진 문장의 밑줄 친 조동사와 의미가 다른 것을 고르시오.

3

You may borrow my textbook for the history class.

① Visitors may not park here.
② You may come with us to the mall.
③ Ms. Taylor may be our homeroom teacher.
④ You may not touch the sculpture.
⑤ May I take a short break now?

4

He must do the laundry today.

① Daniel must wake up early tomorrow.
② The girl must be ten years old.
③ We must leave for the airport right now.
④ Rachel must practice hard for the contest.
⑤ You must take your umbrella because it's raining.

5 다음 우리말을 영작할 때 빈칸에 들어갈 알맞은 것은?

Tim은 수업에 늦게 올지도 모른다.
= Tim ________ be late to class.

① will ② might
③ must ④ used to
⑤ had better

서술형

[6-7] 다음 문장의 밑줄 친 부분을 바르게 고쳐 쓰시오.

6

We had not better make him angrier. He is already too upset.

→ ________________

7

It is Sunday. Students do need not go to school today.

→ ________________

8 다음 우리말을 영작한 것 중 어색한 것은?

① 그는 그의 침실을 청소해야 할 것이다.
= He will have to clean his bedroom.
② 너는 여기서 사진을 찍으면 안 된다.
= You should not take pictures here.
③ 나의 형은 차를 운전할 수 있다.
= My brother can drive a car.
④ 나는 다음 주에 쇼핑을 하러 가고 싶다.
= I would like to go shopping next week.
⑤ 우리는 잔디 위를 걸으면 안 된다.
= We don't have to walk on the grass.

서술형 고난도

[9-10] 다음 빈칸에 공통으로 들어갈 알맞은 말을 쓰시오.

9

- I would like ________ introduce my friend.
- We used ________ play tennis every night.
- You have ________ drink enough water when you exercise.

10

- You ________ better stay home after midnight.
- Sarah ________ to spend a long time on her homework because it was difficult.

[11-12] 다음 밑줄 친 부분과 바꿔 쓸 수 있는 것을 고르시오.

11

Kate wasn't able to hear the doorbell ringing.

① cannot ② couldn't
③ must not ④ didn't have to
⑤ had better not

12

You don't have to move the boxes by yourself.

① aren't able to ② would like to
③ don't need to ④ had better not
⑤ are not going to

[13-14] 다음 글의 빈칸에 들어갈 말이 순서대로 짝지어진 것을 고르시오.

13

Our family ________ have a puppy before. We loved the dog so much, but it died when it was 13. I ________ see my puppy again.

① might – had better
② used to – would like to
③ used to – had better
④ had better – must
⑤ had better – would like to

14

The community center provides table tennis classes. There are enough balls for everyone, so you ________ bring one. You ________ bring your own racket because there aren't any at the center.

① don't have to – should
② must – would
③ must – should
④ have to – used to
⑤ don't have to – would

서술형

[15-16] 다음 두 문장의 의미가 같도록 빈칸에 알맞은 말을 쓰시오.

15

We must save water to protect our environment.
→ We ________ ________ ________ water to protect our environment.

16

Adam can make a paper airplane.
→ Adam ________ ________ ________ ________ a paper airplane.

17 다음 중 어법상 바른 것을 모두 고르시오.

① I had better to sell my old books.
② He was not able to walk straight.
③ You don't have worry about the problem.
④ People should not to go near wild animals.
⑤ Billy used to play soccer a few years ago.

고난도

18 다음 중 짝지어진 두 문장의 의미가 다른 것은?

① You may eat the apple on the table.
→ You can eat the apple on the table.
② The train will arrive very soon.
→ The train is going to arrive very soon.
③ Jinny used to collect teddy bears.
→ Jinny would collect teddy bears.
④ You don't need to think about the past.
→ You need not think about the past.
⑤ These boxes must not block the hallway.
→ These boxes don't have to block the hallway.

서술형

[19-20] 우리말과 같도록 괄호 안의 말을 활용하여 문장을 완성하시오.

19

Sam은 주말마다 잠을 많이 자곤 했다. (sleep, a lot)

= Sam ______________________ every weekend.

20

나는 케이크 한 조각을 먹고 싶다. (eat, a piece of cake)

= I ______________________.

[21-22] 다음 중 어법상 어색한 것을 고르시오.

21 ① David should study math harder.
② You have to listen to your parents.
③ She will finish her homework first.
④ I am going to get a haircut soon.
⑤ He is used to swim well five years ago.

22 ① That man must be the groom.
② I will be back before 8 P.M.
③ You had better not eat too much junk food.
④ Lauren would like sing her favorite songs.
⑤ Anyone can come inside the building.

서술형

23 우리말과 같도록 괄호 안의 말을 알맞게 배열하시오.

그녀는 산책하러 갈 것이다. (to, go, walk, is, for, a, going)

= She ______________________.

서술형

24 우리말과 같도록 주어진 <조건>에 맞게 영작하시오.

그는 그의 친구들을 기다려야 할 것이다.

<조건>	1. have to, wait for를 사용하시오. 2. 8단어로 쓰시오.

= ______________________.

Chapter

03

동사의 종류

동사의 종류에 따라 필수 문장 요소가 달라진다.

UNIT 01 감각동사와 수여동사

1 감각동사: look, sound, smell, taste, feel

주격 보어가 필요한 동사이며, 감각동사의 주격 보어 자리에는 형용사만 온다.

These vegetables **look** *fresh*.
Your soup **smells** very *spicy*.
We **felt** *tired* after the soccer game.

TIP 감각동사 뒤에 명사가 올 때는 전치사 like와 함께 「감각동사 + like + 명사」의 형태로 쓴다.
Mark's story **sounded like** *a lie*.
The cupcake **tastes like** *lemons*.

---

2 수여동사: give, send, buy, cook, ask 등

❶ '-에게 ~을 (해)주다'라는 의미를 나타내며, 간접 목적어(-에게)와 직접 목적어(~을)가 모두 필요한 동사이다.

Katie **gave** *me a teddy bear*.
He will **cook** *his children lunch* tomorrow.

❷ 「수여동사 + 간접 목적어 + 직접 목적어」는 「수여동사 + 직접 목적어 + to/for/of + 간접 목적어」로 바꿔 쓸 수 있다. 이때 쓰는 전치사 to/for/of는 동사에 따라 다르다.

ⓐ to를 쓰는 동사: give, send, bring, pass, show, teach, tell, write, read, lend 등
Ms. Hall **teaches** *students French*.
→ Ms. Hall **teaches** *French* **to** *students*.

ⓑ for를 쓰는 동사: buy, cook, find, make, get, build 등
They **made** *their parents a card*.
→ They **made** *a card* **for** *their parents*.

ⓒ of를 쓰는 동사: ask 등
I **asked** *my friend a favor*.
→ I **asked** *a favor* **of** *my friend*.

Smart Check 다음 빈칸에 들어갈 알맞은 것을 고르시오.

1 His idea sounds ________.
① wonder ② terribly ③ great

2 Could you find my glasses ________ me?
① to ② for ③ of

3 Sally will buy ________.
① the tickets them ② them the tickets ③ the tickets to them

Practice

Answers p.4

A 괄호 안에서 알맞은 것을 고르시오.

1 The flowers in the vase smell (nice / nicely).

2 This cookie (looks / looks like) a star.

3 His new song sounds (amazing / amazingly).

4 Kevin gave (me a movie ticket / a movie ticket me).

5 She built a huge house (to / for) her parents.

vase 명 꽃병
amazing 형 놀라운
huge 형 거대한, 매우 큰

B <보기>의 동사와 괄호 안의 말을 활용하여 빈칸에 쓰시오. (단, 현재시제로 쓰시오.)

<보기>	look	sound	taste	feel

1 Her voice _________ _________. (angry)

2 The cake _________ _________ _________ _________. (a carrot)

3 Jacob always _________ _________. (confident)

4 That kite _________ _________ _________ _________. (an eagle)

voice 명 목소리
confident 형 자신 있는
kite 명 연

C 다음 두 문장의 의미가 같도록 빈칸에 알맞은 말을 쓰시오.

1 Gloria lent him her textbook.
→ Gloria lent _________ _________ _________ _________.

2 Could you get me some water?
→ Could you get _________ _________ _________ _________?

3 She asked the guide some questions.
→ She asked _________ _________ _________ _________ _________.

4 Brad sent his cousin an e-mail.
→ Brad sent _________ _________ _________ _________ _________.

lend 동 빌려주다
textbook 명 교과서
guide 명 안내인, 가이드

D 우리말과 같도록 괄호 안의 말을 활용하여 빈칸에 쓰시오.

1 겨울에는, 공기가 차갑게 느껴진다. (cold)
= In winter, the air _________ _________.

2 종업원은 우리에게 메뉴를 가져다줬다. (the menu)
= The waiter brought _________ _________ _________.

3 놀이터에 있는 아이들은 활동적으로 보인다. (active)
= The kids in the playground _________ _________.

4 나의 아버지는 나에게 진실을 말해주셨다. (the truth)
= My father told _________ _________ _________ _________.

active 형 활동적인, 활발한
playground 명 놀이터, 운동장
truth 명 진실, 사실

UNIT 02 목적격 보어가 필요한 동사

목적어를 보충 설명하는 목적격 보어가 필요한 동사가 있으며, 목적격 보어 자리에는 명사, 형용사, to부정사, 동사원형 등이 온다.

1 목적격 보어로 명사를 쓰는 동사: call, make, name 등

My friends **call** me *a dreamer*.
The movie **made** him *a famous director*.

2 목적격 보어로 형용사를 쓰는 동사: make, keep, find 등

The biology class **made** me *sleepy*.
Regular exercise will **keep** you *healthy*.

3 목적격 보어로 to부정사를 쓰는 동사: want, ask, tell, expect, allow, advise, order 등

I will **tell** Chris *to wash* his hands.
Dad didn't **allow** me *to skip* breakfast.

4 사역동사: make, have, let

'~가 -하게 하다'라는 의미를 나타내며, 사역동사의 목적격 보어 자리에는 동사원형이 온다.

The coach **made** the players *take* a rest.
My parents don't **let** me *play* mobile games.

TIP **help**는 목적격 보어 자리에 동사원형과 **to**부정사가 둘 다 올 수 있고, **get**은 목적격 보어 자리에 **to**부정사만 온다.
I **helped** my brother *(to) do* his homework.
Paul **got** my old computer *to work* again.

5 지각동사: see, watch, hear, listen to, smell, feel 등

'~가 -하는 것을 보다/듣다/냄새 맡다/느끼다'라는 의미를 나타내며, 지각동사의 목적격 보어 자리에는 동사원형이나 V-ing형이 온다. 이때, V-ing형이 오면 동작이 진행 중인 것이 강조된다.

I **saw** Lauren *dance* alone.
Can you **smell** something *burning*?

Smart Check 다음 빈칸에 들어갈 알맞은 것을 고르시오.

1 I advised her ________ at school on time.
① arrive ② to arrive ③ arriving

2 Ron felt someone ________ his shoulder.
① touch ② to touch ③ touches

Practice

Answers p.4

A 괄호 안에서 알맞은 것을 고르시오.

1 His jokes make some people (angry / angrily).
2 The kids saw the butterflies (fly / to fly) away.
3 Henry had me (take / took) his picture.
4 They will help Emily (to paint / painting) the fence.
5 I want my classmates (come / to come) to my birthday party.

joke 명 농담
fence 명 울타리

B 다음 문장의 밑줄 친 부분을 바르게 고쳐 쓰시오.

1 I expect you <u>be</u> successful. → ____________
2 A refrigerator keeps food <u>freshly</u>. → ____________
3 My mother got me <u>put</u> on a sweater. → ____________
4 Jack didn't let me <u>to use</u> his phone. → ____________

successful 형 성공한, 출세한
refrigerator 명 냉장고
fresh 형 신선한

C <보기>의 말을 활용하여 문장을 완성하시오.

<보기>	sing	ride	raise	selfish

1 He helped his son ____________ a bicycle.
2 Julie's friends find her ____________.
3 My parents allowed me ____________ a pet.
4 I heard my neighbor ____________ a song last night.

ride 동 타다
raise 동 키우다, 기르다
selfish 형 이기적인

D 우리말과 같도록 괄호 안의 말을 활용하여 빈칸에 쓰시오.

1 사람들은 그를 천재라고 부른다. (call, a genius)
= People ________ ________ ________ ________.

2 나의 아버지는 내가 세차를 하게 하셨다. (make, wash the car)
= My father ________ ________ ________ ________ ________.

3 의사는 그녀에게 매일 운동하라고 조언했다. (advise, exercise)
= The doctor ________ ________ ________ ________ every day.

4 나는 그들이 연못에 동전을 던지는 것을 봤다. (watch, throw coins)
= I ________ ________ ________ ________ in the pond.

genius 명 천재
advise 동 조언하다
throw 동 던지다
coin 명 동전
pond 명 연못

Writing Exercise

A <보기>와 같이 다음 두 문장을 한 문장으로 연결하시오.

<보기> I watched Jessica. She was talking with her friend.
→ I *watched Jessica talk[talking] with her friend* .

1 The students moved the desks. The teacher made them do it.
→ The teacher ______________________________.

2 She saw a strange man. He was entering the building.
→ She ______________________________.

3 I played outside in the afternoon. My mother allowed me to do it.
→ My mother ______________________________.

4 Alex found a useful book in the library. Lily helped him to do it.
→ Lily ______________________________.

5 My brother took vitamin C. The doctor advised him to do it.
→ The doctor ______________________________.

B 우리말과 같도록 괄호 안의 말을 알맞게 배열하시오.

1 이 비누는 아주 좋은 냄새가 난다. (nice, this, smells, really, soap)
= ______________________________.

2 Carter는 그의 친구가 상자들을 옮기는 것을 도와줬다. (the, friend, carry, his, boxes, helped)
= Carter ______________________________.

3 나의 친구는 나에게 몇몇 사진을 보냈다. (me, friend, sent, to, some, my, photos)
= ______________________________.

4 나는 Eva가 우편물을 가져오게 했다. (bring, got, to, mail, the, Eva)
= I ______________________________.

5 운전자는 우리에게 안전벨트를 착용하라고 말했다. (wear, us, seat belts, told, to)
= The driver ______________________________.

6 그녀의 부모님은 그녀가 폭력적인 영화를 보지 못하게 하신다. (let, violent, movies, don't, watch, her)
= Her parents ______________________________.

C 우리말과 같도록 괄호 안의 말을 활용하여 문장을 완성하시오.

1 그 차는 단맛이 난다. (taste, sweet)
= The tea ______________________.

2 나는 수학 시험이 어렵다고 생각했다. (find, the math test, difficult)
= I ______________________.

3 Alice는 그녀의 여동생에게 담요를 가져다줬다. (bring, a blanket)
= Alice ______________________.

4 저 작은 동물은 쥐처럼 보인다. (look, a mouse)
= That small animal ______________________.

5 그 소설은 Ryan을 인기 있는 작가로 만들었다. (make, a popular writer)
= The novel ______________________.

6 그는 주말에 나에게 아침밥을 만들어준다. (cook, breakfast)
= He ______________________ on weekends.

D 다음 그림을 보고 <보기>의 말과 괄호 안의 말을 활용하여 문장을 완성하시오. (단, 과거시제로 쓰시오.)

<보기>	plant a tree	play badminton	read the textbook

1 

2 

3 

1 The man on the bench ______________________. (watch, people)

2 The girl ______________________ in the garden. (help, her mother)

3 The teacher ______________________. (make, students)

Chapter Test

[1-2] 다음 빈칸에 들어갈 알맞은 것을 고르시오.

1 I cooked some food ________ my younger sister.

① to ② for
③ of ④ on
⑤ from

2 The new neighbor looked ________.

① nicely ② greatly
③ rudely ④ gently
⑤ friendly

서술형

3 괄호 안의 동사를 활용하여 문장을 완성하시오.

Jill's parents expect her ____________ a good grade on the English test. (get)

4 다음 대화의 빈칸에 공통으로 들어갈 알맞은 것은?

A: I have a problem with my computer.
B: You should tell Mr. Hall.
A: Will he help me ________ it?
B: Of course. I once asked him ________ mine, too.

① fix ② fixed
③ to fix ④ fixing
⑤ is fixing

[5-6] 다음 중 밑줄 친 부분이 어법상 바른 것을 고르시오.

5 ① Tourists found the palace beautifully.
② The hard exercise made me strong.
③ I got the child sit still in his chair.
④ Our teacher told us read this novel.
⑤ The helmet keeps the bicycle riders safely.

6 ① The cucumber tasted bitterly to me.
② I saw him to cross the road a minute ago.
③ The librarian made us stay quiet.
④ This cushion feels like soft.
⑤ The doctor advised me taking some pills.

[7-8] 다음 빈칸에 들어갈 말로 어색한 것을 고르시오.

7 The parents ________ their children to go to bed.

① told ② ordered
③ advised ④ made
⑤ asked

8 My friend ________ a pencil to me.

① bought ② lent
③ passed ④ gave
⑤ brought

9 다음 중 밑줄 친 부분의 쓰임이 나머지 넷과 다른 것은?

① What makes you so nervous?
② The movie made him a superstar.
③ My friend made me a necklace.
④ John's comment made everyone angry.
⑤ This comfortable chair makes me sleepy.

10 다음 빈칸에 들어갈 말이 순서대로 짝지어진 것은?

- The host didn't expect many people ________.
- The trainer doesn't let me ________ after 8 P.M.

① come - eat　② come - to eat
③ to come - eat　④ to come - to eat
⑤ to come - eating

고난도

11 다음 중 밑줄 친 부분의 문장 성분이 나머지 넷과 다른 것은?

① I watched the dancer perform on the stage.
② He advised me to take the subway.
③ The owner named the ship *Titanic*.
④ Mr. Jackson read his son a poem.
⑤ The athlete's effort made her the winner.

12 다음 빈칸에 들어갈 수 있는 것을 모두 고르시오.

Did you see Evan ________ in class?

① cry　② to cry
③ to be crying　④ crying
⑤ is crying

서술형

[13-14] 다음 두 문장의 의미가 같도록 문장을 완성하시오.

13

Jeff taught me some Spanish words.
→ Jeff taught ________________________.

14

He built the cats a safe shelter.
→ He built ________________________.

서술형

15 우리말과 같도록 주어진 <조건>에 맞게 영작하시오.

Thomas는 그의 개가 신문을 가져오게 했다.

<조건>
1. get, bring, the newspaper를 활용하시오.
2. 8단어로 쓰시오.

= ________________________________.

서술형

16 우리말과 같도록 괄호 안의 말을 알맞게 배열하시오.

그의 아버지는 그에게 집에 일찍 오라고 명령했다.
(him, early, come, to, ordered, home)

= His dad ________________________
________________________.

서술형

[17-18] 다음 두 문장을 한 문장으로 연결하시오.

17

Something was coming inside the house. Jake heard it.
→ Jake heard something ______________
______________________________.

18

Anne writes her diary every day. The teacher told her to do it.
→ The teacher told Anne ______________
______________________________.

서술형

[19-21] 우리말과 같도록 괄호 안의 말을 활용하여 문장을 완성하시오.

19

그 파이는 복숭아 같은 맛이 난다. (taste, peaches)

= The pie ______________________________.

20

그는 그의 친구에게 노트북을 빌려줬다. (lend, a laptop)

= He ______________________________.

21

Allen은 내가 그 비밀을 지키기를 원했다. (want, keep the secret)

= Allen ______________________________.

서술형 고난도

22 다음 글의 밑줄 친 ⓐ~ⓔ 중 어법상 어색한 것을 찾아 기호를 쓰고 바르게 고쳐 쓰시오.

Last Sunday, I wanted to play outside. But my mom ordered me ⓐto stay inside because my room was dirty. I thought I kept my room ⓑcleanly, but there was a lot of dust on the floor. So, my mom got me ⓒto sweep it up. I expected her ⓓto let me play afterwards, but she still didn't allow me ⓔgo outside. She said it was already too dark.

(1) ______ → ______________
(2) ______ → ______________

[23-24] 다음 중 어법상 어색한 것을 고르시오.

23
① Gina feels terrible today.
② We call her the queen of ice.
③ Your new idea sounds like possible.
④ I heard Laura talking on the phone.
⑤ She teaches math to high school students.

24
① He bought some flowers for his wife.
② Her mom doesn't want her play computer games.
③ The meatball sauce smells wonderful.
④ I sent the teacher my essay by e-mail.
⑤ Ms. Williams helped me finish my homework.

Chapter

04

수동태

수동태는 주어가 어떤 행위의 대상이 되는 것이다.

UNIT 01 | 수동태의 쓰임

1 능동태와 수동태

주어가 행위의 주체가 되는 것을 능동태라고 하고, 주어가 행위의 대상이 되는 것을 수동태라고 한다. 수동태는 「be동사 + p.p.(과거분사)」의 형태로 쓴다.

Sammy **raises** a rabbit. <능동태>
A rabbit **is raised** by Sammy. <수동태>

2 수동태 문장 만드는 법

ⓒ Teenagers ⓑ love ⓐ the band.
→ The band is loved by teenagers.

ⓐ 능동태 문장의 목적어를 수동태 문장의 주어로 쓴다.
ⓑ 능동태 문장의 동사를 「be동사 + p.p.(과거분사)」의 형태로 바꾼다. 이때 능동태 문장의 시제를 그대로 쓴다.
ⓒ 능동태 문장의 주어를 「by + 행위자」의 형태로 바꾼다.

She *designed* this wedding dress.
→ This wedding dress **was designed** by her.

TIP 행위자가 일반인이거나 중요하지 않을 때는 「by + 행위자」를 생략할 수 있다.
Spanish is spoken in Mexico (by people).
This carpet was made in Italy (by someone).

3 수동태의 시제

현재시제	「am/are/is + p.p.」	This elevator **is used** by visitors.
과거시제	「was/were + p.p.」	The fence **was painted** by Julie.
미래시제	「will be + p.p.」	The whole house **will be cleaned** by Mr. Ford.

4 수동태로 쓸 수 없는 동사

❶ 목적어를 가지지 않는 동사: stay, look, appear, disappear, happen, occur 등
A rainbow (~~was appeared~~, **appeared**) in the sky.

❷ 목적어를 가지는 동사 중에서 소유나 상태를 나타내는 동사: have, resemble, fit 등
My friend **has** a pet turtle.
A pet turtle is had by my friend. (×)

Smart Check 다음 빈칸에 들어갈 알맞은 것을 고르시오.

1 That gift box ________ by my little sister.
① made ② was making ③ was made

Practice

Answers p.6

A 괄호 안에서 알맞은 것을 고르시오.

1 The picture was (draw / drawn) by Benny.
2 The Eiffel Tower was (built / building) in 1889.
3 Ten roses (planted / were planted) by the gardener today.
4 Ms. Lopez's car is (check / checked) once a month.
5 The red dress (fits / is fitted) Kelly well.

plant 동 심다
gardener 명 정원사
once a month 한 달에 한 번
fit 동 (모양이나 크기가) 맞다

B 괄호 안의 동사를 알맞은 형태로 바꿔 빈칸에 쓰시오. (단, 현재시제로 쓰시오.)

1 Kids ________ ________ by their parents. (love)
2 The classroom ________ ________ after school. (clean)
3 English and French ________ ________ in Canada. (speak)
4 The Olympic Games ________ ________ every four years. (hold)

after school 방과 후에
hold 동 열다, 개최하다

C 다음 능동태 문장을 수동태로 바꿀 때 빈칸에 알맞은 말을 쓰시오.

1 My mother bakes cupcakes on weekends.
→ Cupcakes ________ ________ by my mother on weekends.
2 A man stole my suitcase on the bus.
→ My suitcase ________ ________ by a man on the bus.
3 I found Brian's notebook in the library.
→ Brian's notebook ________ ________ by me in the library.
4 Betty will eat a sandwich for lunch.
→ A sandwich ________ ________ ________ by Betty for lunch.

steal 동 훔치다
suitcase 명 여행 가방

D 우리말과 같도록 괄호 안의 동사를 활용하여 빈칸에 쓰시오.

1 크리스마스 선물이 나의 할머니에 의해 보내졌다. (send)
= The Christmas gift ________ ________ by my grandmother.
2 그 액션 영화는 다음 달에 개봉될 것이다. (release)
= The action movie ________ ________ ________ next month.
3 정문은 오후 6시에 잠긴다. (lock)
= The main entrance ________ ________ at 6 P.M.
4 '햄릿'은 윌리엄 셰익스피어에 의해 쓰였다. (write)
= *Hamlet* ________ ________ by William Shakespeare.

release 동 개봉하다, 공개하다
lock 동 잠그다

UNIT 02 수동태의 다양한 형태

1 수동태의 부정문

수동태의 부정문은 「주어 + be동사 + not + p.p.」의 형태로 쓴다.

History **isn't taught** by Ms. Brown.
The sofa **wasn't moved** by my father.

2 수동태의 의문문

❶ 의문사가 없을 때는 「be동사 + 주어 + p.p. ~?」의 형태로 쓴다.

Are the flowers **watered** every morning?
Was the accident **caused** by Mark?

❷ 의문사가 있을 때는 「의문사 + be동사 + 주어 + p.p. ~?」의 형태로 쓴다.

Where were those shoes **bought**?
When was the mug **washed**?

TIP 주어가 **who**인 능동태 의문문을 수동태 의문문으로 바꿀 때는 「**By whom** + **be**동사 + 주어 + **p.p.** ~?」의 형태로 쓴다.
Who directed the film?
→ **By whom was** the film **directed**?

3 조동사가 있는 수동태

조동사가 있는 수동태는 「조동사 + be + p.p.」의 형태로 쓴다.

Tall trees **can be found** in rainforests.
Traffic laws **must not be broken**.
Should the essay **be completed** in two days?

Smart Check 다음 빈칸에 들어갈 알맞은 것을 고르시오.

1 The building ________ by a famous architect.
① not was designed ② was not designed ③ be not designed

2 Was the poem ________ by Benjamin?
① written ② write ③ be written

3 ________ diamonds made?
① How do ② Are how ③ How are

4 Some fruits ________ in the refrigerator.
① should be kept ② be should kept ③ be kept should

Practice

Answers p.6

A 괄호 안에서 알맞은 것을 고르시오.

1 (Was / Did) this camera produced in Japan?
2 Seeds (be can carried / can be carried) by the wind.
3 When was the Colosseum (build / built)?
4 The bicycle (wasn't / didn't) repaired by my brother.
5 (Who / By whom) is the floor cleaned every day?

produce 동 생산하다
seed 명 씨앗
carry 동 나르다, 운반하다
floor 명 바닥

B 다음 문장의 밑줄 친 부분을 바르게 고쳐 쓰시오.

1 Where was these pictures taken? → ______________
2 Were the free tickets offer by the museum? → ______________
3 This book didn't translated into Korean. → ______________
4 The guidelines should remember all the time. → ______________

offer 동 제공하다
translate 동 번역하다
guideline 명 지침
all the time 항상

C 다음 능동태 문장을 수동태로 바꿀 때 빈칸에 알맞은 말을 쓰시오.

1 Do you feed your goldfish regularly?
→ ________ your goldfish ________ regularly by you?
2 Who published the magazine?
→ ________ ________ was the magazine ________?
3 People must follow the safety rules.
→ The safety rules ________ ________ ________.
4 Tyler didn't complete the science report.
→ The science report ________ ________ by Tyler.

regularly 부 정기적으로
follow 동 따르다
safety 명 안전
rule 명 규칙
complete 동 완료하다

D 우리말과 같도록 괄호 안의 말을 활용하여 빈칸에 쓰시오.

1 많은 신발들이 이 벽장에 보관될 수 있다. (store)
= A lot of shoes ________ ________ ________ in this closet.
2 창문은 언제 깨졌니? (break)
= When ________ the window ________?
3 일요일에 소포들은 배달되지 않는다. (deliver)
= Packages ________ ________ on Sunday.
4 비밀번호가 Nicole에 의해 바뀌었니? (change)
= ________ the password ________ by Nicole?

store 동 보관하다
closet 명 벽장, 옷장
deliver 동 배달하다
package 명 소포

UNIT 03

주의해야 할 수동태

1 4형식 문장의 수동태

❶ 4형식 문장은 목적어가 두 개이므로 각 목적어를 주어로 하는 두 개의 수동태 문장을 만들 수 있다. 이때 직접 목적어가 주어인 수동태 문장은 간접 목적어 앞에 주로 전치사 to/for/of 중 하나를 쓴다.

Joshua **sent** *me a letter*. → *I* **was sent** a letter by Joshua. <간접 목적어가 주어>
→ *A letter* **was sent to** me by Joshua. <직접 목적어가 주어>

❷ 직접 목적어가 주어인 수동태 문장에서 간접 목적어 앞에 쓰는 전치사는 동사에 따라 다르다.

to를 쓰는 동사	give, send, show, teach, tell, lend 등	A present *was given* **to** her by Henry.
for를 쓰는 동사	buy, cook, make, get, build 등	A delicious meal *was cooked* **for** us by our mom.
of를 쓰는 동사	ask 등	Some questions *were asked* **of** the teacher by him.

TIP **buy, cook, make** 등의 동사가 쓰인 4형식 문장은 주로 직접 목적어를 수동태 문장의 주어로 쓴다.
He bought Maria flowers. → **Flowers** were bought for Maria by him.
Maria was bought flowers by him. (×)

2 5형식 문장의 수동태

❶ 목적격 보어가 명사, 형용사, to부정사인 5형식 문장을 수동태로 바꿀 때는 목적격 보어를 그대로 쓴다.

Her friends **call** her **Bella**. → She **is called Bella** by her friends.

❷ 사역동사가 쓰인 5형식 문장을 수동태로 바꿀 때는 목적격 보어로 쓰인 동사원형을 to부정사로 바꾼다.

Dad **made** me **read** this book. → I **was made to read** this book by Dad.

❸ 지각동사가 쓰인 5형식 문장을 수동태로 바꿀 때는 목적격 보어로 쓰인 동사원형을 V-ing형이나 to부정사로 바꾼다.

They **saw** Paul **sing** on the stage. → Paul **was seen singing**[**to sing**] on the stage by them.

3 by 이외의 전치사를 쓰는 수동태

수동태에서 행위자는 보통 by와 함께 사용하지만, by 이외의 전치사를 쓰는 경우도 있다.

be made of ~으로 만들어지다 (재료 성질이 변하지 않음)	be filled with ~으로 가득 차 있다	be known to ~에게 알려져 있다
be made from ~으로 만들어지다 (재료 성질이 변함)	be covered with ~으로 덮여 있다	be surprised at ~에 놀라다
be interested in ~에 흥미가 있다	be satisfied with ~에 만족하다	

This wine **was made from** nice grapes.
Jejudo **is known to** many foreigners.

Smart Check 다음 빈칸에 들어갈 알맞은 것을 고르시오.

1 James was made ________ his room by his mom.
① clean ② to clean ③ cleaning

Practice

Answers p.6

A 다음 문장의 밑줄 친 부분을 바르게 고쳐 쓰시오.

1 The floor was felt shake by everyone last night. → ____________

2 English is taught of her sister by Diana. → ____________

3 The singer calls the king of jazz by his fans. → ____________

4 The cars in the parking lot are covered to snow. → ____________

shake 동 흔들리다, 흔들다
parking lot 명 주차장

B 다음 빈칸에 to, for, of 중 알맞은 것을 쓰시오.

1 The house was built ________ my dog.

2 The pencil was lent ________ Charlotte by her friend.

3 Some photos were shown ________ me by Dennis.

4 A question was asked ________ the tennis player by the reporter.

reporter 명 기자

C 다음 능동태 문장을 수동태로 바꿀 때 빈칸에 알맞은 말을 쓰시오.

1 I cooked my sister curry.
→ Curry ________ ________ ________ my sister by me.

2 Mom made me help the child.
→ I ________ ________ ________ ________ the child by Mom.

3 The chef keeps the knife sharp.
→ The knife ________ ________ ________ by the chef.

4 Ms. Jones expects the guests to come early.
→ The guests ________ ________ ________ ________ early by Ms. Jones.

chef 명 요리사
keep 동 유지하다
sharp 형 (날이) 잘 드는, 날카로운
expect 동 기대하다

D 우리말과 같도록 괄호 안의 말을 활용하여 빈칸에 쓰시오.

1 나는 지구 과학에 흥미가 있다. (interest)
= I ________ ________ ________ earth science.

2 거실에 있는 탁자는 나무로 만들어졌다. (make)
= The table in the living room ________ ________ ________ wood.

3 Chloe는 나에 의해 바이올린을 연주하는 것이 들렸다. (hear, play)
= Chloe ________ ________ ________ the violin by me.

4 몇몇 조언은 Rachel에 의해 너에게 주어질 것이다. (give)
= Some advice ________ ________ ________ ________ ________ by Rachel.

earth science 명 지구 과학
advice 명 조언

Writing Exercise

A 다음 문장을 괄호 안의 지시대로 바꿔 쓰시오.

1 The war destroyed many cities. (수동태 의문문으로)

→ ____________________?

2 You should open your textbook. (수동태로)

→ ____________________.

3 My brother read my text messages. (수동태 부정문으로)

→ ____________________.

4 People speak English in Singapore. (수동태로)

→ ____________________.

5 He lost his key yesterday. (수동태 의문문으로)

→ ____________________?

6 A famous poet wrote this poem. (수동태로)

→ ____________________.

B 다음 문장의 밑줄 친 부분을 주어로 하는 수동태 문장으로 바꿔 쓰시오.

1 She will give me Ben's address.

→ ____________________.

2 Ms. Evans calls her son a prince.

→ ____________________.

3 I saw a family relax on the grass.

→ ____________________.

4 My mother told me to be quiet.

→ ____________________.

5 I sent Austin a postcard.

→ ____________________.

6 Eva asked her friends to find the lost dog.

→ ____________________.

C 우리말과 같도록 괄호 안의 말을 알맞게 배열하시오.

1 부엌은 매일 청소되어야 한다. (be, must, cleaned)
= The kitchen ______________________ every day.

2 화재는 거대한 빌딩에서 일어났다. (a, building, occurred, huge, in)
= A fire ______________________.

3 마라톤은 폭풍 때문에 취소될 거니? (marathon, be, will, canceled, the)
= ______________________ because of the storm?

4 Alex는 시험 결과에 만족한다. (the, satisfied, is, result, with)
= Alex ______________________ of the test.

5 집안일은 그에 의해 오늘 될 수 있다. (by, done, can, be, him)
= The housework ______________________ today.

6 병은 차가운 물로 가득 차 있다. (cold, is, with, water, filled)
= The bottle ______________________.

D 다음 대화의 밑줄 친 부분을 수동태 문장으로 바꿔 쓰시오.

Mary: How was your trip to Egypt?
John: It was really good, but **1** someone stole my wallet on the last day of trip.
Mary: Oh, no! Was there a lot of cash in it?
John: Not much. So, it was fine. Anyway, I was excited to see the pyramids.
Mary: **2** Did you take many photos?
John: Of course! **3** I will show you the photos.
Mary: I'm so excited!

1 ______________________

2 ______________________?

3 ______________________.

Chapter Test

[1-2] 다음 빈칸에 들어갈 알맞은 것을 고르시오.

1

The mayor _________ by the citizens.

① respects ② respecting
③ respected ④ is respecting
⑤ is respected

2

More trees should _________ in this neighborhood.

① plant ② be plant
③ planted ④ is planted
⑤ be planted

3 다음 중 밑줄 친 부분을 생략할 수 있는 것은?

① I was woken up by the alarm clock.
② Laws must be followed by people.
③ This postcard was sent by Peter.
④ The dishes were washed by my dad.
⑤ We were made to do homework by Mr. Hill.

4 다음 중 어법상 어색한 것은?

① The team will be leading by a new leader.
② A video was shown to us in class.
③ Was the picture taken by Tom?
④ The vase wasn't broken by me.
⑤ Some students were told to keep quiet in the library.

서술형

5 다음 문장에서 틀린 부분을 바르게 고쳐 완전한 문장을 쓰시오.

The desk was covered to dust.

→ _______________________________.

6 다음 우리말을 알맞게 영작한 것은?

그 상품은 그 고객에게 보내질 것이다.

① The product sent to the customer.
② The product is sent to the customer.
③ The product will be sent to the customer.
④ The product will send to the customer.
⑤ The product was sent to the customer.

[7-8] 다음 빈칸에 공통으로 들어갈 알맞은 것을 고르시오.

7

• Molly is satisfied _________ her new hair. • The stadium was filled _________ sports fans.

① in ② of ③ at
④ with ⑤ from

8

• The mushroom soup was cooked _________ my grandfather by me. • These sneakers were bought _________ Timmy by his uncle.

① for ② in ③ to
④ of ⑤ by

9 다음 문장을 능동태로 바르게 바꾼 것은?

The bag wasn't carried by Josh.

① Josh doesn't carry the bag.
② Josh didn't carry the bag.
③ The bag doesn't carry Josh.
④ The bag didn't carry Josh.
⑤ Josh wasn't carried the bag.

서술형

[10-11] 다음 문장을 수동태로 바꿔 쓰시오.

10

Our parents made us go to bed early.
→ ______________________
______________________.

11

Who stole the valuable painting?
→ ______________________
______________________?

12 다음 중 수동태 문장으로 바꿀 수 없는 것은?

① Mark put the lamp on the desk.
② Many people enjoy the warm weather.
③ We will watch the comedy program.
④ The deer disappeared into the forest.
⑤ Mr. Davis builds houses for the elderly people.

13 다음 문장을 수동태로 바르게 바꾼 것을 모두 고르시오.

Jordan told us a sad story.

① We were told a sad story by Jordan.
② We were told of a sad story by Jordan.
③ A sad story was told of us by Jordan.
④ A sad story was told to us by Jordan.
⑤ A sad story was told us by Jordan.

서술형

[14-15] 괄호 안의 동사를 활용하여 문장을 완성하시오.

14

The soccer tournament ____________ yesterday. (hold)

15

My foreign friends ____________ to Korea by me every year. (invite)

16 다음 대화의 빈칸에 들어갈 말이 순서대로 짝지어진 것은?

A: Are you interested ________ piano concerts?
B: Yes. Why do you ask?
A: I ________ two tickets by Matt. Do you want to go with me?
B: Sure! When is the concert?

① of – gave
② of – was given
③ in – gave
④ with – was gave
⑤ in – was given

서술형

[17-19] 우리말과 같도록 괄호 안의 말을 활용하여 문장을 완성하시오.

17

그 판타지 소설은 그 작가에 의해 쓰이지 않았다. (write, the author)

= The fantasy novel ______________________
______________.

18

새로운 발명품이 Harry에 의해 우리에게 보여졌다. (show)

= A new invention ______________________
______________.

19

그 독특한 동굴은 많은 관광객들에게 알려져 있다. (know, many tourists)

= The unique cave ______________________
______________.

고난도

20 다음 중 문장의 태를 잘못 바꾼 것은?

① The project will be finished by us.
→ We will finish the project.
② My classmates elected me a leader.
→ I was elected a leader by my classmates.
③ The printer can be fixed by a repairman.
→ A repairman can fix the printer.
④ A waiter served the desserts.
→ The desserts were served by a waiter.
⑤ He bought his brother a laptop.
→ A laptop was bought his brother by him.

서술형 고난도

21 다음 글의 밑줄 친 ⓐ~ⓔ 중 어법상 어색한 것을 찾아 기호를 쓰고 바르게 고쳐 쓰시오.

Welcome to our museum. All exhibits ⓐare displayed on the third floor. Visitors are asked ⓑto use the elevators, not the stairs. Photos can ⓒbe taking with your camera, but phones must ⓓnot used. The special exhibitions will ⓔbe held only on Wednesdays. We hope you enjoy your visit!

(1) ______ → ______________
(2) ______ → ______________

22 다음 문장을 수동태로 바꿀 때 빈칸에 들어갈 알맞은 것을 모두 고르시오.

I heard Luke and Jerry argue. → Luke and Jerry were heard ________ by me.

① argue ② to argue ③ arguing
④ argued ⑤ to arguing

23 다음 중 어법상 어색한 것의 개수는?

ⓐ The bird was seen to flying in the sky. ⓑ I was surprised in his rude behavior. ⓒ The bottles and cans must be recycled. ⓓ Tina is resembled by her grandmother. ⓔ Where was your watch found?

① 1개 ② 2개 ③ 3개
④ 4개 ⑤ 5개

Chapter

05

to부정사

to부정사는 「to + 동사원형」의 형태로
문장 안에서 명사·형용사·부사 역할을 한다.

UNIT 01 to부정사의 명사적 용법

to부정사는 명사 역할을 할 때 문장 안에서 주어, 목적어, 보어로 쓰인다.

1 주어

to부정사가 주어로 쓰일 때는 주로 주어 자리에 가주어 it을 쓰고 진주어 to부정사(구)를 뒤로 보낸다.

To ride roller coasters is exciting.
→ **It** is exciting **to ride** roller coasters.

TIP 주어로 쓰인 **to**부정사(구)는 항상 단수 취급한다.

2 목적어

동사 want, hope, wish, decide, plan 등의 목적어로 쓰인다.

I *want* **to become** healthier.
Harry *promised* **to finish** his report today.

TIP **to**부정사의 부정형: 「**not to** + 동사원형」
My parents decided **not to buy** a new car.

3 보어

My goal is **to learn** another language.
Mr. Miller's wish is **to own** a huge house.

4 의문사 + to부정사

「의문사 + to부정사」는 문장 안에서 명사처럼 쓰이며, 「의문사 + 주어 + should + 동사원형」으로 바꿔 쓸 수 있다.

what + to부정사 무엇을 ~할지	when + to부정사 언제 ~할지
where + to부정사 어디에(서)/어디로 ~할지	how + to부정사 어떻게 ~할지

Could you tell me **what to do** now?
→ Could you tell me **what I should do** now?

Smart Check 다음 빈칸에 들어갈 알맞은 것을 고르시오.

1 We agreed ________ in touch with each other.
① keep ② to keep ③ keeping

2 She didn't know ________ nice shoes, so I recommended Lakeline Mall.
① what to buy ② when to buy ③ where to buy

Practice

Answers p.7

A 다음 문장의 밑줄 친 부분을 바르게 고쳐 쓰시오.

1 I agreed help Jenny with her essay. → ____________

2 To take care of babies are difficult. → ____________

3 Ethan promised to be not late again. → ____________

4 This is impossible to make Susan laugh. → ____________

take care of ~을 돌보다
promise 동 약속하다
impossible 형 불가능한

B 다음 문장을 가주어 it을 사용한 문장으로 바꿔 쓰시오.

1 To swim in the deep sea is not easy.
→ ________ is not easy ____________________.

2 To travel to different countries is interesting.
→ ________ is interesting ____________________.

3 To drink lots of water is good for your health.
→ ________ is good for your health ____________________.

deep sea 명 깊은 바다, 심해
interesting 형 흥미로운
health 명 건강

C 다음 두 문장의 의미가 같도록 문장을 완성하시오.

1 The man doesn't know where he should hang his coat.
→ The man doesn't know ____________ his coat.

2 Please tell me when I should water the flowers.
→ Please tell me ____________ the flowers.

3 We decided what we should do during summer vacation.
→ We decided ____________ during summer vacation.

4 Christina isn't sure how she should get to the bank.
→ Christina isn't sure ____________ to the bank.

hang 동 걸다, 매달다
during 전 ~ 동안
get 동 가다, 이르다

D 우리말과 같도록 괄호 안의 말을 활용하여 빈칸에 쓰시오.

1 그의 계획은 더 많은 고전 소설을 읽는 것이다. (be, read)
= His plan ________ ________ ________ more classic novels.

2 Adam은 내년에 외국에 가기를 바란다. (hope, go)
= Adam ________ ________ ________ abroad next year.

3 밤에 자전거를 타는 것은 위험하다. (ride)
= ________ is dangerous ________ ________ a bicycle at night.

classic 형 고전의
dangerous 형 위험한

UNIT 02

to부정사의 형용사적 용법

to부정사는 형용사 역할을 할 때 명사나 대명사를 수식하거나 「be동사 + to부정사」의 형태로 주어를 설명한다.

1 (대)명사 수식

❶ to부정사는 '~할, ~하는'의 의미로 명사나 대명사를 뒤에서 수식한다.

It's *time* **to eat** dinner.
I don't have *money* **to buy** new clothes.

❷ 「-thing/-body/-one + 형용사 + to부정사」
-thing/-body/-one으로 끝나는 대명사를 형용사와 to부정사가 동시에 수식할 때는 to부정사를 형용사 뒤에 쓴다.

Is there *anything* **cold to drink** on the menu?
We need *someone* **strong to carry** those boxes.

❸ 「(대)명사 + to부정사 + 전치사」
「to부정사 + 전치사」가 수식하는 명사나 대명사는 to부정사 뒤에 있는 전치사의 목적어이다. 이때, 전치사를 반드시 쓴다.

Lisa didn't bring *a pen* **to write with.** (← write with a pen)
My family is looking for *an apartment* **to live in.** (← live in an apartment)

2 be동사 + to부정사

예정	~할 예정이다	He **is to graduate** from middle school next year.
가능	~할 수 있다	Nobody **was to be seen** in the classroom.
의무	~해야 한다	You **are to return** the books by tomorrow.
운명	~할 운명이다	We **were** never **to see** Benjamin again.
의도	~하려고 하다	If you **are to win** the speech contest, you have to practice hard.

Smart Check 다음 빈칸에 들어갈 알맞은 것을 고르시오.

1 My little sister wants a toy ________.
① to play ② to play with ③ with to play

2 Sandra couldn't find anything ________.
① to wear warm ② wear to warm ③ warm to wear

3 The students ________ the final exam soon.
① be to take ② are take ③ are to take

Practice

Answers p.7

A <보기>의 동사를 활용하여 문장을 완성하시오.

<보기>	solve	wear	eat	watch

1 I have a lot of jeans ____________.

2 Lisa found some videos ____________ in her free time.

3 We need someone smart ____________ this problem.

4 There were many delicious dishes ____________ at the buffet.

solve 동 해결하다, 풀다
jeans 명 청바지
buffet 명 뷔페

B 다음 빈칸에 알맞은 전치사를 <보기>에서 한 번씩만 골라 쓰시오.

<보기>	in	on	with	to

1 Are there any benches to sit ________?

2 My friend lent me a pencil to write ________.

3 Bangkok is an exciting city to live ________.

4 Yesterday, I needed somebody to talk ________.

exciting 형 흥미진진한, 신나는

C 밑줄 친 부분의 의미를 나타내는 기호에 연결하시오.

1 You are to listen carefully to the teacher in class. • • ⓐ 예정

2 He was never to return to his country again. • • ⓑ 의무

3 Maria is to leave South Korea next month. • • ⓒ 운명

4 If you are to be a lawyer, you should study harder. • • ⓓ 의도

carefully 부 주의 깊게
return 동 돌아가다
lawyer 명 변호사

D 우리말과 같도록 괄호 안의 말을 활용하여 빈칸에 쓰시오.

1 Matthew는 공유할 유용한 무언가를 갖고 있다. (useful, share)
= Matthew has ________ ________ ________ ________.

2 나는 함께 농구를 할 많은 친구들이 있다. (play, with)
= I have many friends ________ ________ basketball ________.

3 Colt씨는 곧 공항에 도착할 예정이다. (arrive)
= Ms. Colt ________ ________ ________ at the airport soon.

useful 형 유용한
share 동 공유하다

Chapter 05 to부정사

Hackers Grammar Smart Level 2

UNIT 03 | to부정사의 부사적 용법

to부정사는 부사 역할을 할 때 동사, 형용사, 부사, 문장 전체를 수식하며, 다양한 의미를 나타낸다.

1 목적: ~하기 위해

목적의 의미를 강조하기 위해 to 대신 in order to나 so as to를 쓸 수 있다.

I went to the market **to buy** some eggs.
= I went to the market **in order to**[**so as to**] **buy** some eggs.

2 감정의 원인: ~해서, ~하니

주로 감정을 나타내는 형용사(glad, pleased, sad, sorry, surprised, disappointed 등) 뒤에 쓰인다.

We were *glad* **to hear** the good news.
Charlie was *disappointed* **to lose** the soccer game.

3 판단의 근거: ~하다니

You were wise **to bring** an umbrella.
She must be kind **to help** me with my homework.

4 결과: (…해서 결국) ~하다

My cousin grew up **to be** a dentist.
They ran to the station, only **to miss** their train.
→ 부정적인 내용의 결과를 말할 때 to부정사 앞에 only를 쓰기도 한다.

5 형용사 수식: ~하기에

Some mushrooms aren't *safe* **to eat**.
The lecture was *difficult* **to understand**.

Smart Check 다음 밑줄 친 to부정사의 쓰임을 고르시오.

1 Sammy turned on the computer to play online games.
① 목적 ② 판단의 근거 ③ 형용사 수식

2 I was surprised to see my teacher on the street.
① 목적 ② 감정의 원인 ③ 결과

3 The building wasn't easy to find.
① 감정의 원인 ② 결과 ③ 형용사 수식

Practice

Answers p.7

A 괄호 안의 동사를 활용하여 문장을 완성하시오.

1 I went to the pharmacy ____________ medicine. (buy)

2 He must be honest ____________ everyone the truth. (tell)

3 This kind of frog is dangerous ____________. (touch)

4 They joined a tap dancing class, only ____________ it difficult. (find)

pharmacy 명 약국
medicine 명 약
truth 명 사실, 진실
join 동 가입하다

B 주어진 문장을 우리말로 해석하시오.

1 All of the questions were easy to answer.
= ______________________________.

2 I'm pleased to see you at this festival.
= ______________________________.

3 She must be clever to understand this poem.
= ______________________________.

question 명 질문
pleased 형 기쁜
clever 형 똑똑한, 영리한

C <보기>와 같이 to부정사를 이용하여 다음 두 문장을 한 문장으로 연결하시오.

<보기> I told you the bad news. I was sorry.
→ I was sorry *to tell you the bad news*.

1 I know you are well. I am happy.
→ I am happy ______________________________.

2 Amy worries about everything. She must be foolish.
→ Amy must be foolish ______________________________.

3 They met each other in Paris. They were surprised.
→ They were surprised ______________________________.

sorry 형 유감스러운
worry 동 걱정하다
foolish 형 어리석은

D 우리말과 같도록 괄호 안의 말을 활용하여 빈칸에 쓰시오.

1 나의 어머니는 저녁을 준비하기 위해 식료품을 사셨다. (prepare, dinner)
= My mother bought groceries ________ ________ ________ ________ ________.

2 그의 손글씨는 읽기에 불가능하다. (impossible, read)
= His handwriting is ________ ________ ________.

3 Jessica는 자라서 가수가 되었다. (be, a singer)
= Jessica grew up ________ ________ ________ ________.

groceries 명 식료품
handwriting 명 손글씨

UNIT 04 | to부정사의 의미상 주어, to부정사 구문

1 to부정사의 의미상 주어

to부정사가 나타내는 행위의 주체가 문장의 주어와 다를 때 의미상 주어를 「for/of + 목적격」의 형태로 to부정사 앞에 쓴다.

❶ to부정사의 의미상 주어는 보통 「for + 목적격」의 형태로 쓴다.

It is hard **for him** *to make* new friends.

It is impossible **for Anna** *to finish* the homework today.

❷ to부정사의 의미상 주어가 사람의 성격·성질을 나타내는 형용사(kind, nice, polite, rude, wise, selfish, foolish, careless 등) 뒤에 쓰일 때는 「of + 목적격」의 형태로 쓴다.

It was *nice* **of you** *to give* me a present.

It was *careless* **of her** *to make* the same mistake again.

2 too + 형용사/부사 + to부정사

'…하기에 너무 ~한/하게'라는 의미로, 「so + 형용사/부사 + that + 주어 + can't + 동사원형」으로 바꿔 쓸 수 있다.

Sarah is **too** sleepy **to concentrate**.
→ Sarah is **so** sleepy **that** she **can't concentrate**.

The tea was **too** hot *for him* **to drink**.
→ *The tea* was **so** hot **that** *he* **couldn't drink** *it*.
→ 문장의 주어가 to부정사의 목적어인 경우 that절에 반드시 목적어를 쓴다.

3 형용사/부사 + enough + to부정사

'…할 만큼 충분히 ~한/하게'라는 의미로, 「so + 형용사/부사 + that + 주어 + can + 동사원형」으로 바꿔 쓸 수 있다.

Paul was brave **enough to tell** the truth.
→ Paul was **so** brave **that** he **could tell** the truth.

These books are easy **enough** *for kids* **to read**.
→ *These books* are **so** easy **that** *kids* **can read** *them*.

Smart Check 다음 빈칸에 들어갈 알맞은 것을 고르시오.

1 It is easy ________ to remember others' names.
① for me ② of me ③ me

2 Hannah was ________ short to reach the cupboard.
① so ② too ③ enough

3 The stadium is large ________ to hold 80,000 people.
① so ② too ③ enough

Practice

Answers p.8

A 괄호 안에서 for나 of 중 알맞은 것을 고르시오.

1 It is good (for / of) you to eat a lot of vegetables.
2 It is wise (for / of) Julie to follow her mom's advice.
3 It was kind (for / of) him to lend me his jacket.
4 It is possible (for / of) me to do two things at once.

vegetable 명 채소
wise 형 현명한
advice 명 조언
at once 동시에

B 다음 문장의 밑줄 친 부분을 바르게 고쳐 쓰시오.

1 Sophia was too nervous <u>that</u> sing on the stage. → ______
2 It is selfish <u>for</u> him to only think about himself. → ______
3 The wallet is <u>enough small</u> to fit in a pocket. → ______
4 The place is <u>so</u> noisy for me to hear your voice. → ______

nervous 형 긴장한
selfish 형 이기적인
pocket 명 주머니

C 다음 두 문장의 의미가 같도록 빈칸에 알맞은 말을 쓰시오.

1 I was so tired that I couldn't walk home.
→ I was ______ ______ ______ ______ home.

2 Alice is brave enough to catch the spider.
→ Alice is ______ ______ ______ ______ ______ ______ the spider.

3 Martin arrived too late to see the concert.
→ Martin arrived ______ ______ ______ ______ ______ ______ the concert.

4 Ben is so strong that he can lift the table.
→ Ben is ______ ______ ______ ______ the table.

brave 형 용감한
lift 동 들어 올리다

D 우리말과 같도록 괄호 안의 말을 활용하여 빈칸에 쓰시오.

1 나는 지금 너를 돕기에 너무 바쁘다. (busy, help)
= I am ______ ______ ______ ______ you now.

2 나의 남동생은 모델이 될 만큼 충분히 키가 크다. (tall, be)
= My brother is ______ ______ ______ ______ a model.

3 Lena가 우리를 초대하다니 친절했다. (kind, invite)
= It was ______ ______ ______ ______ ______ us.

4 그가 좋은 아파트를 찾는 것은 어렵다. (difficult, find)
= It is ______ ______ ______ ______ ______ a nice apartment.

invite 동 초대하다

Writing Exercise

A to부정사를 이용하여 다음 두 문장을 한 문장으로 연결하시오.

1 I will go to Canada. I will see my cousins there.
→ I will go to Canada ________ ________ ________ ________.

2 Molly went to the post office. She sent a package there.
→ Molly went to the post office ________ ________ ________ ________.

3 Cars can't pass on that road. The road isn't that wide.
→ That road isn't ________ ________ ________ ________ ________ ________ ________.

4 She takes walks with her dog. It is her hobby.
→ Her hobby is ________ ________ ________ ________ ________ ________.

5 The players trained hard. But they lost the game.
→ The players trained hard, only ________ ________ ________ ________.

6 Mark was disappointed. He didn't get any presents on Christmas.
→ Mark was disappointed ________ ________ ________ ________ ________ on Christmas.

B 우리말과 같도록 괄호 안의 말을 활용하여 빈칸에 쓰시오.

1 더운 날에 아이스크림을 먹는 것은 굉장히 좋다. (eat, ice cream)
= ________ is wonderful ________ ________ ________ ________ on a hot day.

2 Josh는 볼 흥미로운 무언가가 있다. (interesting, watch)
= Josh has something ________ ________ ________.

3 내가 너에게 이 기계를 어떻게 사용해야 할지 보여줄게. (use, this machine)
= Let me show you ________ ________ ________ ________ ________.

4 학교에, Clara는 말할 많은 친구들이 있다. (many friends, talk to)
= In school, Clara has ________ ________ ________ ________ ________.

5 만약 네가 성공하려고 한다면, 너는 매일 계획을 세워야 한다. (succeed)
= If you ________ ________ ________, you should make plans every day.

6 부엌에 있는 저 의자는 수리하기에 너무 오래됐다. (old, repair)
= That chair in the kitchen is ________ ________ ________ ________.

C 우리말과 같도록 괄호 안의 말을 알맞게 배열하시오.

1 나는 너에게 이 시를 읽어주고 싶다. (you, to, poem, read, this)
= I want ______________________.

2 Ella는 그녀의 피부를 보호하기 위해 모자를 썼다. (her, to, skin, protect)
= Ella put on a hat ______________________.

3 그가 변화에 적응하는 것은 어렵다. (adapt, him, to, for, change, to)
= It is difficult ______________________.

4 그들은 그 행사를 개최할 장소를 찾고 있다. (hold, to, place, the, event, a)
= They are looking for ______________________.

5 Wilson씨는 그의 차를 어디에 주차해야 할지 모른다. (his, park, where, car, to)
= Mr. Wilson doesn't know ______________________.

6 그렇게 자유롭게 돈을 쓰다니 너는 부자인 것이 틀림없다. (money, be, rich, to, must, spend)
= You ______________________ so freely.

D 다음 그림을 보고 too나 enough와 괄호 안의 말을 활용하여 문장을 완성하시오.

1

2

3

1 The suitcase is ______________________ many things. (big, carry)

2 The smartphone is ______________________. (him, expensive, buy)

3 The weather is ______________________ shorts. (her, warm, wear)

Chapter Test

[1-2] 다음 빈칸에 들어갈 알맞은 것을 고르시오.

1

It is fun ________ board games.

① play ② played
③ be playing ④ to play
⑤ to playing

2

Do you have paper ________?

① write ② write on
③ writing on ④ to writing on
⑤ to write on

[3-4] 다음 중 어법상 어색한 것을 고르시오.

3 ① Her writing is difficult to understand.
② Tom was shocked to hear the terrible news.
③ It is easy of her to bake blueberry muffins.
④ I am planning to do the laundry tonight.
⑤ She is to enter high school next year.

4 ① Did you decide when to go to the library?
② We need to sleep for at least seven hours.
③ My favorite thing is to read a book in bed.
④ You are to be quiet in the hallway.
⑤ Do you have something to eat sweet?

5 다음 빈칸에 공통으로 들어갈 알맞은 것은?

• It is kind ________ you to give me information about the school.
• It was foolish ________ him to forget his key.

① to ② for ③ of
④ with ⑤ from

6 다음 중 어법상 바른 것은?
① It was hard of him to follow the lecture.
② The room isn't enough big to hold everyone.
③ Jim wants visit the new museum with me.
④ We are too hungry to walk anymore.
⑤ To finish it in 15 minutes are impossible.

서술형

[7-8] 다음 두 문장의 의미가 같도록 빈칸에 알맞은 말을 쓰시오.

7

I'm not sure how to turn on the washing machine.
→ I'm not sure ________ ________ ________ ________ ________ the washing machine.

8

Johnny walked up to the stage to give a speech.
→ Johnny walked up to the stage ________ ________ ________ ________ a speech.

Answers p.8

[9-10] 다음 문장을 우리말로 가장 알맞게 해석한 것을 고르시오.

9

I went to the bathroom in order to take a shower.

① 나는 샤워를 하기 위해 욕실로 갔다.
② 나는 샤워를 욕실에서 하고 싶었다.
③ 나는 욕실로 가기 위해 샤워를 했다.
④ 나는 욕실에서 샤워를 할 예정이다.
⑤ 나는 욕실로 가서 샤워를 할 수 있었다.

10

Thomas bought a new scarf, only to lose it.

① Thomas는 목도리를 잃어버려서 새 것을 샀다.
② Thomas는 새 목도리를 샀지만, 결국 그것을 잃어버렸다.
③ Thomas는 목도리를 잃어버렸지만, 결국 새 것을 샀다.
④ Thomas는 목도리를 잃어버려서 새 것을 사고 싶었다.
⑤ Thomas는 새 목도리를 사기 위해 목도리를 잃어버렸다.

11 다음 중 밑줄 친 부분을 바르게 고친 것은?

① My wish is to becoming a good teacher.
→ become
② Tina was so sleepy to go to the gym.
→ very
③ I don't have any pencils to write.
→ to writing
④ The view is too amazing that we can't leave.
→ so
⑤ Can you tell me when to bring for the class?
→ how

서술형

[12-13] 괄호 안의 말을 활용하여 문장을 완성하시오.

12

Patrick was too sick ________ to school. (go)

13

We didn't know ________ after school. (what, do)

14 다음 중 짝지어진 두 문장의 의미가 다른 것은?

① To grow a plant is not easy.
→ It is not easy to grow a plant.
② It is too cold for me to go out.
→ It is so cold that I can go out.
③ I don't know where I should put my bag.
→ I don't know where to put my bag.
④ She is wise enough to give advice.
→ She is so wise that she can give advice.
⑤ I always take a bus to go to school.
→ I always take a bus in order to go to school.

서술형 고난도

15 다음 글의 밑줄 친 ⓐ~ⓔ 중 어법상 어색한 것을 찾아 기호를 쓰고 바르게 고쳐 쓰시오.

My plan was ⓐto meet my friends at the restaurant. However, I was ⓑtoo tired that I couldn't go there. So, my friends decided ⓒto gathering at my place. We ordered our favorite food ⓓto eat for dinner. It was nice ⓔof them to change the plan for me.

(1) ____ → ________
(2) ____ → ________

서술형

16 우리말과 같도록 주어진 <조건>에 맞게 영작하시오.

네가 그를 용서하다니 너그러웠다.

<조건>	1. 가주어 it을 사용하시오. 2. generous, forgive를 포함하시오. 3. 8단어로 쓰시오.

= ______________________________.

서술형

17 우리말과 같도록 괄호 안의 말을 알맞게 배열하시오.

그 수프는 내가 먹기에 너무 뜨겁다. (eat, for, to, the, is, too, me, soup, hot)

= ______________________________.

서술형

[18-19] 우리말과 같도록 괄호 안의 말을 활용하여 문장을 완성하시오.

18

그 어르신이 길을 건너는 것을 돕다니 너는 친절하다. (kind, help)

= You are ______________________ the elderly man cross the road.

19

Paula는 네 개의 언어를 말할 만큼 충분히 똑똑하다. (smart, speak)

= Paula is ______________________ four languages.

고난도

[20-21] 주어진 문장의 밑줄 친 to부정사와 용법이 같은 것을 고르시오.

20

We all agreed to meet up at 5 P.M.

① It's time to wake the children up.
② Jeff was disappointed to fail the science test.
③ You must be nice to volunteer every month.
④ His plan is to watch a movie tonight.
⑤ Lisa doesn't have any dress to wear for her uncle's wedding.

21

He needed something to drink after the workout.

① Andrew grew up to be a brave soldier.
② To play sports is not interesting to me.
③ I will build a house to live in someday.
④ He was sad to see Jenny with her boyfriend.
⑤ She plans to go abroad for her vacation.

서술형

[22-23] to부정사를 이용하여 다음 두 문장을 한 문장으로 연결하시오.

22

• James is looking for a comic book. • He will read it tomorrow.

→ James is looking for ______________________ tomorrow.

23

• I got many presents on my birthday. • I was glad.

→ I was glad ______________________ on my birthday.

Chapter 06

동명사

동명사는 「동사원형 + -ing」의 형태로 문장 안에서 명사 역할을 한다.

UNIT 01 동명사의 쓰임

동명사는 「동사원형 + -ing」의 형태로 문장 안에서 명사처럼 주어, 목적어, 보어로 쓰인다.

1 주어

주어로 쓰인 동명사(구)는 항상 단수 취급한다.

Eating vegetables *is* necessary.
Knitting a sweater *takes* a lot of time.

2 목적어

동명사는 동사나 전치사의 목적어로 쓰인다.

Emily *imagined* **being** a ballerina.
I'm worried *about* **getting** up early tomorrow.

TIP 동명사의 부정형은 동명사 앞에 **not**을 붙여 만든다.
I'm sorry for **not keeping** the promise.

3 보어

Jake's hobby is **collecting** foreign stamps.
Her job is **taking** pictures of wild animals.

4 동명사 관용 표현

go + V-ing ~하러 가다	It is no use + V-ing ~해도 소용없다
cannot help + V-ing ~하지 않을 수 없다	on + V-ing ~하자마자
be busy + V-ing ~하느라 바쁘다	feel like + V-ing ~하고 싶다
be worth + V-ing ~할 가치가 있다	be good at + V-ing ~하는 것을 잘하다

My mom **was busy preparing** dinner.
He **feels like going** camping during the holiday.

Smart Check 다음 빈칸에 들어갈 알맞은 것을 고르시오.

1 ________ in the ocean at night isn't safe.
① Swims ② Swimming ③ To swimming

2 Samantha is good at ________ jewelry.
① made ② to make ③ making

Practice

Answers p.9

A 괄호 안에서 알맞은 것을 고르시오.

spend 동 (시간을) 보내다
fish 동 낚시하다

1 (Spend / Spending) time with my dog is really fun.
2 My father goes (fish / fishing) once a month.
3 Her dream is (traveled / traveling) all over the world.
4 Carter was angry about (to lose / losing) the race.

B 밑줄 친 동명사의 쓰임을 <보기>에서 골라 그 기호를 쓰시오.

prize 명 상, 상품
contest 명 대회, 경기
be famous for ~으로 유명하다

<보기>	ⓐ 주어	ⓑ 동사의 목적어	ⓒ 전치사의 목적어	ⓓ 보어

1 Helen finished painting the fence. [ ]
2 His goal is winning the first prize in the contest. [ ]
3 Climbing up the high mountain is not easy. [ ]
4 Paul is famous for playing the cello well. [ ]

C <보기>와 같이 동명사를 이용하여 다음 두 문장을 한 문장으로 연결하시오.

in public 공개적으로
be afraid of ~을 두려워하다

<보기> Some people can't live in a big city. It is stressful for them.
→ *Living in a big city* is stressful for some people.

1 Eric writes novels. It is his hobby.
→ Eric's hobby is ____________________.

2 I don't want to speak in public. I'm afraid of it.
→ I'm afraid of ____________________.

3 You should get enough sleep. It is important for your health.
→ ____________________ is important for your health.

D 우리말과 같도록 괄호 안의 말을 활용하여 빈칸에 쓰시오.

historical 형 역사의

1 그 역사 박물관은 다시 방문할 가치가 있다. (visit)
= The historical museum ________ ________ ________ again.

2 Jackson씨의 계획은 다음 달에 새 차를 사는 것이다. (buy, a new car)
= Ms. Jackson's plan is ________ ________ ________ ________
next month.

3 집에 도착하자마자, 나는 샤워를 했다. (arrive, home)
= ________ ________ ________, I took a shower.

UNIT 02 동명사와 to부정사를 목적어로 쓰는 동사

1 동명사를 목적어로 쓰는 동사

enjoy finish avoid keep mind give up stop quit practice deny imagine …

Diane *enjoys* **listening** to K-pop.
Do you *mind* **turning** on the heater?

2 to부정사를 목적어로 쓰는 동사

want hope wish decide plan need expect promise agree …

Thomas *wants* **to visit** Busan this summer.
She *promised* **to watch** the movie with me.

3 동명사와 to부정사를 모두 목적어로 쓰는 동사

❶ 의미 차이가 없는 경우

like love hate prefer begin start continue …

It *started* **raining**[**to rain**] in the afternoon.

❷ 의미 차이가 있는 경우

forget + 동명사 forget + to부정사	(과거에) ~한 것을 잊다 (미래에) ~할 것을 잊다	I *forgot* **buying** some eggs and milk. I *forgot* **to buy** some eggs and milk.
remember + 동명사 remember + to부정사	(과거에) ~한 것을 기억하다 (미래에) ~할 것을 기억하다	He *remembers* **meeting** her last year. *Remember* **to meet** me in the theater.
regret + 동명사 regret + to부정사	~한 것을 후회하다 ~하게 되어 유감이다	I *regret* **telling** them the truth. I *regret* **to tell** you the bad news.
try + 동명사 try + to부정사	(시험 삼아) ~해보다 ~하려고 노력하다	Let's *try* **pushing** this green button. *Try* **to exercise** more regularly.

TIP 「stop + 동명사」(~하는 것을 멈추다)에서 동명사는 stop의 목적어이며, 「stop + to부정사」(~하기 위해 멈추다)에서 to부정사는 부사적 용법으로 쓰여 목적을 나타낸다.

My brother *stopped* **drinking** coffee.
My brother *stopped* **to drink** coffee.

Smart Check 다음 빈칸에 들어갈 알맞은 것을 고르시오.

1 Sam forgot ________ the front door, so his cat ran away.
① close ② closing ③ to close

Practice

Answers p.9

A 괄호 안의 동사를 알맞은 형태로 바꿔 문장을 완성하시오.

1 (ask)
① Don't forget ___________ him to turn off the lights before leaving.
② I forgot ___________ you about your holiday plans yesterday.

2 (go)
① I avoid ___________ to crowded places.
② Luke is planning ___________ abroad next year.

3 (send)
① My mother doesn't remember ___________ me packages last month.
② I'll remember ___________ you the pictures after the trip.

4 (hide)
① My younger sister denied ___________ my favorite doll.
② Everyone needed ___________ for the surprise birthday party.

5 (look for)
① Angela stopped ___________ her necklace in the middle of the road.
② Because it became too dark, he stopped ___________ his dog.

turn off 끄다
crowded 형 붐비는
package 명 소포
look for ~을 찾다

B 다음 빈칸에 알맞은 말을 <보기>에서 한 번씩만 골라 알맞은 형태로 바꿔 쓰시오.

<보기>	find	spend	receive	throw

1 He regrets ___________ too much money last Sunday.

2 Ms. Jones expects ___________ the award.

3 The baseball player practiced ___________ the ball all day.

4 I tried ___________ my lost cell phone, but I couldn't.

receive 동 받다
award 명 상
lost 형 잃어버린

C 우리말과 같도록 괄호 안의 말을 활용하여 문장을 완성하시오.

1 아기는 갑자기 울기 시작했다. (begin, cry)
= The baby suddenly ______________________.

2 나는 TV 없이 사는 것을 상상할 수 없다. (imagine, live)
= I can't ______________________ without TV.

3 Rachel은 어렸을 때 중국에 방문했던 것을 기억한다. (remember, visit)
= Rachel ______________________ China when she was little.

4 그들은 같은 실수를 하지 않기로 약속했다. (promise, not, make)
= They ______________________ the same mistake.

suddenly 부 갑자기
without 전 ~ 없이

Writing Exercise

A <보기>와 같이 다음 두 문장의 의미가 같도록 동명사를 이용하여 문장을 완성하시오.

<보기> I'll never forget that I spent time with my grandmother.
→ I'll never forget *spending time with my grandmother*.

1 It is not easy to become rich and famous.
→ ________________ is not easy.

2 Ellie travels by train. It is her hobby.
→ Ellie's hobby is ________________.

3 It is important to brush your teeth three times a day.
→ ________________ three times a day is important.

4 Mr. Smith is busy. He is replying to many e-mails.
→ Mr. Smith is busy ________________.

5 He remembers that he didn't turn off the oven after baking.
→ He remembers ________________ after baking.

B 우리말과 같도록 괄호 안의 말을 활용하여 문장을 완성하시오.

1 우리는 TV에서 스포츠 경기를 보는 것을 즐긴다. (enjoy, watch)
= We ________________ sports games on TV.

2 그녀는 David의 파티에 가기를 원한다. (want, go)
= She ________________ to David's party.

3 사람들은 미래를 위해 에너지를 절약할 필요가 있다. (need, save)
= People ________________ energy for the future.

4 Albert는 요즘 그의 친구와 한국어를 말하는 것을 연습한다. (practice, speak)
= Albert ________________ Korean with his friend these days.

5 너는 이 책을 읽는 것을 끝냈니? (finish, read)
= Did you ________________ this book?

6 나는 그 새로운 스마트폰 모델을 사기로 결정했다. (decide, buy)
= I ________________ the new smartphone model.

7 콘서트에서, Helen은 두 시간 동안 계속 서 있었다. (keep, stand)
= At the concert, Helen ________________ for two hours.

Answers p.9

C 우리말과 같도록 괄호 안의 말을 알맞게 배열하시오.

1 시험 결과에 대해 불평해도 소용없다. (use, it, complaining, no, is)
= ______________________ about the test result.

2 Jeff는 그 재미있는 이야기를 들었을 때 웃지 않을 수 없었다. (help, laughing, couldn't)
= Jeff ______________________ when he heard the funny story.

3 대부분의 아이들은 동물원에 가는 것을 좋아한다. (like, the, zoo, to, going)
= Most children ______________________.

4 Jonathan은 그녀에게 그의 공책을 가져다 줄 것을 잊었다. (bring, his, to, notebook, forgot, her)
= Jonathan ______________________.

5 Anna는 소방관인 것을 자랑스러워 한다. (of, firefighter, a, proud, is, being)
= Anna ______________________.

6 사무실에 있는 사람들은 오후 6시에 일하는 것을 멈췄다. (people, working, in, office, the, stopped)
= ______________________ at 6 P.M.

D 다음 그림을 보고 <보기>의 말을 활용하여 문장을 완성하시오.

<보기>	get a shot	stay home	play with a ball	run a marathon

1

The dog enjoys ______________________.

2

Jake hopes ______________________.

3

Scott loves ______________________.

4

Molly is scared of ______________________.

Chapter Test

[1-2] 다음 빈칸에 들어갈 알맞은 것을 고르시오.

1

I finished ________ in my diary.

① write ② wrote
③ writing ④ to write
⑤ to writing

2

On ________ at school, she went to the library.

① arrive ② to arrive
③ to arriving ④ arrived
⑤ arriving

3 다음 우리말을 영작할 때 빈칸에 들어갈 알맞은 것은?

Hannah는 바다에서 서핑을 해보았다. = Hannah tried ________ in the ocean.

① surf ② surfed
③ surfing ④ to surf
⑤ to surfing

4 다음 빈칸에 들어갈 수 있는 것을 모두 고르시오.

It rained heavily, but I continued ________.

① walk ② walking
③ to walk ④ walked
⑤ to walking

[5-6] 다음 중 어법상 어색한 것을 고르시오.

5 ① Shaking your legs is a bad habit.
② The train began to move slowly.
③ His goal is getting an award for his movie.
④ I avoid put off my assignments.
⑤ Josh thought about living in New York.

6 ① My little brother likes watching cartoons.
② The restaurant is famous for to use fresh vegetables.
③ You should quit worrying about small things.
④ He needs to go to the hospital immediately.
⑤ I hate to speak badly of my friends.

서술형

7 우리말과 같도록 주어진 <조건>에 맞게 영작하시오.

나는 뜨거운 물을 마시고 싶다.

<조건> 1. feel like, drink를 활용하시오. 2. 6단어로 쓰시오.

= ________________________________.

서술형

8 다음 문장에서 어법상 어색한 부분을 찾아 쓰고 바르게 고쳐 쓰시오.

She remembers to go to the museum when she was a child.

________________ → ________________

서술형

[9-11] 괄호 안의 동사를 활용하여 문장을 완성하시오.

9 Tim agreed __________ more housework on weekends. (do)

10 I'm afraid of __________ in front of a large crowd. (speak)

11 Jenny forgot __________ a pencil yesterday, so she bought another one today. (buy)

[12-13] 다음 중 어법상 바른 것을 고르시오.

12 ① Peter is interested in study science.
② Mr. White's job is to analyzing data.
③ Building a ship requires a lot of time.
④ The thief denied to steal the wallet.
⑤ I hope going to Paris for vacation.

13 ① He is busy writing his report.
② I really wanted buying the smartwatch.
③ We stopped to eat junk food for our health.
④ She gave up to telling her son what to do.
⑤ Please remember bringing me your notebook tomorrow.

14 다음 빈칸에 들어갈 말로 어색한 것은?

Laura ________ chatting with her friends.

① wishes ② avoids
③ loves ④ keeps
⑤ enjoys

[15-16] 다음 글의 빈칸에 들어갈 말이 순서대로 짝지어진 것을 고르시오.

15 Yesterday, Harry exercised hard although he didn't feel good. As a result, he got sick. He regretted ________ too hard. He decided ________ to the hospital.

① exercise - to go
② to exercise - going
③ to exercise - to go
④ exercising - to go
⑤ exercising - going

16 Kate and I are best friends. We enjoy ________ with each other. We are going to go on a trip to London together, and we expect ________ a great time there.

① be - have
② to be - having
③ to be - to have
④ being - having
⑤ being - to have

서술형 고난도

17 다음 글의 밑줄 친 ⓐ~ⓔ 중 어법상 어색한 것을 찾아 기호를 쓰고 바르게 고쳐 쓰시오.

> My hobby is ⓐcollecting coins from other countries. I hoped ⓑtraveling to Germany to collect some coins, but I gave up ⓒgoing there because of school. Fortunately, my uncle lives in Germany, and he promised ⓓto send me some coins. I'm very excited about ⓔto get them.

(1) ______ → ____________________

(2) ______ → ____________________

고난도

18 주어진 문장의 밑줄 친 부분과 쓰임이 같은 것은?

> Jane enjoys learning new languages.

① Riding a horse was scary.
② My sister denied wearing my coat.
③ His plan is reading a book on the weekend.
④ Eating healthy food is good for your body.
⑤ My dream is becoming an astronaut.

서술형

[19-20] 동명사를 이용하여 다음 두 문장을 한 문장으로 연결하시오.

19

> Aaron didn't see his grandmother yesterday. He regrets it.
> → Aaron regrets ____________________
> ____________________.

20

> I met my old friend. It made me cry.
> → ____________________ made me cry.

서술형

[21-22] 우리말과 같도록 괄호 안의 말을 활용하여 문장을 완성하시오.

21

> 그 가수는 콘서트를 위해 춤추는 것을 연습했다. (practice, dance)

= The singer ____________________ for the concert.

22

> 그 영화는 두 번 볼 가치가 있다. (worth, watch)

= The movie ____________________ twice.

23 다음 중 짝지어진 두 문장의 의미가 다른 것은?

① Mom began washing the dishes.
→ Mom began to wash the dishes.
② He prefers going to school by bus.
→ He prefers to go to school by bus.
③ I tried opening the water bottle.
→ I tried to open the water bottle.
④ We love riding bicycles at the park.
→ We love to ride bicycles at the park.
⑤ James hates waking up early in the morning.
→ James hates to wake up early in the morning.

서술형

24 우리말과 같도록 괄호 안의 말을 알맞게 배열하시오.

> 그 사실들을 부인해도 소용없다.
> (is, no, the, it, use, facts, denying)

= ____________________.

Chapter 07

분사

분사는 동사가 V-ing형이나 p.p.형으로 쓰여
문장 안에서 형용사 역할을 하는 것이다.

UNIT 01 현재분사와 과거분사

1 분사의 쓰임

분사는 V-ing(현재분사)나 p.p.(과거분사)의 형태로, 형용사처럼 명사를 수식하거나 문장 안에서 보어로 쓰인다.

The **smiling** baby looks happy.
Harry heard his name **called**.

TIP 명사를 수식하는 분사가 구를 이루어 쓰이면 명사 뒤에 온다.
Do you know that *boy* **singing on the stage**?

2 현재분사와 과거분사

❶ 현재분사는 능동(~하는)·진행(~하고 있는)의 의미를 나타내고, 과거분사는 수동(~된, ~당한)·완료(~된)의 의미를 나타낸다.

The girl **wearing** a blue blouse is my friend.
Look at those **falling** leaves.

These are the uniforms **worn** by our team.
The woman swept up the **fallen** leaves.

❷ 분사가 수식하거나 설명하는 대상이 감정을 일으키는 원인일 때는 현재분사를 쓰고, 감정을 느낄 때는 과거분사를 쓴다.

surprising 놀라운 - surprised 놀란	interesting 흥미로운 - interested 흥미로워하는
amazing 놀라운 - amazed 놀란	boring 지루한 - bored 지루해하는
tiring 피곤한 - tired 피곤해하는	pleasing 기쁜 - pleased 기뻐하는
exciting 신나는 - excited 신이 난	disappointing 실망스러운 - disappointed 실망스러워하는

The news was **surprising**. Everyone was **surprised**.
We watched a very **disappointing** movie. We were **disappointed**.

❸ 현재분사는 진행시제를 만들기도 하고, 과거분사는 완료시제와 수동태를 만들기도 한다.

Butterflies *are* **flying** in the field.
Justin *has* **lived** here since he was five.
This building *was* **designed** by a famous architect.

TIP 현재분사는 형용사 역할을 하고, 동명사는 명사 역할을 한다.
There is a **sleeping** *cat* on my bed.
Luke *enjoys* **sleeping** on the sofa.

Smart Check 다음 빈칸에 들어갈 알맞은 것을 고르시오.

1 Let's help the ________ girl.
① cries ② crying ③ cried

2 I bought the ________ in France.
① bag made ② made bag ③ bag making

Practice

Answers p.10

A 괄호 안에서 알맞은 것을 고르시오.

1 The (breaking / broken) glass on the floor is dangerous.
2 I saw my friends (arguing / argued) with each other.
3 We were (amazing / amazed) at the size of the stadium.
4 Chris is the boy (dancing / danced) in front of the people.

glass 명 유리
floor 명 바닥
argue 동 말다툼하다
stadium 명 경기장

B 괄호 안의 동사를 알맞은 형태로 바꿔 빈칸에 쓰시오.

1 Who is that kid ________ alone in the classroom? (sit)
2 Everyone tried hard to find the ________ cat. (lose)
3 The girl ________ the window is Betty. (clean)
4 Anna was ________ with her father's gift. (please)
5 Is there any milk ________ in the refrigerator? (leave)

hard 부 열심히
leave 동 남아 있다
refrigerator 명 냉장고

C 밑줄 친 부분의 쓰임과 같은 것을 <보기>에서 골라 그 기호를 쓰시오.

<보기>	ⓐ There are some ducks swimming in the pond. ⓑ I like watching e-sports games.

1 Kevin played tennis all day. It was very tiring. [ ]
2 Did you finish decorating your room? [ ]
3 Mike's hobby is reading mystery novels. [ ]
4 The boring movie made me sleepy. [ ]

pond 명 연못
decorate 동 꾸미다

D <보기>와 같이 분사를 이용하여 다음 두 문장을 한 문장으로 연결하시오.

<보기>	I ate a Mexican dish. It was called burrito. → I ate a Mexican dish *called* *burrito*.

1 Mom got me some eggs. They were boiled.
→ Mom got me some ________ ________.

2 Do you know the man? He is smiling at us.
→ Do you know the man ________ ________ ________?

3 Jenny saw her dog. It was running in the garden.
→ Jenny saw her dog ________ ________ ________ ________.

4 I'm wearing a bracelet. It is made of gold.
→ I'm wearing a bracelet ________ ________ ________.

dish 명 요리
boil 동 삶다
bracelet 명 팔찌

UNIT 02

분사구문

1 분사구문

❶ 분사구문은 분사를 이용하여 「접속사 + 주어 + 동사」 형태의 부사절을 부사구로 바꾼 것이다.

❷ 분사구문은 부사절의 접속사와 주어를 생략하고 부사절의 동사를 V-ing형으로 바꿔서 만든다.

When she arrived at the airport, she called me.
→ **Arriving** at the airport, she called me.

While I jog in the park, I listen to music.
→ **Jogging** in the park, I listen to music.

TIP 분사구문의 부정형은 분사 앞에 **not**을 붙여 만든다.
Not being hungry, he skipped breakfast.

2 분사구문의 다양한 의미

시간	when ~할 때 while ~하는 동안 before ~하기 전에 after ~한 후에	**Entering** the room, he turned on the light. (← When he entered the room)
이유	because/as/since ~하기 때문에	**Having** enough money, I can buy this laptop. (← Because I have enough money)
동시동작	while/as ~하면서	**Sweeping** the floor, she found an earring. (← While she swept the floor)
조건	if 만약 ~한다면	**Taking** the subway line 2, you can get to city hall. (← If you take the subway line 2)
양보	although/though 비록 ~이지만	**Although being** tired, he didn't take a break. (← Although he was tired) TIP 양보를 나타내는 분사구문은 주로 접속사를 생략하지 않는다.

Smart Check 다음 밑줄 친 부사절을 분사구문으로 바꿀 때 빈칸에 알맞은 말을 쓰시오.

1 When they saw their favorite actor, they screamed.
→ ________ ________ ________ ________, they screamed.

2 Since I didn't feel well, I went to the hospital.
→ ________ ________ ________, I went to the hospital.

3 While she sat on the sofa, she read a book.
→ ________ ________ ________ ________, she read a book.

Practice

Answers p.10

A 괄호 안에서 알맞은 것을 고르시오.

1 (Listen / Listening) to the radio, I washed the dishes.

2 (Being / Been) tall, Jacob can reach the top shelf.

3 (To turn / Turning) to the right, you'll see the bank.

4 (Knowing not / Not knowing) how to bake, Laura asked her mom.

top 형 맨 위의
shelf 명 선반
turn 동 돌다

B 다음 밑줄 친 부사절을 분사구문으로 바꿀 때 빈칸에 알맞은 말을 쓰시오.

1 When they saw a dolphin in the ocean, they felt amazed.
→ ________ a dolphin in the ocean, they felt amazed.

2 Because I don't have enough time, I should hurry to get to school.
→ ________ ________ enough time, I should hurry to get to school.

3 While she cleaned her room, she found some old photos.
→ ________ her room, she found some old photos.

4 Since he was very hungry, he ate a lot of food.
→ ________ very hungry, he ate a lot of food.

dolphin 명 돌고래
ocean 명 바다
hurry 동 서두르다

C 다음 밑줄 친 부분을 접속사 after, because, if를 이용하여 부사절로 바꿔 쓰시오.

1 Taking this bus, you can get to the theater.
→ ______________________________, you can get to the theater.

2 Coming home from school, he fell asleep.
→ ______________________________, he fell asleep.

3 Being good at singing, I will audition for the band.
→ ______________________________, I will audition for the band.

fall asleep 잠들다
audition 동 오디션을 보다

D 우리말과 같도록 괄호 안의 말을 활용하여 빈칸에 쓰시오.

1 만약 너는 점심을 먹지 않으면, 곧 배고파질 것이다. (eat, lunch)
= ________ ________ ________, you'll be hungry soon.

2 그녀는 좋은 소식을 들었기 때문에, 매우 행복했다. (hear, the good news)
= ________ ________ ________ ________, she was very happy.

3 그는 거리를 걸으면서, 그의 선생님을 만났다. (walk, on the street)
= ________ ________ ________ ________, he met his teacher.

4 나는 많은 친구들이 있기 때문에, 외롭지 않다. (have, many friends)
= ________ ________ ________, I'm not lonely.

soon 부 곧
lonely 형 외로운

Writing Exercise

A 괄호 안의 동사를 알맞은 형태로 바꿔 빈칸에 쓰시오.

1 (surprise)
① The student gave a ____________ answer. It was creative.
② They were ____________ at Henry's success.

2 (interest)
① Megan is ____________ in space. She wants to be an astronaut.
② We should find ____________ things to do in our free time.

3 (excite)
① The ____________ boy played outside all day.
② I like bungee jumping. It is very ____________.

4 (bore)
① He is ____________ with the long and difficult lecture.
② This book is ____________, so I can't continue reading it.

5 (disappoint)
① Christine was ____________ to lose the game.
② His foolish mistake was ____________.

B 우리말과 같도록 괄호 안의 말을 활용하여 문장을 완성하시오.

1 너는 이 게시판에 붙여진 메모를 봤니? (post, on this board)
= Did you see the memo ______________________________?

2 끓고 있는 물을 조심하세요. (boil, water)
= Please watch out for the ______________________________.

3 독일에서 만들어진 차들은 인기 있다. (make, in Germany)
= Cars ______________________________ are popular.

4 나는 그 혼란스러운 퍼즐을 풀 수 없었다. (confuse, puzzle)
= I couldn't solve the ______________________________.

5 그 배우를 기다리고 있는 팬들이 많이 있다. (wait, for the actor)
= There are many fans ______________________________.

C <보기>와 같이 우리말과 같도록 괄호 안의 말을 활용하여 문장을 완성하시오.

<보기> 나는 바람을 느끼면서, 눈을 감았다. (feel the wind)
= While *I felt the wind*, I closed my eyes.
= *Feeling the wind*, I closed my eyes.

1 그는 뱀을 봤을 때, 달아났다. (see a snake)
= When __________, he ran away.
= __________, he ran away.

2 그는 할 숙제가 있었기 때문에, TV 보는 것을 멈췄다. (have homework to do)
= Because __________, he stopped watching TV.
= __________, he stopped watching TV.

3 나는 수영복이 없었기 때문에, 수영장에서 수영할 수 없었다. (have a swimsuit)
= As __________, I couldn't swim in the pool.
= __________, I couldn't swim in the pool.

4 그녀는 집에 도착했을 때, 창문이 깨진 것을 발견했다. (arrive home)
= When __________, she found the window broken.
= __________, she found the window broken.

5 우리는 산을 오르면서, 도시의 아름다운 경치를 볼 수 있다. (climb the mountain)
= While __________, we can see the beautiful view of the city.
= __________, we can see the beautiful view of the city.

D 다음 그림을 보고 <보기>의 말을 활용하여 문장을 완성하시오.

<보기> drop on the ground fill with flowers listen to music play the guitar

1 A man __________ has long red hair.

2 A girl is looking at the coins __________.

3 There is a garden __________.

4 __________, a woman is doing jump rope.

Chapter Test

[1-2] 다음 빈칸에 들어갈 알맞은 것을 고르시오.

1 The trip to London was ________.

① excite ② excites
③ to excite ④ exciting
⑤ excited

2 ________ home, she changed her clothes.

① Arrive ② Arrives
③ Arriving ④ Arrived
⑤ To arriving

[3-4] 다음 빈칸에 들어갈 말이 순서대로 짝지어진 것을 고르시오.

3
• Their love for each other was ________.
• Dave was ________ during the play.

① touch - boring ② touching - boring
③ touching - bored ④ touched - bored
⑤ touched - boring

4
• Did you see the ________ frog?
• Only the people ________ to the party can enter the hall.

① jumping - invite ② jumped - invited
③ jumping - inviting ④ jumped - inviting
⑤ jumping - invited

서술형

[5-6] 다음 문장의 밑줄 친 부분을 분사구문으로 바꿔 쓰시오.

5
When she saw the flower, she smiled.
→ ________________, she smiled.

6
Because he has a toothache, he will go to the dentist.
→ ________________, he will go to the dentist.

7 다음 중 어법상 옳은 것은?

① The research on sharks was interested.
② Hear the news, he ran to his home.
③ Nobody likes the bored TV show.
④ I wore a sweater knitted by my aunt.
⑤ I met a man calling Timothy.

서술형

8 다음 문장에서 어법상 어색한 부분을 찾아 쓰고 바르게 고쳐 쓰시오.

Played soccer, I hurt my leg.

________________ → ________________

서술형

9 우리말과 같도록 주어진 <조건>에 맞게 문장을 완성하시오.

그 탁자 가까이에 서서, 나는 주스를 조금 마셨다.

<조건>	1. stand, near를 활용하시오. 2. 접속사를 쓰지 마시오.

= ______________________, I drank some juice.

서술형

10 괄호 안의 동사를 활용하여 빈칸에 알맞은 말을 쓰시오.

Jim can't carry his bag because of his ________ arm. (break)

[11-12] 다음 중 어법상 어색한 것을 고르시오.

11 ① I had an amazed dream last night.
② Did you hear the shocking rumor?
③ The sleeping cat is under the sofa.
④ The girl acting on the stage is my sister.
⑤ They are eating the food cooked by me.

12 ① Shaving his chin, he sang a song.
② Washing not your hands, you can get sick.
③ Entering the room, I saw all my friends.
④ Being surprised, we couldn't say anything.
⑤ Living in the country, she can see many cows.

서술형

13 우리말과 같도록 괄호 안의 말을 활용하여 분사구문을 완성하시오.

그들은 열쇠가 없었기 때문에, 그 서랍을 열 수 없었다. (have, a key)

= ______________________, they couldn't open the drawer.

14 주어진 문장의 밑줄 친 부분과 쓰임이 다른 것은?

Who is the woman walking down the street?

① Do you know the boy talking to John?
② Her hobby is collecting sneakers.
③ The result of the game was disappointing.
④ Let's take care of the crying baby.
⑤ The author wrote an interesting novel.

서술형

[15-16] 우리말과 같도록 괄호 안의 말을 활용하여 빈칸에 쓰시오.

15

그녀는 그 버스에서 내리면서, 넘어졌다. (get off, the bus)

= ________ ________ ________ ________ ________ ________, she fell down.
= ________ ________ ________ ________, she fell down.

16

그는 그의 실수를 깨달았기 때문에, 사과했다. (realize, mistake)

= ________ ________ ________ ________ ________, he apologized.
= ________ ________ ________, he apologized.

고난도

[17-18] 다음 밑줄 친 부분과 바꿔 쓸 수 있는 것을 고르시오.

17

Turning to the left, you will find the library.

① Since you turn to the left
② And you turn to the left
③ Although you turn to the left
④ Because you turn to the left
⑤ If you turn to the left

18

Seeing the bus, she ran to the bus stop.

① And she saw the bus
② If she sees the bus
③ When she saw the bus
④ Although she saw the bus
⑤ Since she sees the bus

서술형 고난도

19 다음 글의 밑줄 친 ⓐ~ⓔ 중 어법상 어색한 것을 찾아 기호를 쓰고 바르게 고쳐 쓰시오.

After the math test, I was sure that I would get a ⓐsatisfied score. However, ⓑtalking with my friends, I felt something was wrong. My answers ⓒwritten on the test paper were different from my friends' answers. ⓓCompared the answers with my friends, I felt ⓔdisappointed.

(1) ______ → ____________________
(2) ______ → ____________________

서술형

[20-22] 분사를 이용하여 다음 두 문장을 한 문장으로 연결하시오.

20

I was hit by a car. It was coming toward me.
→ I was hit by ____________________.

21

Kelly was afraid of the dog. It was barking.
→ Kelly was afraid of the ____________________.

22

Ronald wants to eat the doughnut. It is filled with chocolate.
→ Ronald wants to eat ____________________
____________________.

23 다음 중 어법상 바른 것의 개수는?

ⓐ Feeling cold, she wore her coat.
ⓑ Traveled alone, he felt lonely.
ⓒ Tim was pleasing with his birthday gifts.
ⓓ Do not touch the broken vase.
ⓔ The ice cream bought by my dad tasted sweet.

① 1개 ② 2개 ③ 3개
④ 4개 ⑤ 5개

Chapter

08

대명사

대명사는 앞에서 언급된 특정한 명사를
반복하지 않기 위해 대신해서 쓰는 말이다.

UNIT 01 | 부정대명사 I

특별히 정해지지 않은 막연한 사람이나 사물을 가리키는 대명사로, 일부 부정대명사는 형용사로도 쓰인다.

1 one

앞에서 언급된 명사와 같은 종류의 불특정한 대상을 가리킬 때 쓰며, 복수형은 ones이다.

This *skirt* doesn't fit me, so I want to try that **one**.

TIP 앞에서 언급된 특정한 대상을 가리킬 때는 **it**이나 **they/them**을 쓴다.
This *skirt* doesn't fit me, so I can't wear **it**.

2 another: 하나 더, 또 다른 (하나)

This pen is out of ink. Can you lend me **another**?

3 other: (불특정한) 다른 (사람들/것들)

대명사로 쓰일 때는 주로 복수형인 others로 쓴다. 「the + other(s)」는 '나머지 (전부)'라는 의미이다.

Victoria always makes **others** happy.

The students have to solve **other** *problems*, too.

4 some, any: 약간(의), 조금(의), 몇몇(의)

some은 주로 긍정문과 권유·요청을 나타내는 의문문에 쓰고, any는 주로 부정문과 의문문에 쓴다.

We're making **some** *coffee*. Would you like to have **some**?

I couldn't see **any** *signs* on the road. Did you see **any**?

5 여럿 중 일부를 나타내는 표현

one ~, the other -	(둘 중) 하나는 ~, 나머지 하나는 -	She has two foreign friends. **One** is American, and **the other** is Chinese.
one ~, another -, the other ...	(셋 중) 하나는 ~, 다른 하나는 -, 나머지 하나는 …	I bought three flowers. **One** is a rose, **another** is a daisy, and **the other** is a lily.
some ~, others -	(여럿 중) 몇몇은 ~, 다른 사람들/것들은 -	**Some** like comedy movies, and **others** like thriller movies.
some ~, the others -	(여럿 중) 몇몇은 ~, 나머지 전부는 -	Eight people are in the lobby. **Some** are wearing glasses, and **the others** aren't wearing glasses.

Smart Check 다음 빈칸에 들어갈 알맞은 것을 고르시오.

1 Some students are playing basketball, and ________ are sitting on the benches.
① another ② others ③ the other

Practice

Answers p.12 

A 괄호 안에서 알맞은 것을 고르시오.

1 This hat is too small for you. You need a bigger (one / other).

2 Mary has two cats. One is black, and (others / the other) is white.

3 I'm still thirsty. Can I get (another / other) glass of water?

4 Is this ring yours? I found (one / it) under the chair.

5 He likes table tennis, but he doesn't like (another / other) sports.

thirsty 형 목이 마른, 갈증이 나는
table tennis 명 탁구

B 다음 빈칸에 알맞은 말을 <보기>에서 한 번씩만 골라 쓰시오.

<보기>	ones	another	other	others

1 In my class, some play the piano, and ________ play the violin.

2 You can use my pencils. The ________ on the desk are mine.

3 I have been to France, Germany, and many ________ countries.

4 After Nathan ate a hamburger, he ordered ________.

country 명 나라, 국가
order 동 주문하다

C 다음 빈칸에 some과 any 중 알맞은 것을 쓰시오.

1 The guests don't need ________ help with their luggage.

2 Ben is going to meet ________ friends at the park.

3 I don't have ________ time to work out.

4 Would you like ________ orange juice?

luggage 명 짐, 수하물
work out 운동하다

D 우리말과 같도록 빈칸에 알맞은 말을 쓰시오.

1 나의 옷장에 있는 많은 코트 중에, 나는 갈색의 것이 좋다.
= Among the many coats in my closet, I like the brown ________.

2 다른 사람들을 도와주다니 William은 친절하다.
= It is kind of William to help ________.

3 상자 안에 펜 일곱 자루가 있다. 몇몇은 파란색이고, 나머지 전부는 빨간색이다.
= Seven pens are in the box. ________ are blue, and ________ are red.

4 선반에 책 세 권이 있다. 한 권은 소설이고, 다른 한 권은 요리책이고, 나머지 한 권은 만화책이다.
= There are three books on the shelf. ________ is a novel, ________ is a cookbook, and ________ is a comic book.

closet 명 옷장
cookbook 명 요리책

UNIT 02 | 부정대명사 Ⅱ

1 **all**: 모두, 모든 (것)

❶ 대명사로 쓰여 사람을 나타낼 때는 복수 취급하고 사물이나 상황을 나타낼 때는 단수 취급한다.

All *were* surprised at the news.
All *is* fine today.

❷「all (of) + 명사」의 형태로 쓸 때는 all (of) 뒤의 명사에 동사를 수일치시킨다.

All (**of**) **his money** *was* stolen yesterday.
All (**of**) **the leaves** in that mountain *are* turning red.

2 **both**: 둘 다

복수 취급하며,「both of + 복수명사」나「both + 복수명사」의 형태로도 쓴다.

Wendy has two younger sisters. **Both** *like* playing with her.
Both of them *enjoy* going on a picnic.
Both (**of the**) **kids** *are* good at riding a bike.

3 **each**: 각각(의)

단수 취급하며,「each of + 복수명사」나「each + 단수명사」의 형태로도 쓴다.

I read three books last month. **Each** *was* very impressive.
Each of the members *has* a different opinion.
Each participant *is* wearing a name tag.

TIP **each other**는 '(둘 사이에) 서로', **one another**는 '(셋 이상 사이에) 서로'라는 의미의 대명사이다.
Monica and Peter like **each other**.
The team members hugged **one another**.

4 **every**: 모든

단수 취급하며,「every + 단수명사」의 형태로만 쓴다.

Every door *was* painted by Mr. Lopez.

Smart Check 다음 빈칸에 들어갈 알맞은 것을 고르시오.

1 They are twin brothers. Both ________ musical instruments well.
① play ② plays ③ is playing

2 Each ________ a different personality.
① person has ② person have ③ people have

Practice

Answers p.12

A 괄호 안에서 알맞은 것을 고르시오.

1 (All / Every) the students arrived at school on time.
2 (Both / Each) of my parents work for the same company.
3 After the party, the host gave (both / each) guest a present.
4 (Both / Every) driver must follow the traffic laws.
5 Both of the bags on the sofa (is / are) my brother's.

company 명 회사
host 명 주인, 주최측
traffic law 교통 법규

B 우리말과 같도록 빈칸에 알맞은 말을 쓰시오.

1 이 거리에 있는 각각의 집은 다른 지붕 색을 가지고 있다.
= ________ house on this street has a different roof color.

2 그 개들 둘 다 공을 가지고 노는 것을 좋아한다.
= ________ of the dogs love playing with balls.

3 모든 숙제는 어제 완료되었다.
= ________ the homework was completed yesterday.

different 형 다른
complete 동 완료하다

C 밑줄 친 부분이 어법상 맞으면 O를 쓰고, 틀리면 바르게 고쳐 쓰시오.

1 Please read every questions carefully. → ________
2 All of the stars in the sky is shining. → ________
3 Each of the coins in the box have a different size. → ________
4 Both boys are running in the playground. → ________
5 Every restaurant on Second Street open at 11 A.M. → ________

shine 동 빛나다, 반짝이다
coin 명 동전

D 우리말과 같도록 괄호 안의 말을 활용하여 빈칸에 쓰시오.

1 Michael과 Emily는 서로를 알고 있다. (know)
= Michael and Emily ________ ________ ________.

2 여자들 둘 다 사진 속에서 아름답게 웃고 있다. (woman)
= ________ ________ ________ smiling beautifully in the picture.

3 병들 각각은 우유로 가득 차 있다. (the bottle)
= ________ ________ ________ ________ ________ filled with milk.

4 시험 전, 모든 학생들은 불안해했다. (student, be)
= Before the exam, ________ ________ ________ ________ nervous.

be filled with ~으로 가득 차 있다
nervous 형 불안해하는

UNIT 03 재귀대명사

재귀대명사는 '~ 자신, ~ 자체'의 의미로, 인칭대명사의 소유격이나 목적격에 -self(단수)/-selves(복수)를 붙인 형태이다.

1 재귀대명사의 용법

❶ 재귀 용법
동사나 전치사의 목적어가 주어와 같은 대상일 때 목적어로 재귀대명사를 쓴다. 이때 재귀대명사는 생략할 수 없다.

Samuel drew **himself** in art class.
I was angry at **myself** after losing the game.

❷ 강조 용법
문장의 주어나 목적어를 강조하기 위해 강조하는 말 바로 뒤나 문장 맨 뒤에 재귀대명사를 쓴다. 이때 재귀대명사는 생략할 수 있다.

You should answer the question (**yourself**).
She doesn't like *chocolate* (**itself**), but she likes chocolate cakes.

2 재귀대명사를 쓰는 관용 표현

by oneself 혼자서, 홀로	introduce oneself 자기 소개를 하다
for oneself 혼자 힘으로, 스스로	enjoy oneself 즐거운 시간을 보내다
in itself 그 자체가, 본질적으로	talk to oneself 혼잣말을 하다
beside oneself 제정신이 아닌	seat oneself 앉다
between ourselves 우리끼리 이야기지만	hurt oneself 다치다
help oneself (to) (~을) 마음껏 먹다	cut oneself 베이다
make oneself at home (집에서처럼) 편히 쉬다/지내다	burn oneself 불에 데다

He went jogging **by himself** today.
They were **beside themselves** with worry.
Please **help yourself to** the ice cream.
Natalie and I **enjoyed ourselves** at the concert.

Smart Check 다음 빈칸에 들어갈 알맞은 것을 고르시오.

1 I cut ________ on a piece of glass.
① me ② myself ③ my

2 My grandmother planted these orange trees ________.
① herself ② itself ③ myself

3 The children wanted to solve the riddle ________ themselves.
① in ② for ③ beside

Practice

Answers p.12

A 괄호 안에서 알맞은 것을 고르시오.

1 Did you paint the wall (myself / yourself)?
2 Please make (you / yourself) at home.
3 Julie gave (me / myself) some advice.
4 Edward was very proud of (itself / himself).
5 They kept (themself / themselves) warm near the fire.

wall 명 벽
advice 명 충고

B 밑줄 친 부분을 생략할 수 있으면 O를 쓰고, 생략할 수 없으면 X를 쓰시오.

1 The little girl looked at herself in the mirror. → ________
2 Jonathan doesn't like milk itself so much. → ________
3 My mother made the bracelet herself. → ________
4 He introduced himself in front of many people. → ________

mirror 명 거울

C 다음 빈칸에 알맞은 말을 <보기>에서 한 번씩만 골라 쓰시오.

<보기>	by	in	enjoy	talk to

1 The diamond ________ itself is so beautiful.
2 Feeling lonely, Gloria often ________ herself.
3 I went shopping ________ myself last weekend.
4 Did they ________ themselves at the film festival?

film 명 영화

D 우리말과 같도록 괄호 안의 말을 활용하여 빈칸에 쓰시오.

1 Matthew는 축구를 하는 동안 다쳤다. (hurt)
= Matthew ________ ________ while he played soccer.

2 우리는 바이러스로부터 우리 자신을 안전하게 지켜야 한다. (keep, safe)
= We have to ________ ________ ________ from the virus.

3 사람들은 분노로 제정신이 아니었다. (be)
= People ________ ________ ________ with anger.

4 나는 스스로를 돌볼 만큼 충분히 나이가 많다. (take care of)
= I'm old enough to ________ ________ ________ ________.

anger 명 분노, 화
take care of ~을 돌보다

Writing Exercise

A 다음 빈칸에 알맞은 말을 <보기>에서 한 번씩만 골라 문장을 완성하시오.

<보기>	one	the other	any	all	both	each	myself	herself

1 I would like to introduce ________.

2 I love Paris and Rome. ________ cities have many tourist sites.

3 ________ of the characters has a different feature.

4 Do you have ________ good ideas for the history project?

5 In the morning, ________ of the roads are crowded with cars.

6 My friend lent me a red pen, but I needed a blue ________.

7 Amy went to the shopping mall to get ________ some clothes.

8 Mr. Jackson has two daughters. One is a reporter, and ________ is a scientist.

B 우리말과 같도록 괄호 안의 말을 활용하여 빈칸에 쓰시오.

1 나의 옷장에 또 다른 스카프가 있다. (be, scarf)
= There ________ ________ ________ in my closet.

2 그 선수들은 그들 자신에게 실망했다. (disappointed in)
= The players were ________ ________ ________.

3 나의 반 친구들과 나는 현장 학습에서 즐거운 시간을 보냈다. (enjoy)
= My classmates and I ________ ________ on the field trip.

4 이 집은 큰 방 한 개와 작은 것 두 개를 가지고 있다. (small)
= This house has one big room and ________ ________ ________.

5 Linda는 그녀의 정원에서 많은 야채들을 재배한다. 몇몇은 당근이고, 다른 것들은 양파다. (carrots, onions)
= Linda grows many vegetables in her garden. ________ ________ ________, and ________ ________ ________.

C 우리말과 같도록 괄호 안의 말을 알맞게 배열하시오.

1 내가 저녁을 준비하는 동안 너는 편히 쉬어도 된다. (make, home, can, yourself, at, you)
= ________________________ while I prepare dinner.

2 두 버스 다 너를 박물관으로 데려다 줄 것이다. (buses, take, of, both, will, the)
= ________________________ you to the museum.

3 그는 직접 나에게 놀라운 소식을 말해줬다. (told, me, himself, he)
= ________________________ the surprising news.

4 모든 가게는 공휴일에 문을 닫는다. (is, store, closed, every)
= ________________________ on the national holiday.

5 저에게 약간의 소금을 건네주시겠어요? (pass, salt, me, some)
= Would you ________________________?

D 다음 그림을 보고 빈칸에 알맞은 말을 쓰시오.

1

2

3

1 The boy and the girl are smiling at ________ ________.

2 There are six cars on the road. ________ are black, and ________ ________ are white.

3 While my father was shaving, he cut ________.

Chapter Test

[1-3] 다음 빈칸에 들어갈 알맞은 것을 고르시오.

1

She wanted a black watch as a present, but she received a brown ________.

① all
② one
③ any
④ both
⑤ others

2

My smartphone is broken. I'll take ________ to the repair shop.

① it
② one
③ some
④ them
⑤ other

3

If you're still thirsty, you may take ________ bottle of water.

① other
② both
③ another
④ each of
⑤ the others

4 다음 중 밑줄 친 부분을 생략할 수 있는 것은?

① They blamed <u>themselves</u> for the problem.
② You should love <u>yourself</u> more.
③ We <u>ourselves</u> fixed the copy machine.
④ I tell <u>myself</u> to cheer up every day.
⑤ The intelligent child taught <u>himself</u> to read when he was three years old.

서술형

[5-6] 우리말과 같도록 빈칸에 알맞은 말을 쓰시오.

5

각각의 책은 올바른 위치에 놓여야 한다.

= ________ ________ should be put in the right place.

6

James는 언제나 다른 사람들을 격려한다.

= James always encourages ________.

[7-8] 다음 빈칸에 공통으로 들어갈 알맞은 것을 고르시오.

7

- ________ people are playing baseball, and the others are standing beside.
- My uncle baked ________ bread for his neighbors.

① any
② some
③ each
④ both
⑤ others

8

- I don't need ________ help with my assignment.
- Do you have ________ idea about what to do today?

① any
② some
③ every
④ all
⑤ other

[9-10] 다음 중 어법상 어색한 것을 고르시오.

9 ① Both of the boys enjoy math class.
② He wants another shirt in a different color.
③ Would you like some strawberry ice cream?
④ All of us were surprised by the news.
⑤ Each student need to bring a musical instrument.

10 ① Susan and I like each other.
② Please introduce yourself to us.
③ Some kids are drawing, and others are singing.
④ I have any reasons for being late to the class.
⑤ Every window was cleaned last week.

서술형

11 우리말과 같도록 주어진 <조건>에 맞게 영작하시오.

그녀의 아들들 둘 다 선생님이다.

<조건>
1. 부정대명사를 사용하시오.
2. sons, be, teachers를 활용하시오.
3. 6단어로 쓰시오.

= ______________________________.

12 다음 (A)~(C)에 들어갈 말이 바르게 짝지어진 것은?

Patrick has three foreign friends at school. ___(A)___ is from France, ___(B)___ came from China, and ___(C)___ is Italian.

	(A)	(B)	(C)
①	One	other	the other
②	One	another	others
③	One	another	the other
④	Some	another	the other
⑤	Some	other	others

[13-14] 다음 글의 빈칸에 들어갈 말이 순서대로 짝지어진 것을 고르시오.

13 My puppy usually plays with two toys. ________ is a ball, and ________ is a doll.

① One - other
② One - the other
③ Another - the other
④ Another - other
⑤ The other - others

14 I borrowed ten books from the library. ________ are classics, and ________ are biographies.

① Others - some
② Others - the others
③ Some - other
④ Some - the others
⑤ Some - any

15 다음 중 밑줄 친 부분이 어법상 바른 것은?

① We should protect <u>us</u> from danger.
② All of the trees in the garden <u>is</u> tall and green.
③ She was proud of <u>herself</u> after the contest.
④ Each of them <u>have</u> the same kind of laptop.
⑤ Some passed the exam, and <u>other</u> failed.

서술형

[16-17] 우리말과 같도록 재귀대명사를 이용하여 빈칸에 쓰시오.

16 그녀는 자주 혼잣말을 한다.

= She often ________ ________ ________.

17 나는 그 경기 중에 다쳤다.

= I ________ ________ during the game.

[18-19] 다음 글을 읽고 주어진 질문에 답하시오.

When Chloe was younger, she was afraid of riding a bicycle. However, she decided to trust ⓐherself and learned how to ride. Now, (A) Chloe has a good time when she rides her bicycle every weekend.

고난도

18 위 글의 밑줄 친 ⓐ의 용법과 같은 것은?

① The kid can wear the pants himself.
② The cat took the snack from the cupboard itself.
③ She herself thinks that her English is bad.
④ Mr. Jones himself baked the cake.
⑤ Ronald always talks about himself.

서술형

19 위 글의 밑줄 친 (A)와 의미가 같도록 빈칸에 알맞은 말을 쓰시오.

→ Chloe ________ ________ when she rides her bicycle every weekend.

20 다음 대화의 빈칸에 들어갈 말이 순서대로 짝지어진 것은?

A: I want to buy some sunflowers. How much are they?
B: Each of them ________ four dollars.
A: That is expensive. What about the others?
B: The other flowers ________ two dollars each.

① cost - is　② cost - are
③ costs - is　④ costs - are
⑤ costing - being

서술형 고난도

21 다음 글의 밑줄 친 ⓐ~ⓔ 중 어법상 어색한 것을 찾아 기호를 쓰고 바르게 고쳐 쓰시오.

Yesterday, Cathy invited three friends to her birthday party. ⓐAll her friends gave her gifts, and every ⓑgifts was precious. ⓒOne was a necklace, and ⓓthe others were rings. Cathy was satisfied with the presents, and she couldn't wait to wear ⓔones.

(1) ______ → ________________
(2) ______ → ________________

서술형

22 다음 빈칸에 알맞은 말을 <보기>에서 한 번씩만 골라 쓰시오.

<보기> one　some　both

(1) Ms. Taylor wants to buy a microwave because she doesn't have ________.
(2) He couldn't choose between the two books. ________ were written by his favorite author.
(3) I made chocolate chip cookies. Do you want to try ________?

서술형

23 다음 문장에서 어법상 어색한 부분을 찾아 쓰고 바르게 고쳐 쓰시오.

All the milk have gone bad because the refrigerator is broken.

________________ → ________________

Chapter

09

관계사

관계사는 두 문장을 연결하는 접속사 역할을 하며,
관계사가 이끄는 절은 앞 문장의 명사를 꾸민다.
관계사에는 관계대명사와 관계부사가 있다.

UNIT 01

관계대명사

1 관계대명사

❶ 접속사와 대명사 역할을 하며, 관계대명사가 이끄는 절은 선행사(앞 문장의 명사)를 수식한다.

I saw *a man*. *He* was wearing a hat.
→ I saw *a man* **who** was wearing a hat.
선행사 관계대명사절

❷ 관계대명사는 선행사의 종류와 관계절 안에서의 관계대명사의 역할에 따라 형태가 달라진다.

선행사 \ 관계대명사의 격	주격	목적격	소유격
사람	who	who(m)	whose
사물, 동물	which	which	

2 주격 관계대명사 who, which

I know *a girl*. *She* lives in Canada.
→ I know *a girl* **who** lives in Canada.
→ 주격 관계대명사절의 동사는 선행사에 수일치시킨다.

They ate *the cake*. *It* was in the fridge.
→ They ate *the cake* **which** was in the fridge.

TIP **who는 '누가'라는 의미의 의문사로도 쓰인다.**
I don't remember **who** drew this painting.

3 목적격 관계대명사 who(m), which

She is *the singer*. My mother likes *her* the most.
→ She is *the singer* **who(m)** my mother likes the most.

The phone broke. Peter bought *it* last week.
→ *The phone* **which** Peter bought last week broke.

4 소유격 관계대명사 whose

Ron is looking for *a house*. *Its* door is white.
→ Ron is looking for *a house* **whose** door is white.

Smart Check 다음 빈칸에 들어갈 알맞은 것을 고르시오.

1 The reporter interviewed a ballerina ________ is famous worldwide.
① who ② whom ③ which

Practice

Answers p.13

A 다음 문장의 선행사에는 동그라미를 치고, 관계대명사에는 밑줄을 치시오.

1 I know the man who delivers letters to me.

2 They met the designer whose shoes are popular.

3 He has a watch which was made in Switzerland.

deliver 동 배달하다

B 다음 빈칸에 알맞은 말을 <보기>에서 한 번씩만 골라 쓰시오.

<보기>	who	which	whom	whose

1 I have an older sister ________ works at the bank.

2 Ariana remembered the boy ________ she met at the library.

3 Look at the tree ________ leaves turned red and yellow.

4 Tyler ate the chocolate cookies ________ were on the table.

leaf 명 나뭇잎
turn 동 (~한 상태로) 변하다

C 관계대명사를 이용하여 다음 두 문장을 한 문장으로 연결하시오.

1 They're on a plane. It is going to Sydney.
→ They're on a plane ______________________.

2 Julian is the boy. Stella introduced him to me.
→ Julian is the boy ______________________.

3 People are healthy. They eat and exercise regularly.
→ People ______________________ are healthy.

4 I like the girl. Her eyes are blue.
→ I like the girl ______________________.

introduce 동 소개하다
healthy 형 건강한

D 우리말과 같도록 관계대명사와 괄호 안의 말을 활용하여 빈칸에 쓰시오.

1 그는 그를 도와줄 수 있는 누군가를 찾고 있다. (someone, can, help)
= He is searching for ________ ________ ________ ________
________.

2 나의 아버지는 내가 정말 많이 존경하는 사람이다. (the person, respect)
= My father is ________ ________ ________ ________ ________
so much.

3 Amy는 색상이 독특한 스마트폰을 가지고 있다. (a smartphone, color, unique)
= Amy has ________ ________ ________ ________ ________
________.

search 동 찾다
unique 형 독특한

UNIT 02 관계대명사 that/what, 주의해야 할 관계대명사의 쓰임

1 관계대명사 that

❶ 선행사와 상관없이 주격이나 목적격 관계대명사로 쓰인다.

He is *the architect* **that**[**who**] designed the new mall.

I'd like to visit *the city* **that**[**which**] I saw in the movie.

❷ 선행사에 다음이 포함될 때 주로 관계대명사 that을 쓴다.

사람 + 사물/동물	The news is about *a man and a dog* **that** survived the fire.
최상급, 서수	Irene was *the last person* **that** left the room.
the only, the same, the very	I'll buy *the same shoes* **that** you have.
-thing으로 끝나는 대명사	My parents believed *everything* **that** I said.
all, every, no 등	The bread was *all* **that** she could buy.

2 관계대명사 what

선행사를 포함하고 있으며, '~한 것'이라는 의미이다. the thing(s) which[that]으로 바꿔 쓸 수 있다.

What I want to drink is a glass of lemonade.

→ **The thing which**[**that**] I want to drink is a glass of lemonade.

3 관계대명사의 생략

❶ 목적격 관계대명사 who(m), which, that은 생략할 수 있다.

Lena is the girl (**who**(**m**)[**that**]) I met on the street.

The book (**which**[**that**]) you're reading is mine.

❷ 「주격 관계대명사 + be동사」는 생략할 수 있다.

Look at the child (**who**[**that**] **is**) chasing a pigeon.

4 전치사 + 관계대명사

관계대명사가 전치사의 목적어인 경우, 전치사는 관계대명사절의 맨 뒤나 관계대명사 바로 앞에 온다.

I know *the girl*. You were talking **about** *her*.

→ I know *the girl* (**who**(**m**)[**that**]) you were talking **about**.

→ I know *the girl* **about whom** you were talking.

↳ 관계대명사 바로 앞에 전치사가 올 때는 목적격 관계대명사를 생략할 수 없고, 관계대명사 who나 that을 쓸 수 없다.

Smart Check 다음 빈칸에 들어갈 알맞은 것을 고르시오.

1 Let's take the bus ________ comes first.

① who ② that ③ what

Practice

Answers p.13

A 괄호 안에서 알맞은 것을 고르시오.

1 (That / What) makes me happy is your smile.
2 She is the very person (that / what) donated money.
3 Sandra can't understand (that / what) the teacher is saying.
4 This is the bakery (that / what) I go to every morning.

donate 동 기부하다

B 다음 문장에서 생략할 수 있는 부분에 밑줄을 치시오.

1 The boy who is dancing on the stage is my brother.
2 This is the restaurant which I've wanted to visit.
3 Ashley wore a jacket that she bought yesterday.
4 We went to the national museum which was built in 1985.

stage 명 무대
national 형 국립의

C 관계대명사를 이용하여 다음 두 문장을 한 문장으로 연결할 때 빈칸에 알맞은 말을 쓰시오.

1 I need a piece of paper. I can write on it.
→ I need a piece of paper ________ I can write ________.

2 Brian is my friend. I like to talk with him.
→ Brian is my friend ________ ________ I like to talk.

3 Laura visited the city. She used to live in that city.
→ Laura visited the city ________ ________ she used to live.

4 We are going to the party. We were invited to it.
→ We are going to the party ________ we were invited ________.

used to ~하곤 했다

D 우리말과 같도록 괄호 안의 말을 알맞게 배열하시오.

1 나에게 중요한 것은 시험의 결과이다. (for, is, important, what, me)
= ____________________ is the result of the test.

2 그가 이전에 당신이 말했던 그 배우인가요? (actor, about, talked, you, the)
= Is he ____________________ before?

3 펜싱은 내가 즐기는 유일한 스포츠이다. (the, I, that, sport, enjoy, only)
= Fencing is ____________________.

4 나는 Eric이 함께 노는 그 소년을 안다. (who, the, plays, Eric, boy, with)
= I know ____________________.

result 명 결과
actor 명 배우

UNIT 03 관계부사

1 관계부사

접속사와 부사 역할을 하며, 관계부사가 이끄는 절은 선행사를 수식한다. 관계부사는 장소, 시간, 이유, 방법을 나타내며, 「전치사 + 관계대명사」로 바꿔 쓸 수 있다.

	선행사	관계부사	「전치사 + 관계대명사」
장소	the place, the house, the city 등	where	at/on/in/to + which
시간	the time, the day, the year 등	when	at/on/in/during + which
이유	the reason	why	for + which
방법	the way	how	in + which

❶ where

This is *the hotel*. Gary stayed *at this hotel* for a week.
→ This is *the hotel* **where**[**at which**] Gary stayed for a week.

❷ when

She celebrates *the day*. The baby was born *on that day*.
→ She celebrates *the day* **when**[**on which**] the baby was born.

❸ why

The teacher heard *the reason*. Tina was late *for that reason*.
→ The teacher heard *the reason* **why**[**for which**] Tina was late.

❹ how

the way와 how는 둘 중 하나만 쓸 수 있다.

Tell me *the way*. You made the pie *in that* way.
→ Tell me **how** you made the pie.
→ Tell me *the way* (**in which**) you made the pie.

Smart Check 다음 빈칸에 들어갈 알맞은 것을 고르시오.

1 2018 is the year ________ the Winter Olympics was held in Korea.
① where ② when ③ how

2 This is the market ________ my family buys fruits.
① where ② why ③ how

3 Andy doesn't know the reason ________ I'm angry at him.
① where ② how ③ why

Practice

Answers p.13

A 괄호 안에서 알맞은 것을 고르시오.

1 Saturday is the day (when / why) we go to the beach.

2 Please teach me (why / how) I can stay healthy.

3 I remember all the places (when / where) I traveled last month.

4 My mother explained the reason (when / why) I can't go out at night.

healthy 형 건강한
explain 동 설명하다

B 다음 빈칸에 알맞은 말을 <보기>에서 한 번씩만 골라 쓰시오.

<보기>	where	when	why	how

1 11 o'clock is the time ________ Julia goes to bed.

2 He knows the reason ________ the singer became popular.

3 This is the house ________ Vincent van Gogh lived.

4 I will show you ________ I got a good grade in science.

go to bed 자다
grade 명 성적

C 관계부사를 이용하여 다음 두 문장을 한 문장으로 연결하시오.

1 Olivia told us the reason. She started to learn ballet for this reason.
→ Olivia told us the reason ____________________.

2 Tomorrow is the day. Adam is going abroad to study on that day.
→ Tomorrow is the day ____________________.

3 Beijing is the city. The Great Wall is in that city.
→ Beijing is the city ____________________.

4 This is the way. The CEO succeeded in business in that way.
→ This is ____________________.

CEO 최고 경영자
succeed 동 성공하다
business 명 사업

D 우리말과 같도록 관계부사와 괄호 안의 말을 활용하여 빈칸에 쓰시오.

1 이곳은 내가 종종 옷을 사는 가게이다. (the shop, often, buy clothes)
= This is ______ ______ ______ ______ ______
______ ______.

2 5월은 장미가 피는 달이다. (the month, roses bloom)
= May is ______ ______ ______ ______ ______.

3 나는 그녀가 역으로 갈 수 있는 방법을 그녀에게 말해줄 것이다. (can, get to the station)
= I'll tell her ______ ______ ______ ______ ______
______ ______.

bloom 동 꽃이 피다

Writing Exercise

A 다음 빈칸에 알맞은 말을 <보기>에서 한 번씩만 골라 쓰시오.

<보기>	who	which	whose	that	what	where	when	why

1 I heard the reason ________ Leah doesn't like Carter.

2 He is the chef ________ restaurant is always crowded.

3 The movie is about a boy and a dog ________ grew up together.

4 The end of the story was different from ________ people expected.

5 The doll ________ my uncle gave me looks cute.

6 This is the park ________ I take a walk every morning.

7 Yesterday was the day ________ Hailey arrived in Korea.

8 The man ________ caused the car accident was arrested.

B 다음 문장에서 생략된 부분을 넣어 완전한 문장을 쓰시오. (단, that은 쓰지 마시오.)

1 The girl watering the plant is Sophia.

→ ____.

2 Grace found the smartwatch she lost last week.

→ ____.

3 He read a novel written by Shakespeare.

→ ____.

4 The police officer we saw on the news was brave.

→ ____.

5 They are eating the sandwiches sold on the street.

→ ____.

6 I miss the teacher I met in the second grade.

→ ____.

C 우리말과 같도록 괄호 안의 말을 알맞게 배열하시오.

1 거북이는 아주 오래 사는 동물이다. (lives, an, which, animal, long, really)
= A turtle is ______________________________.

2 네가 너의 스케치북에 그린 것을 내가 봐도 되니? (drew, your, what, in, sketchbook, you)
= May I look at ______________________________?

3 1월 1일은 새로운 해가 시작되는 날이다. (when, the, begins, year, day, new, the)
= January 1 is ______________________________.

4 내가 지난여름에 갔던 그 섬은 아름다웠다. (I, last, the, where, summer, island, went)
= ______________________________ was beautiful.

5 너는 시장에서 원하는 것은 어떤 것이든지 골라도 된다. (want, anything, the, you, market, that, in)
= You can pick ______________________________.

6 Henry는 숙제를 끝낼 수 없었던 이유를 설명했다. (he, the, reason, finish, homework, couldn't, why, the)
= Henry explained ______________________________.

D 다음은 Katie의 친구들에 대한 설명이다. 관계대명사를 이용하여 문장을 완성하시오. (단, that은 쓰지 마시오.)

Jonathan	He likes to draw cartoons.
Lily	She is good at playing the guitar.
Evan	Katie met him at the tennis club.
Caroline	Katie goes to school with her every day.

1 Jonathan is the boy ______________________________.

2 Lily is the girl ______________________________.

3 Evan is the boy ______________________________.

4 Caroline is the girl with ______________________________.

Chapter Test

[1-3] 다음 빈칸에 들어갈 알맞은 것을 고르시오.

1

Sarah is the girl ________ is in my class.

① who ② which ③ whose
④ whom ⑤ what

2

1990 is the year ________ he first met his wife.

① how ② where ③ when
④ which ⑤ why

3

Look at the old man and his dog ________ are crossing the bridge.

① whom ② where ③ why
④ that ⑤ whose

4 다음 우리말을 알맞게 영작한 것은?

Kathy는 그녀가 초대받았던 그 파티에 갔다.

① Kathy went to the party she was invited.
② Kathy went to the party to she was invited.
③ Kathy went to the party who she was invited to.
④ Kathy went to the party which she was invited to.
⑤ Kathy went to the party to that she was invited.

서술형

[5-6] 다음 두 문장의 의미가 같도록 빈칸에 알맞은 관계부사를 쓰시오.

5

We are looking for a hotel at which we can stay during vacation.
→ We are looking for a hotel ________ we can stay during vacation.

6

John found out the reason for which his sister was angry.
→ John found out the reason ________ his sister was angry.

[7-8] 다음 중 어법상 어색한 것을 고르시오.

7

① I heard why she refused to join the club.
② Can you tell me the way how I can use the copy machine?
③ Let's go to a pool where everyone can swim safely.
④ He visited the city in which he was born.
⑤ I forgot the time when the movie starts.

8

① He came up with an idea which was creative.
② Tell me everything that you know about Jim.
③ Kelly found the bag she was searching for.
④ The person from whom I borrowed the book is Josh.
⑤ She will buy a bicycle which color is blue.

서술형

[9-10] 우리말과 같도록 괄호 안의 말을 활용하여 빈칸에 쓰시오.

9

나는 정직한 사람들을 좋아한다. (be, honest)

= I like people ________ ________ ________.

10

어제는 Logan이 시험에 통과한 날이었다. (pass, the exam)

= Yesterday was the day ________ ________ ________ ________ ________.

[11-12] 다음 빈칸에 들어갈 말이 순서대로 짝지어진 것을 고르시오.

11

- The bird ________ is resting in the nest is cute.
- Reading a newspaper is ________ I do every morning.

① what - what ② what - that
③ which - what ④ which - that
⑤ that - that

12

- Bamboo is the only plant ________ pandas eat.
- We saw a tree ________ leaves were very large.

① that - whose ② which - which
③ that - which ④ which - who
⑤ who - whose

서술형

13 다음 빈칸에 알맞은 말을 <보기>에서 한 번씩만 골라 쓰시오.

<보기> who that what

(1) Let us know anything ________ you need.

(2) My friends were surprised at ________ they found in the box.

(3) The lady ________ is waving at us is my aunt.

14 다음 중 어법상 바른 것은?

① A lemon is a fruit who is sour and yellow.
② My cat lost the toy mouse with that it plays.
③ This is the apartment when my family lives.
④ Listening to music is which he loves.
⑤ You are the first guest that visited our home.

15 다음 빈칸에 공통으로 들어갈 알맞은 것은?

- Mr. Stevens bought a camera ________ is very useful.
- I told my teacher the reason for ________ I didn't bring my homework.

① what ② that ③ which
④ who ⑤ why

16 다음 중 밑줄 친 부분을 생략할 수 없는 것은?

① Dylan is the only one <u>that</u> I trust.
② He's the comedian <u>whom</u> we talked about.
③ The kid <u>who is</u> running in the playground looks excited.
④ She has a brother <u>that</u> graduated from elementary school.
⑤ The after-school program <u>which</u> I wanted to join was canceled.

고난도

17 다음 중 밑줄 친 who의 쓰임이 나머지 넷과 다른 것은?

① Dean is a student who is interested in science.
② We couldn't find out who left all the presents.
③ I thanked everyone who gave me a hand.
④ The man who is wearing jeans looks so young.
⑤ Angela is a lovely girl who lives next door.

서술형

[18-19] 알맞은 관계사를 이용하여 다음 두 문장을 한 문장으로 연결하시오.

18

I'm going to a river. It has a wonderful bridge.
→ I'm going to a river ______________
______________.

19

Tony is the friend. I go to the gym with him.
→ Tony is the friend ______________
______________.

서술형

20 주어진 <조건>에 맞게 다음 두 문장을 한 문장으로 연결하시오.

My mom still remembers the time. We went to her favorite singer's concert at that time.

<조건> 1. 관계부사를 사용하시오.
2. the time을 사용하시오.

= ______________
______________.

서술형

[21-23] 다음 문장에서 어법상 어색한 부분을 찾아 쓰고 바르게 고쳐 쓰시오.

21

A small bracelet was all whose Janet purchased.

______________ → ______________

22

The man is blamed for which he did.

______________ → ______________

23

January is the month where my sister was born.

______________ → ______________

고난도

24 다음 빈칸에 들어갈 관계사가 나머지 넷과 다른 것은?

① We didn't believe ________ Mark said.
② ________ the teacher taught us was difficult to understand.
③ My uncle gave me ________ I wanted for my birthday.
④ Jim remembers ________ he saw on the street last night.
⑤ Sammy is a girl ________ dream is to become a singer.

Chapter

10

접속사

접속사는 단어와 단어, 구와 구, 절과 절을 연결하는 말이다.

UNIT 01 | 시간/이유/결과를 나타내는 접속사

1 시간을 나타내는 접속사

❶ when(~할 때), as(~하고 있을 때, ~하면서), while(~하는 동안), as soon as(~하자마자)

When I was an elementary school student, I was short.
Jackson met Miranda **as** he was going home.
Do not watch TV **while** you're having dinner.
He turned on the lights **as soon as** he entered the room.

❷ before(~하기 전에), after(~한 후에)

My brother did his homework **before** he played computer games.
After Erica finishes jogging, she always drinks lemonade.

❸ until[till](~할 때까지), since(~한 이후로)

We couldn't go on a picnic **until[till]** the rain stopped.
I have known him **since** I was 14 years old.

TIP 시간을 나타내는 부사절에서는 미래시제 대신 현재시제를 쓴다.
She'll wash the dishes *before* her parents (~~will come~~, **come**) back.

2 이유를 나타내는 접속사

because, since, as(~하기 때문에)

I got a high score on the math test **because** I studied hard.
Since she had the flu, she didn't come to school today.
As Eric told a lie before, they don't trust him.

TIP '~ 때문에'라는 의미의 **because of** 뒤에는 명사(구)가 온다.
I woke up early **because of** *the noise*.

3 결과를 나타내는 접속사

❶ so(그래서)

Mr. Bennett missed the bus, **so** he was late for the meeting.

❷ so ~ that …(너무 ~해서 …한)

The weather was **so** cold **that** I wore a coat.

Smart Check 다음 빈칸에 들어갈 알맞은 것을 고르시오.

1 ________ today is Sunday, the bank isn't open.
① When ② Since ③ After

2 Someone called my name ________ I was walking down the street.
① while ② so ③ that

Practice

Answers p.15

A 괄호 안에서 알맞은 것을 고르시오.

1 (When / So) I was asleep, I heard someone shouting outside.
2 He was tired (until / because) he played soccer for two hours.
3 Natalie has lived in Seoul (as / since) she was five years old.
4 (Before / Until) I went to school, I dropped by the pharmacy.
5 The wind is too strong, (as soon as / so) the windows are shaking.

drop by ~에 들르다
pharmacy 명 약국
shake 동 흔들리다

B 다음 빈칸에 가장 알맞은 말을 <보기>에서 한 번씩만 골라 쓰시오.

<보기>	as soon as	before	until	since	so

1 ____________ I arrive home, I'm going to take a shower.
2 The kids stayed awake ____________ the TV show ended.
3 ____________ Olivia likes Jacob, she keeps looking at him.
4 My bedroom was too cold ____________ I turned on the heater.
5 We didn't want to cook, ____________ we ordered hamburgers.

stay awake 자지 않고 깨어 있다
turn on ~을 켜다

C 다음 문장의 밑줄 친 부분을 바르게 고쳐 쓰시오.

1 They will open the store after they <u>will prepare</u> everything.
→ ____________

2 I was very excited <u>because of</u> the concert was fantastic.
→ ____________

3 Lucas was so busy <u>when</u> he couldn't go to Emily's party.
→ ____________

prepare 동 준비하다
fantastic 형 환상적인

D 우리말과 같도록 괄호 안의 말을 활용하여 빈칸에 쓰시오.

1 내가 병원에 입원했던 동안, 많은 친구들이 왔다. (stay)
= ________ ________ ________ in the hospital, many friends came.

2 우리는 눈 때문에 여행을 취소했다. (the snow)
= We canceled our trip ________ ________ ________ ________.

3 모기가 너무 빠르게 날고 있어서 나는 그것을 잡을 수 없다. (fast)
= The mosquito is flying ________ ________ ________ I can't catch it.

4 너는 몸 상태가 나아질 때까지 휴식을 취하는 것이 낫겠다. (feel better)
= You had better rest ________ ________ ________ ________.

cancel 동 취소하다
mosquito 명 모기
rest 동 휴식을 취하다

Chapter 10 접속사

Hackers Grammar Smart Level 2

UNIT 02 조건/양보를 나타내는 접속사, 접속사 that

1 조건을 나타내는 접속사

❶ if(만약 ~한다면)

If you're hungry, I can make you some soup.

❷ unless(= if ~ not)(만약 ~하지 않는다면)

Unless I save more money, I can't buy the camera.
= **If** I do**n't** save more money, I can't buy the camera.

TIP 조건을 나타내는 부사절에서는 미래시제 대신 현재시제를 쓴다.
If you (~~will follow~~, **follow**) the arrow, you'll find the park.

2 양보를 나타내는 접속사

although[though](비록 ~이지만)

Although[**Though**] he turned on the air conditioner, it is still hot.

3 that(~이라는 것)

that이 이끄는 명사절은 문장 안에서 주어, 목적어, 보어로 쓰인다.

❶ 주어
that절이 주어로 쓰일 때는 주로 주어 자리에 가주어 it을 쓰고 진주어 that절을 뒤로 보낸다.

That he won the first prize in the competition is surprising.
= **It** is surprising **that** he won the first prize in the competition.

❷ 목적어
that절이 동사 think, believe, say, hear 등의 목적어로 쓰일 때는 that을 생략할 수 있다.

We believe (**that**) Anna lied to all of us.

❸ 보어

The issue is **that** global warming is getting serious.

Smart Check 다음 빈칸에 들어갈 알맞은 것을 고르시오.

1 I couldn't speak well on the stage ________ I practiced a lot.
① that ② although ③ if

2 If you ________ up all night, you'll be very sleepy tomorrow.
① to stay ② will stay ③ stay

3 Ms. Evans thinks ________ her son wants to raise a dog.
① that ② unless ③ though

Practice

Answers p.15

A 괄호 안에서 알맞은 것을 고르시오.

1 (If / Unless) you have any questions, please ask me.

2 (If / Unless) there is a heavy storm, the flight won't be canceled.

3 (If / Although) Anna studied hard, she didn't pass the exam.

4 Justin won't come to the party unless you (invite / don't invite) him.

5 If you (send / will send) the letter today, I'll get it tomorrow.

flight 명 항공편
pass 동 통과하다

B 다음 두 문장의 의미가 같도록 문장을 완성하시오.

1 The air pollution will get worse if we don't protect our environment.
→ The air pollution will get worse ______________________.

2 Unless you have a ticket, you can't enter the concert hall.
→ ______________________, you can't enter the concert hall.

3 If Leah doesn't listen to the teacher's advice, she will regret it.
→ ______________________, she will regret it.

air pollution 대기 오염
protect 동 보호하다
environment 명 환경
regret 동 후회하다

C 밑줄 친 that절의 역할을 <보기>에서 골라 그 기호를 쓰시오.

<보기>	ⓐ 주어	ⓑ 목적어	ⓒ 보어

1 I think that Bryan is the best soccer player on our team. [ ]

2 It is disappointing that you made the same mistake. [ ]

3 The fact is that we can't get to the class on time. [ ]

4 Claire heard that her friend will move to another school. [ ]

fact 명 사실
get 동 도착하다
on time 제시간에

D 우리말과 같도록 괄호 안의 말을 활용하여 빈칸에 쓰시오.

1 만약 눈이 많이 온다면, 우리는 거기에 갈 수 없을 것이다. (snow)
= ________ ________ ________ a lot, we won't be able to go there.

2 비록 그녀는 큰 집에 살지 않지만 그녀의 집에 만족한다. (live)
= ________ ________ ________ ________ in a big house, she is satisfied with her house.

3 각각의 구성원이 서로 다른 의견을 가지고 있다는 것은 흥미로웠다. (interesting)
= ________ ________ ________ ________ each member had a different opinion.

be satisfied with ~에 만족하다
opinion 명 의견

UNIT 03 | 명령문 + and/or, 상관접속사

1 명령문 + and/or

❶ 「명령문 + and ~」(…해라, 그러면 ~)
이때 명령문은 조건을 나타내는 접속사 if를 이용하여 바꿔 쓸 수 있다.

Take this bus, **and** you'll get to the mall.
→ **If** you **take** this bus, you'll get to the mall.

❷ 「명령문 + or ~」(…해라, 그렇지 않으면 ~)
이때 명령문은 조건을 나타내는 접속사 if ~ not이나 unless를 이용하여 바꿔 쓸 수 있다.

Call your parents, **or** they'll worry about you.
→ **If** you **don't call** your parents, they'll worry about you.
→ **Unless** you **call** your parents, they'll worry about you.

2 상관접속사

두 개 이상의 단어가 짝을 이뤄 문법적으로 대등한 단어와 단어, 구와 구, 절과 절을 연결하는 말이다.

❶ both A and B(A와 B 둘 다)

Oliver can speak **both** *Italian* **and** *French*.

❷ not only A but (also) B(= B as well as A)(A뿐만 아니라 B도)

Amanda is **not only** *selfish* **but** (**also**) *mean*.
= Amanda is *mean* **as well as** *selfish*.

❸ either A or B(A나 B 둘 중 하나)

I'd like to buy **either** *a desktop* **or** *a laptop*.

❹ neither A nor B(A도 B도 아닌)

She could **neither** *laugh* **nor** *cry*.

TIP **both A and B 뒤에는 항상 복수동사를 쓰고, 나머지 상관접속사 뒤에 오는 동사는 B에 수일치시킨다.**
Both *my mom* **and** *dad* (~~works~~, **work**) at a bank.
Neither *this movie* **nor** *that movie* (~~are~~, **is**) moving.

Smart Check 다음 빈칸에 들어갈 알맞은 것을 고르시오.

1 Tell me your phone number, ________ I'll call you tonight.
① or ② but ③ and

2 He's interested in ________ drawing pictures and writing novels.
① both ② not only ③ either

3 Chris can go to school either by bus ________ on foot.
① nor ② or ③ also

Practice

Answers p.15

A 괄호 안에서 알맞은 것을 고르시오.

1 Wear a jacket, (and / or) you'll catch a cold.

2 Go upstairs, (and / or) you'll find the teachers' room.

3 (Both / Neither) Kyle and Jackson are going to the museum.

4 I would like to have either chicken (or / nor) beef.

catch a cold 감기에 걸리다
upstairs 뷰 위층으로
teacher's room 교무실
beef 명 소고기

B 다음 두 문장의 의미가 같도록 빈칸에 알맞은 말을 쓰시오.

1 Unless you come to class on time, you'll be in trouble.
→ Come to class on time, ________ you'll be in trouble.

2 If you exercise regularly, you'll get in shape.
→ Exercise regularly, ________ you'll get in shape.

3 The documentary is interesting as well as educational.
→ The documentary is ________ ________ educational ________ ________ interesting .

4 This sofa isn't comfortable. This sofa isn't cheap, either.
→ This sofa is ________ comfortable ________ cheap.

get in shape 좋은 몸 상태를 유지하다
educational 형 교육적인

C 다음 빈칸에 알맞은 형태의 be동사를 쓰시오. (단, 현재시제로 쓰시오.)

1 Neither this book nor those pencils ________ mine.

2 Either my brother or I ________ going to water the plants.

3 Both New York and Paris ________ popular with many tourists.

4 Not only Chloe but also her sister ________ friendly to everyone.

water 동 물을 주다
plant 명 식물
tourist 명 관광객
friendly 형 친절한

D 우리말과 같도록 괄호 안의 말을 활용하여 문장을 완성하시오.

1 불을 꺼라, 그러면 너는 에너지를 절약할 수 있다. (save energy)
= Turn off the lights, ________________________________.

2 Wilson씨는 성실할 뿐만 아니라 관대하기도 하다. (diligent, generous)
= Mr. Wilson is ________________________________.

3 조심해서 걸어라, 그렇지 않으면 너는 빙판에서 미끄러질 것이다. (slip on the ice)
= Walk carefully, ________________________________.

4 학생들은 시험에서 검은색 펜이나 파란색 펜 둘 중 하나를 사용해야 한다. (a black pen, a blue pen)
= Students should use ________________________________ on the test.

save 동 절약하다
generous 형 관대한
slip 동 미끄러지다

Writing Exercise

A 다음 빈칸에 가장 알맞은 말을 <보기>에서 골라 쓰시오.

<보기>	because he had a fever	if you like reading books
	until her friends arrived	although I ate dinner
	as soon as I called him	when my dog sees a stranger

1 ________________, it barks loudly.

2 Mr. Jackson couldn't go to work ________________.

3 ________________, I still feel hungry.

4 Sharon had to wait too long ________________.

5 You can join our book club ________________.

6 He answered the phone ________________.

B 우리말과 같도록 <보기 1>의 접속사와 <보기 2>의 말을 활용하여 문장을 완성하시오.

<보기 1>	as	before	after	since	because of	unless

<보기 2>	drink hot tea	make a decision	get older
	be young	the rain	change one's attitude

1 너는 따뜻한 차를 마신 후에 기분이 나아질 것이다.
= You'll feel better ________________.

2 Ward씨는 비 때문에 오늘 조심해서 운전해야 한다.
= Ms. Ward should drive carefully today ________________.

3 만약 그가 그의 태도를 바꾸지 않는다면, 그는 성공하지 못할지도 모른다.
= He might not be able to succeed ________________.

4 사람들은 나이 들면서, 그들의 건강에 대해 더 걱정한다.
= ________________, they care about their health more.

5 내가 어렸을 때 이후로 나의 집 뒤에 큰 나무가 있어왔다.
= There has been a big tree behind my house ________________.

6 나는 결정을 내리기 전에 모든 정보를 확인해야 한다.
= I have to check all the information ________________.

Answers p.15

C 우리말과 같도록 괄호 안의 말을 활용하여 문장을 완성하시오.

1 이 의자는 너무 불편해서 나는 그것을 반품할 것이다. (uncomfortable, return)
= This chair is ______________________.

2 더 크게 말해라, 그렇지 않으면 나는 너의 목소리를 들을 수 없을 것이다. (hear, voice)
= Speak louder, ______________________.

3 William은 러시아가 세계에서 가장 큰 나라인 것을 알고 있다. (Russia, big, country)
= William knows ______________________ in the world.

4 신중하게 생각해라, 그러면 너는 실수하지 않을 것이다. (make mistakes)
= Think carefully, ______________________.

5 이 시는 어려워서, 많은 사람들이 그것을 이해할 수 없다. (many, understand)
= This poem is difficult, ______________________.

6 만약 네가 그에게 미안하다고 말하지 않는다면, 그는 너에게 실망할 것이다. (not, say sorry to)
= ______________________, he will be disappointed with you.

D 다음은 학생 네 명의 말할 수 있는 언어, 취미, 성격을 나타내는 표이다. 괄호 안의 말을 활용하여 문장을 완성하시오.

	language	hobby	personality
Daniel	English, Spanish	flute, soccer	honest, confident
Matthew	Spanish, Italian	violin, soccer	shy, friendly
Jessica	English, Italian	piano, tennis	active, brave
Nancy	French, Italian	violin, badminton	gentle, friendly

1 ______________________ speak Spanish. (both)

2 ______________________ is friendly. (not only)

3 ______________________ enjoys playing soccer. (neither)

4 ______________________ likes playing the violin. (as well as)

Chapter Test

[1-3] 다음 빈칸에 들어갈 가장 알맞은 것을 고르시오.

1 ________ I left home late, I arrived on time.

① That ② Since ③ Because
④ If ⑤ Although

2 Buy the ticket now, ________ you'll have to pay more for it later.

① or ② and ③ but
④ so ⑤ unless

3 ________ you aren't taking the bus, you should get out of the line.

① Unless ② If ③ After
④ That ⑤ So

4 다음 중 밑줄 친 부분의 쓰임이 어색한 것은?

① Tim doesn't have many friends because he is shy.
② Please stay seated until the nurse calls your name.
③ Though Janice didn't have enough money, she couldn't buy the skirt.
④ I visited the N Seoul Tower while I was in Seoul.
⑤ As his sister was sleeping, he couldn't listen to music on a speaker.

서술형

[5-6] 다음 두 문장의 의미가 같도록 빈칸에 알맞은 말을 쓰시오.

5 Jim can play not only the piano but also the flute.
→ Jim can play ________ ________ ________ ________ ________ ________ ________.

6 Take a rest, and you'll feel better.
→ ________ ________ ________ ________ ________, you'll feel better.

7 다음 중 어법상 어색한 것은?

① He got up after the sun came up.
② Not only Jess but also Kate like K-pop.
③ I think that Sam is the kindest boy in my class.
④ This English book is so easy that kids can understand it.
⑤ As soon as Josh reached Busan, he went to the beach.

8 다음 밑줄 친 since와 의미가 같은 것은?

Since my grandfather is wise, I often ask him for advice.

① That ② Though ③ Until
④ And ⑤ Because

서술형

[9-11] 우리말과 같도록 괄호 안의 말을 활용하여 빈칸에 쓰시오.

9 만약 네가 공부를 열심히 하지 않는다면, 너는 시험에 떨어질 것이다. (study, hard)

= ________ ________ ________ ________, you will fail the test.

10 Lauren과 그녀의 친구 둘 다 어제 학교에 늦었다. (be, late)

= ________ ________ ________ ________ ________ ________ ________ for school yesterday.

11 Eric은 그의 엄마가 오시기 전에 방 청소를 끝낼 것이다. (mom, come)

= Eric will finish cleaning the room ________ ________ ________ ________.

12 다음 빈칸에 들어갈 말이 순서대로 짝지어진 것은?

- I won't talk to him ________ he doesn't apologize.
- The building was damaged ________ the earthquake.

① if - because
② if - because of
③ unless - because
④ unless - because of
⑤ till - because

13 다음 중 밑줄 친 as의 의미가 나머지 넷과 다른 것은?

① As the baby is cute, he is loved by everyone.
② As she was tired, she quickly fell asleep.
③ As we are on the top of the mountain, we feel cold.
④ As he was washing the dishes, he listened to the radio.
⑤ As my computer was broken, I couldn't do my homework.

14 다음 중 어법상 바른 것은?

① Unless Josh doesn't come home early, his parents will get angry.
② Drink some water, and you will be thirsty later.
③ The rock festival will be canceled if it will rain.
④ The weather was too hot that I bought a fan.
⑤ You have to be careful when you cross a road.

서술형

[15-16] 알맞은 접속사를 이용하여 다음 두 문장을 한 문장으로 연결하시오.

15 The novel was great. So, Jimmy read it three times.
→ Jimmy read the novel three times ____________ it was great.

16 Alice lied to me. However, I still trust her.
→ ____________ Alice lied to me, I still trust her.

고난도

17 다음 빈칸에 들어갈 접속사가 나머지 넷과 다른 것은?

① ________ I couldn't hear from my friend anymore, I felt sad.
② ________ the song makes me happy, I love it.
③ ________ they lost the baseball match, they were glad to participate.
④ ________ Tom was hungry, he ate more than usual.
⑤ ________ the artist's works were beautiful, she became famous.

18 주어진 문장의 밑줄 친 that과 쓰임이 같은 것은?

> That you forgot my birthday is disappointing.

① It is surprising that we won the contest.
② I think that the washing machine is broken.
③ The problem is that his health is getting worse.
④ She believed that she could get a good grade.
⑤ The truth is that the politician is hiding something.

서술형

19 다음 문장에서 어법상 어색한 부분을 찾아 쓰고 바르게 고쳐 쓰시오.

> Neither Thomas and Jenny takes the after-school class.

________________ → ________________

서술형

20 다음 세 문장의 의미가 같도록 빈칸에 알맞은 말을 쓰시오.

> Finish your meal, or you can't have any dessert.
> → ________ you don't finish your meal, you can't have any dessert.
> → ________ you finish your meal, you can't have any dessert.

[21-22] 다음 빈칸에 공통으로 들어갈 알맞은 것을 고르시오.

21

> • Be nice to them, ________ they'll like you.
> • Both cats ________ dogs are mammals.

① and ② so ③ after
④ or ⑤ that

22

> • He stayed in bed ________ he was sick.
> • Sam and I've been friends ________ we were 13.

① because ② although ③ since
④ until ⑤ if

서술형 고난도

23 다음 빈칸에 알맞은 접속사를 <보기>에서 한 번씩만 골라 쓰시오.

> <보기> because if though

(1) I have a lot of free time ________ the summer vacation has begun.
(2) Nobody bought his painting ________ it was excellent.
(3) We can give you a hand ________ you want.

Chapter

11

비교구문

둘 이상의 대상의 성질·상태·수량 등을 서로 견주어 비교하는 것을 비교구문이라고 한다. 형용사나 부사를 그대로 사용하거나 형태를 바꿔 원급, 비교급, 최상급 비교를 표현할 수 있다.

UNIT 01 원급/비교급/최상급 비교

1 「as + 원급 + as」: …만큼 ~한/하게

비교하는 두 대상의 정도가 비슷하거나 같음을 나타낸다.

Yesterday was **as cloudy as** today.

Kevin jumps **as high as** I do. = Kevin jumps **as high as** me.

→ as나 than 뒤의 「주어 + 동사」는 목적격으로 바꿔 쓸 수 있다.

TIP **「not + as[so] + 원급 + as」: …만큼 ~하지 않은/않게**

This room is **not as[so] big as** that room.

2 「비교급 + than」: …보다 더 ~한/하게

비교하는 두 대상 간 정도의 차이를 나타낸다.

Your hand is **smaller than** mine.

Janet is speaking **more loudly than** you.

TIP **비교급 앞에 much, even, far, a lot 등을 써서 '훨씬'이라는 의미로 비교급을 강조할 수 있다.**

Cars are **much** *safer* than motorcycles.

3 「the + 최상급」: 가장 ~한/하게

셋 이상의 비교 대상 중 하나의 정도가 가장 높음을 나타내며, 보통 in이나 of를 사용하여 비교 범위를 나타낸다.

Marie is **the tallest** girl *in her school*. <in + 장소/집단>

This watch was **the most luxurious** *of the three*. <of + 비교 대상>

4 비교급과 최상급 만드는 법

비교급/최상급 만드는 법		원급 - 비교급 - 최상급
대부분의 형용사/부사	+ -er/-est	great - great**er** - great**est**
-e로 끝나는 형용사/부사	+ -r/-st	nice - nice**r** - nice**st**
「자음 + y」로 끝나는 형용사/부사	y를 i로 바꾸고 + -er/-est	tasty - tast**ier** - tast**iest**
「단모음 + 단자음」으로 끝나는 형용사/부사	마지막 자음을 한 번 더 쓰고 + -er/-est	hot - hot**ter** - hot**test**
대부분의 2음절 이상인 형용사/부사	more/most + 원급	useful - **more** useful - **most** useful
「형용사 + ly」 형태의 부사		gladly - **more** gladly - **most** gladly
불규칙하게 변하는 형용사/부사	good/well - **better** - **best** bad/badly/ill - **worse** - **worst**	many/much - **more** - **most** little - **less** - **least**

Smart Check 다음 빈칸에 들어갈 알맞은 것을 고르시오.

1 Reading a book is as ________ as watching TV.

① more interesting ② most interesting ③ interesting

Practice

Answers p.16

A 괄호 안에서 알맞은 것을 고르시오.

1 His smartphone is (new / newer) than mine.

2 I arrived at the party as (late / later) as Sharon did.

3 Gold is (very / much) more valuable than bronze.

4 Mount Everest is (higher / the highest) mountain in the world.

valuable 형 값비싼, 가치가 큰
bronze 명 청동

B 괄호 안의 말을 알맞은 형태로 바꿔 문장을 완성하시오.

1 A turtle can't move as ________________ as a rabbit. (quickly)

2 A sofa is ________________ than a bench. (comfortable)

3 Michelle is ________________ student in this class. (smart)

4 I usually sleep ________________ than my brother. (little)

quickly 부 빠르게
comfortable 형 편안한, 편한
usually 부 보통

C 괄호 안의 말을 활용하여 다음 문장을 한 문장으로 바꿔 쓰시오.

1 My sister is 9 years old. I am 14 years old. (young)
→ My sister is ________________ me.

2 The black jacket is $100. The white jacket is also $100. (expensive)
→ The white jacket is ________________ the black jacket.

3 Thomas can lift a 15-kg box. Anthony can lift a 10-kg box. (strong)
→ Thomas is ________________ Anthony.

4 Friday was 25℃. Saturday was 23℃. Sunday was 28℃. (hot)
→ Sunday was ________________ of the three days.

young 형 어린, 젊은
lift 동 들어 올리다

D 우리말과 같도록 괄호 안의 말을 활용하여 빈칸에 쓰시오.

1 나는 나의 가장 친한 친구만큼 부지런하지 않다. (diligent)
= I'm ________ ________ ________ ________ my best friend.

2 Helen은 나보다 더 밝게 웃는다. (brightly)
= Helen smiles ________ ________ ________ I do.

3 저것은 이 도시에서 가장 유명한 건물이다. (famous, building)
= That is ________ ________ ________ ________ in this city.

4 공연 전, 주연 배우는 나머지 사람들보다 훨씬 더 불안해했다. (nervous)
= Before the performance, the main actor was ________ ________
________ ________ the others.

diligent 형 부지런한
brightly 부 밝게
famous 형 유명한
performance 명 공연

UNIT 02 비교구문을 이용한 표현

1 **「배수사 + as + 원급 + as」**: …보다 -배 더 ~한/하게

「배수사 + 비교급 + than」으로 바꿔 쓸 수 있다.

This rope is **three times as long as** that one.
= This rope is **three times longer than** that one.

Your bag is **five times as heavy as** her bag.
= Your bag is **five times heavier than** her bag.

---

2 **「as + 원급 + as + possible」**: 가능한 한 ~한/하게

「as + 원급 + as + 주어 + can[could]」로 바꿔 쓸 수 있다.

The students go to the library **as often as possible.**
= The students go to the library **as often as they can.**

I had to eat lunch **as quickly as possible.**
= I had to eat lunch **as quickly as I could.**

---

3 **「the + 비교급, the + 비교급」**: ~하면 할수록 더 …하다

The more you exercise, **the healthier** you will be.
The more famous the restaurant became, **the more crowded** it was.

---

4 **「비교급 + and + 비교급」**: 점점 더 ~한/하게

She's getting **better and better** after the surgery.
Computer skills are becoming **more and more important.**
→ 비교급이 「more + 원급」의 형태인 경우 「more and more + 원급」으로 쓴다.

---

5 **「one of the + 최상급 + 복수명사」**: 가장 ~한 것들 중 하나

Beethoven is **one of the greatest composers** in history.
It was **one of the most difficult questions.**

Smart Check 다음 빈칸에 들어갈 알맞은 것을 고르시오.

1 ________ we are, the more chances we have.
① The younger ② The young ③ The youngest

2 I want to try the menu as ________ as possible.
① sooner ② soon ③ soonest

Practice

Answers p.16

A 괄호 안에서 알맞은 것을 고르시오.

1 Eric can run (twice as / as twice) fast as you.

2 Bella is speaking (loudly as / as loudly as) possible.

3 Last Friday was one of the chilliest (day / days) in December.

4 The (long / longer) I stayed at the hotel, the (much / more) I liked it.

5 The movie became (more and more / most and most) interesting.

loudly 부 큰 소리로
chilly 형 추운, 쌀쌀한

B 괄호 안의 말을 알맞은 형태로 바꿔 빈칸에 쓰시오.

1 ________ ________ ________ he got, the busier he was. (popular)

2 My grandparents are five times ________ ________ me. (old)

3 The more hamburgers I had, ________ ________ I got. (full)

4 As the tornado moved, it grew ________ ________ ________. (large)

popular 형 인기 있는
full 형 배부른
tornado 명 토네이도, 회오리바람

C 다음 두 문장의 의미가 같도록 문장을 완성하시오.

1 I'll text you as soon as possible.
→ I'll text you ________________.

2 His test score is three times as high as mine.
→ His test score is ________________ mine.

3 The soccer players kicked the balls as hard as possible.
→ The soccer players kicked the balls ________________.

text 동 문자 메시지를 보내다
score 명 점수
kick 동 (발로) 차다

D 우리말과 같도록 괄호 안의 말을 활용하여 빈칸에 쓰시오.

1 해가 뜨면서, 점점 더 밝아지고 있다. (bright)
= As the sun rises, it's getting ________________.

2 코끼리는 인간보다 30배 더 빨리 음식을 먹는다. (fast)
= Elephants eat food ________________ humans.

3 우리는 가능한 한 안전하게 여행하기를 바란다. (safely)
= We hope to travel ________________.

4 너는 더 많은 책을 읽을수록 더 현명해질 것이다. (many books, wise)
= ________________ you read, ________________ you will be.

rise 동 (해·달이) 뜨다, 오르다
human 명 인간
safely 부 안전하게
wise 형 현명한

Writing Exercise

A 다음 빈칸에 알맞은 말을 <보기>에서 한 번씩만 골라 알맞은 형태로 바꿔 쓰시오.

<보기>	bad	tall	small	long	neatly	comfortable

1 Betty's hair is ____________________ than Angela's.

2 Mercury is ____________________ planet in the solar system.

3 I would like to buy a ____________________ sofa than this one.

4 He put all of his shoes on the floor ____________________ possible.

5 Kevin is 180 cm. Brian is also 180 cm. Brian is ____________________ Kevin.

6 I didn't take the medicine last night. I feel even ____________________ than yesterday.

B 우리말과 같도록 괄호 안의 말을 활용하여 문장을 완성하시오.

1 David는 그의 반에서 가장 재미있는 소년이다. (funny, boy)
= David is ________________________________ in his class.

2 나는 나무 꼭대기에 닿기 위해 가능한 한 높게 뛰었다. (high)
= I jumped ________________________________ to reach the top of the tree.

3 루브르 박물관은 프랑스에서 가장 인기 있는 관광지들 중 하나이다. (popular, tourist site)
= The Louvre is ________________________________ in France.

4 대기 오염은 점점 더 악화되고 있다. (get, bad)
= The air pollution is ________________________________.

5 역사 수업은 영어 수업만큼 흥미롭지 않다. (interesting)
= The history class is ________________________________ the English class.

6 네가 파티에 더 많은 친구들을 초대하면 할수록 더 많은 음식이 필요할 것이다. (many friends, many food)
= ____________________ you invite to the party, ____________________ you will need.

C 다음은 여러 도시의 특징을 비교하는 표이다. 괄호 안의 말을 활용하여 빈칸에 알맞은 말을 쓰시오.

도시	Seoul	Paris	Hanoi	Toronto
면적	605 km^2	105 km^2	3,359 km^2	630 km^2
인구	9,963,000	2,148,000	8,053,663	2,731,571
8월 평균 기온	29°C	25.5°C	31.5°C	22°C

1 Toronto is __________ __________ Paris. (large)

2 Seoul's population is __________ __________ of the four. (big)

3 Seoul is __________ __________ Paris in August. (warm)

4 Hanoi is __________ __________ __________ __________ Toronto. (not, cool)

D 다음 그림을 보고 괄호 안의 말을 활용하여 문장을 완성하시오.

1

2

3

4

1 The doughnut costs ____________________ a cup of coffee. (much)

2 ____________________ Aaron grew, ____________________ he became. (tall, thin)

3 The textbook is ____________________ the notebook. (three, thick)

4 Naomi runs ____________________ of the three. (fast)

Chapter Test

[1-3] 다음 빈칸에 들어갈 알맞은 것을 고르시오.

1

This action movie is ________ than that horror movie.

① long ② longer
③ more long ④ most long
⑤ longest

2

My brother is the ________ in my family.

① short ② shorter
③ shortest ④ more short
⑤ most short

3

The black dog is ________ as the white one.

① big ② bigger
③ as twice big ④ twice as big
⑤ twice as bigger

4 다음은 세 권의 책을 비교하는 표이다. 다음 표를 바르게 설명한 것은?

책	A	B	C
가격	$10	$30	$15
무게	300 g	200 g	500 g

① Book A is the heaviest book of all.
② Book B is the most expensive of the three.
③ Book B is heavier than Book A.
④ Book C is as cheap as Book A.
⑤ Book C is lighter than Book B.

서술형

[5-7] 우리말과 같도록 괄호 안의 말을 활용하여 문장을 완성하시오.

5

그 소설은 점점 더 유명해졌다. (famous)

= The novel became ____________________.

6

너는 가능한 한 일찍 올 수 있니? (early)

= Can you come ____________________?

7

금성은 태양계에서 가장 밝은 행성이다. (bright)

= Venus is ____________________ planet in the solar system.

8 다음 빈칸에 들어갈 말로 어색한 것은?

Serena speaks French ________ more fluently than me.

① much ② even ③ a lot
④ far ⑤ very

9 다음 빈칸에 공통으로 들어갈 알맞은 것은?

• My dad loves me as ________ as my mom does.
• The yellow skirt fits you ________ more perfectly than the gray skirt.

① even ② very ③ much
④ a lot ⑤ many

Answers p.17

[10-11] 다음 중 어법상 어색한 것을 고르시오.

10 ① It's getting darker and darker outside.
② Today is more cold than yesterday.
③ Henry is as tall as his teacher.
④ Cheetahs are a lot faster than horses.
⑤ This question is the most difficult on the test.

11 ① Jenna is the smarter of all my friends.
② The more you laugh, the happier you will become.
③ I am not so friendly as James is.
④ The thief ran away as quickly as possible.
⑤ This documentary is more interesting than a comedy show.

서술형

[12-13] 괄호 안의 말을 활용하여 다음 두 문장을 한 문장으로 바꿔 쓰시오.

12
- The blue bag is 30 dollars.
- The red bag is 30 dollars.

→ The blue bag costs ______________ the red bag. (much)

13
- Tim is 15 years old.
- His father is 45 years old.

→ Tim's father is ______________ Tim. (three, old)

서술형

[14-15] 다음 문장에서 어법상 어색한 부분을 찾아 쓰고 바르게 고쳐 쓰시오.

14

Diana's hair is longest than mine.

__________ → __________

15

He is one of the most talented actor in Korea.

__________ → __________

서술형

16 우리말과 같도록 주어진 <조건>에 맞게 영작하시오.

이 의자는 소파만큼 편하지 않다.

<조건>
1. this chair, comfortable, the sofa를 사용하시오.
2. 부정형을 축약하지 마시오.
3. 원급을 사용하시오.

= ______________________________.

17 다음 중 밑줄 친 부분을 바르게 고친 것은?
① Now, I feel best than an hour ago.
→ the best
② You may take a nap as more as you want.
→ most
③ The runner was the slower in the marathon.
→ the slowest
④ Sweaters are warm than t-shirts.
→ more warm
⑤ My sister's allowance is least than mine.
→ little

서술형

[18-19] 다음 두 문장의 의미가 같도록 빈칸에 알맞은 말을 쓰시오.

18

You should stretch as often as possible.
→ You should stretch ________ ________ ________ ________ ________.

19

Her room is three times bigger than mine.
→ Her room is ________ ________ ________ ________ ________ mine.

20 다음 빈칸에 들어갈 말이 순서대로 짝지어진 것은?

- My voice is ________ loud as yours.
- Vegetables are much healthier ________ junk food.

① as - so ② as - than
③ so - than ④ so - as
⑤ than - so

서술형 고난도

21 다음 글의 밑줄 친 ⓐ~ⓔ 중 어법상 어색한 것을 찾아 기호를 쓰고 바르게 고쳐 쓰시오.

When Sarah took her first dance class, she was surprised because everyone danced ⓐfar better than her. The ⓑbestest dancer in the class was Simon. Sarah wanted to dance as ⓒmore beautifully as Simon, so she asked him how to dance well. Simon said he has already taken the class ⓓten times longer than Sarah. He advised her to take the class ⓔas long as possible.

(1) ______ → ______________
(2) ______ → ______________

22 다음 중 어법상 바른 것은?

① The carrot cake is most popular in our bakery.
② Thailand is more hotter than Canada.
③ Tom's score was low than Christian's.
④ This TV screen is not as wide as that one.
⑤ My sister is generous than me.

23 다음 빈칸에 들어갈 말이 순서대로 짝지어진 것은?

As I studied more, my grades became higher.
→ ________ I studied, ________ my grades became.

① More - higher ② More - the higher
③ The more - higher ④ The more - more high
⑤ The more - the higher

고난도

24 다음 중 짝지어진 두 문장의 의미가 다른 것의 개수는?

ⓐ Give me a call as soon as possible.
→ Give me a call as soon as you can.
ⓑ Airplanes are much safer than cars.
→ Cars are as safe as airplanes.
ⓒ Kate is not as polite as her sister.
→ Kate is not so polite as her sister.
ⓓ If you leave sooner, you will arrive earlier.
→ The sooner you leave, the earlier you will arrive.
ⓔ This desk is four times heavier than that chair.
→ That chair is four times as heavy as this desk.

① 1개 ② 2개 ③ 3개
④ 4개 ⑤ 5개

Chapter

12

가정법

가정법은 사실과 반대되거나 실현 가능성이
거의 없는 일을 가정하여 말하는 것이다.

UNIT 01 가정법 과거, 가정법 과거완료

1 가정법 과거

'만약 ~한다면 …할 텐데'의 의미로 현재의 사실과 반대되거나 실현 가능성이 거의 없는 일을 가정할 때 쓴다.

If	+	주어	+	동사의 과거형 (be동사는 were)	~,	주어	+	would, could, might	+	동사원형	…

If Jake **knew** how to swim, he **wouldn't need** a life jacket.
(← As Jake doesn't know how to swim, he needs a life jacket.)

If I **were** 15 years old, I **could watch** that movie.
(← As I am not 15 years old, I can't watch that movie.)

If the computer **weren't** broken, I **could surf** the Internet.
(← As the computer is broken, I can't surf the Internet.)

TIP 가정법은 실현 가능성이 거의 없는 일을 가정할 때 쓰고, 조건문은 현재나 미래에 일어날 수 있는 상황을 나타낼 때 쓴다. 조건문의 부사절에서는 미래를 나타내더라도 현재시제를 쓴다.

If Tom **had** time, he **would take** a break. <가정법: Tom이 시간이 있을 가능성이 거의 없음>
If Tom **has** time, he **will take** a break. <조건문: Tom이 시간이 있을 가능성이 있음>

2 가정법 과거완료

'만약 ~했더라면 …했을 텐데'의 의미로 과거의 사실과 반대되는 일을 가정할 때 쓴다.

If	+	주어	+	had p.p.	~,	주어	+	would, could, might	+	have p.p.	…

If Cindy **had studied** hard, she **would have passed** the exam.
(← As Cindy didn't study hard, she didn't pass the exam.)

If the puzzle **had not been** difficult, we **could have solved** it.
(← As the puzzle was difficult, we couldn't solve it.)

Smart Check 다음 빈칸에 들어갈 알맞은 것을 고르시오.

1 If Ronald ________ an umbrella, he wouldn't get wet.
① have ② has ③ had

2 If I ________ taller, I could join the basketball team.
① am ② are ③ were

3 If you had taken the medicine, you ________ better.
① will get ② would have gotten ③ will have gotten

Practice

Answers p.18

A 괄호 안에서 알맞은 것을 고르시오.

1 If it (is / were) sunny, we would go on a picnic outside.

2 If this necklace weren't expensive, Julie (can / could) buy it.

3 If Jill had invited me, I (will go / would have gone) to her house.

4 If Adam (knew / had known) how to ski, he could go skiing with his friends.

outside 부 밖에서
necklace 명 목걸이

B 괄호 안의 말을 활용하여 가정법 문장을 완성하시오.

1 If the heater ______________, this room wouldn't be so cold. (work)

2 If I had woken up earlier, I ______________ to school. (will, not, run)

3 If the bag ______________ heavy, he could carry it. (be, not)

4 If I had had enough money, I ______________ you some. (can, lend)

work 동 작동하다
enough 형 충분한

C 다음 문장을 가정법 문장으로 바꿔 쓰시오.

1 As Brian is hurt, he can't play soccer.
→ If Brian ______________, he could play soccer.

2 As Gloria didn't get an A, she wasn't satisfied with herself.
→ If Gloria had gotten an A, she ______________ with herself.

3 As you didn't tell me your problem, you couldn't get advice.
→ If you had told me your problem, you ______________ advice.

hurt 형 다친
problem 명 문제
advice 명 조언

D 우리말과 같도록 괄호 안의 말을 활용하여 빈칸에 쓰시오.

1 만약 내가 너라면, Jacob에게 사과할 텐데. (be, apologize)
= If I ________ you, I ________ ________ to Jacob.

2 만약 우리가 역에 늦게 도착했더라면, 기차를 놓쳤을 텐데. (arrive, miss)
= If we ________ ________ late at the station, we ________ ________ ________ the train.

3 만약 나의 오빠가 바쁘지 않았더라면, 나와 함께 더 놀 수 있었을 텐데. (be, play)
= If my brother ________ ________ ________ busy, he ________ ________ ________ more with me.

4 만약 박물관이 월요일에 문을 연다면, Amy는 그 전시를 볼 텐데. (open, see)
= If the museum ________ on Monday, Amy ________ ________ the exhibit.

apologize 동 사과하다
miss 동 놓치다
exhibit 명 전시

UNIT 02

I wish 가정법, as if 가정법

1 I wish 가정법

❶ 「I wish + 가정법 과거」는 '~하면 좋을 텐데'라는 의미로 현재 이룰 수 없거나 실현 가능성이 거의 없는 일을 소망할 때 쓴다.

I wish	+	주어	+	동사의 과거형 (be동사는 were)

I wish I **were** stronger than my brother.
(← I'm sorry that I am not stronger than my brother.)

I wish I **could speak** Chinese fluently.
(← I'm sorry that I can't speak Chinese fluently.)

❷ 「I wish + 가정법 과거완료」는 '~했더라면 좋았을 텐데'라는 의미로 과거에 이루지 못한 일에 대한 아쉬움을 나타낼 때 쓴다.

I wish	+	주어	+	had p.p.

I wish I **had been** more careful.
(← I'm sorry that I wasn't more careful.)

I wish James **had not lied** to me.
(← I'm sorry that James lied to me.)

2 as if 가정법

❶ 「as if + 가정법 과거」는 '마치 ~인 것처럼'이라는 의미로 주절의 시제와 같은 시점의 사실과 반대되는 일을 가정한다.

주어	+	동사	+	as if	+	주어	+	동사의 과거형 (be동사는 were)

He talks **as if** he **were** a doctor.
(← In fact, he isn't a doctor.)

❷ 「as if + 가정법 과거완료」는 '마치 ~이었던 것처럼'이라는 의미로 주절의 시제보다 앞선 시점의 사실과 반대되는 일을 가정한다.

주어	+	동사	+	as if	+	주어	+	had p.p.

Jessica speaks **as if** she **had finished** her homework.
(← In fact, Jessica didn't finish her homework.)

Smart Check 다음 빈칸에 들어갈 알맞은 것을 고르시오.

1 I wish I ________ in New York now.
① am ② were ③ had been

2 Jonathan acts as if he ________ the answer.
① known ② know ③ knew

Practice

Answers p.18

A 괄호 안에서 알맞은 것을 고르시오.

1 I'm not good at singing. I wish I (sang / had sung) well.

2 Fred acts as if he (saw / had seen) the thief. But he didn't see anyone.

3 It's too hot outside, so Hannah feels as if she (were / has been) in the desert.

4 I wish I (won / had won) a gold medal, but I got a silver medal.

act 동 행동하다
thief 명 도둑
desert 명 사막

B 괄호 안의 동사를 활용하여 가정법 문장을 완성하시오.

1 I didn't listen to my mother's advice. I wish I ____________ her advice. (take)

2 I need to print something right now. I wish I ____________ how to use this printer. (know)

3 Steven seems as if he ____________ his wallet. In fact, he didn't lose it. (lose)

take 동 받아들이다
print 동 출력하다
seem 동 (~처럼) 보이다

C 다음 문장을 가정법 문장으로 바꿀 때 빈칸에 알맞은 말을 쓰시오.

1 In fact, the car wasn't repaired.
→ The car looks as if it ________ ________ ________.

2 I'm sorry that I can't go to the jazz festival.
→ I wish I ________ ________ to the jazz festival.

3 In fact, Lisa isn't a magician.
→ Lisa acts as if she ________ a magician.

4 I'm sorry that I didn't buy you a new backpack.
→ I wish I ________ ________ you a new backpack.

repair 동 수리하다
magician 명 마술사

D 우리말과 같도록 괄호 안의 말을 활용하여 가정법 문장을 완성하시오.

1 나의 부모님이 나와 함께 더 많은 시간을 보내면 좋을 텐데. (spend)
= ______________________ more time with me.

2 연설은 마치 흥미로운 것처럼 들린다. (be)
= The speech sounds ______________________ interesting.

3 Lucas는 마치 그 책을 이미 읽었던 것처럼 말한다. (read)
= Lucas talks ______________________ the book already.

4 내가 제시간에 보고서를 제출했더라면 좋았을 텐데. (turn)
= ______________________ in the report on time.

speech 명 연설
already 부 이미
turn in ~을 제출하다

Writing Exercise

A 다음 문장을 가정법 문장으로 바꿔 쓰시오.

1 As the test wasn't easy, Robert couldn't get a perfect score.
→ If ______________________.

2 As you aren't in Paris, you can't meet Alexa.
→ If ______________________.

3 As Daniel didn't have free time, he wouldn't go to the gym.
→ If ______________________.

4 As I'm not a millionaire, I can't buy a yacht.
→ If ______________________.

5 I'm sorry that you feel so disappointed.
→ I wish ______________________.

6 In fact, the girl doesn't have questions to ask.
→ The girl seems as if ______________________.

B 우리말과 같도록 괄호 안의 말을 활용하여 가정법 문장을 완성하시오.

1 Ashley는 마치 아이인 것처럼 종종 행동한다. (act, be a child)
= Ashley often ______________________.

2 내가 나의 반 친구들보다 더 빨리 달릴 수 있다면 좋을 텐데. (run faster, classmates)
= I wish ______________________.

3 만약 내가 어제 그를 만났더라면, 그와 이야기를 많이 했을 텐데. (see, talk with)
= If ____________ yesterday, I ____________ a lot.

4 만약 오늘이 토요일이라면, 나의 아버지는 일하러 가지 않으실 텐데. (be, go to work)
= If ____________ today, my father ____________.

5 그 남자는 마치 그 사고에 대해 아무것도 몰랐던 것처럼 말한다. (talk, know nothing)
= The man ______________________ about the accident.

Answers p.18

C 우리말과 같도록 괄호 안의 말을 알맞게 배열하시오.

1 내가 오디션에서 더 자신감 있었더라면 좋았을 텐데. (more, had, been, confident, I)
= I wish ______________________ at the audition.

2 Noah는 마치 모든 비밀을 아는 것처럼 보인다. (if, seems, as, knew, he)
= Noah ______________________ all of the secrets.

3 만약 비가 그친다면, 우리는 밖에서 자전거를 탈 수 있을 텐데. (bicycles, we, outside, could, ride)
= If it stopped raining, ______________________.

4 만약 네가 더 주의 깊게 찾았더라면, 너의 반지를 찾았을 텐데. (had, more, searched, if, carefully, you)
= ______________________, you would have found your ring.

D <보기>의 말을 활용하여 문장을 완성하시오.

<보기>	see it with you	be a famous singer
	will play with my friends	keep the salad in the fridge

1 *A*: Ms. Jones talks as if she ______________________.
B: Not really. In fact, she has few fans.

2 *A*: How was the movie? I'm sorry that I didn't see it.
B: It was interesting. I wish I ______________________.

3 *A*: The salad went bad because of hot weather.
B: Oh, I see. If I ______________________, it could have lasted longer.

4 *A*: If I didn't have homework, I ______________________.
B: I'm sure you can finish it soon.

Chapter Test

[1-2] 다음 빈칸에 들어갈 알맞은 것을 고르시오.

1

If John ________ rich, he would buy a big house for his family.

① be ② is
③ being ④ were
⑤ has been

2

If Angela had not been sick, she ________ on the picnic with us yesterday.

① go ② went
③ will go ④ has gone
⑤ would have gone

3 다음 빈칸에 공통으로 들어갈 알맞은 것은?

• If I ________ a writer, I would write a children's book.
• Jimmy speaks as if he ________ generous.

① be ② am ③ is
④ was ⑤ were

서술형

4 다음 두 문장의 의미가 비슷하도록 빈칸에 알맞은 말을 쓰시오.

Janet talks as if ________ ________ ________ ________.
→ In fact, Janet can't swim well.

[5-6] 다음 중 밑줄 친 부분이 어법상 어색한 것을 고르시오.

5
① I wish I had a nice smartwatch.
② They speak as if they didn't know me.
③ If I had left earlier, I wouldn't have been late.
④ My uncle talks as if he had visited the U.S. before.
⑤ If we fixed the computer, we could have played games together.

6
① I wish we had met each other sooner.
② If Peter had read the book, he would have liked it.
③ My mom treats me as if I were a child.
④ If I were you, I would have done the homework now.
⑤ If she had not watched TV, she would have slept more.

서술형

[7-8] 우리말과 같도록 괄호 안의 말을 활용하여 빈칸에 쓰시오.

7

만약 Ted가 우리 집에 왔더라면, 우리는 함께 공부했을 텐데. (study, together)

= If Ted had come to my house, we ________ ________ ________ ________.

8

Tina가 나에게 친절하면 좋을 텐데. (be, kind)

= I wish ________ ________ ________ to me.

서술형

[9-10] 다음 문장을 가정법 문장으로 바꿔 쓰시오.

9

As the store doesn't have the sneakers, Matt can't buy them.
→ If the store ____________________,
____________________.

10

I'm sorry that I didn't see the shooting star.
→ I wish ____________________
____________________.

[11-12] 다음 빈칸에 들어갈 말이 순서대로 짝지어진 것을 고르시오.

11

• I don't have enough money to buy a flower basket. I wish I ________ more money.
• If she had known that the sauce was spicy, she ________ it.

① have - didn't choose
② had - wouldn't have chosen
③ had - didn't choose
④ had had - wouldn't choose
⑤ had had - wouldn't have chosen

12

• Anna talks as if she ________ taller than me. In fact, she isn't.
• If it rained today, we ________ home.

① is - stayed
② is - would stay
③ were - would stay
④ were - would have stayed
⑤ had been - would have stayed

13 다음 우리말을 알맞게 영작한 것은?

만약 네가 여기 있다면, 이 아름다운 풍경을 볼 텐데.

① If you were here, you see this beautiful view.
② If you were here, you saw this beautiful view.
③ If you were here, you would see this beautiful view.
④ If you had been here, you would see this beautiful view.
⑤ If you had been here, you would have seen this beautiful view.

14 다음 중 밑줄 친 부분이 어법상 바른 것은?

① I wish Josh <u>joined</u> our school band last week.
② If you <u>had seen</u> me on stage, you would have been proud.
③ If Jenny <u>is</u> not tired, she would go camping.
④ They talk as if they <u>are</u> players on the team.
⑤ If Tom had not been so nervous, he <u>would give</u> a better speech yesterday.

서술형

[15-16] 괄호 안의 동사를 알맞은 형태로 바꿔 문장을 완성하시오.

15

I can't speak French at all. I wish I ____________ how to speak French. (know)

16

If Kelly ____________ lunch, she would have had more energy. (eat)

고난도

17 다음 문장을 가정법 문장으로 바르게 바꾸지 못한 것은?

① I'm sorry that I left the party so soon.
→ I wish I didn't leave the party so soon.

② As the players didn't practice enough, they lost the game.
→ If the players had practiced enough, they wouldn't have lost the game.

③ As Mr. Williams isn't a doctor, he can't treat his own father.
→ If Mr. Williams were a doctor, he could treat his own father.

④ I'm sorry that I can't decide what to buy.
→ I wish I could decide what to buy.

⑤ As Emily worked hard every day, she could open her own store.
→ If Emily had not worked hard every day, she couldn't have opened her own store.

18 다음 대화의 빈칸에 들어갈 말이 순서대로 짝지어진 것은?

> *A*: Why did you catch a cold?
> *B*: I didn't wear a coat last night. If I ________ my coat, I ________ a cold.

① bring - catch
② brought - wouldn't catch
③ brought - wouldn't have caught
④ had brought - wouldn't catch
⑤ had brought - wouldn't have caught

서술형

[19-20] 다음 문장에서 어법상 어색한 부분을 찾아 쓰고 바르게 고쳐 쓰시오.

19

> If I were in Busan now, I could have met you.

________________ → ________________

20

> If Jane had known that yesterday was your birthday, she would give you a present.

________________ → ________________

21 다음 문장을 가정법 문장으로 바르게 바꾼 것은?

> As my phone doesn't work, I can't call you.

① If my phone works, I can call you.
② If my phone doesn't work, I can't call you.
③ If my phone worked, I can call you.
④ If my phone worked, I could call you.
⑤ If my phone had worked, I could have called you.

고난도

22 다음 중 밑줄 친 부분을 바르게 고치지 못한 것은?

① Mr. Smith speaks as if he knows everything. (→ knew)
② If we have known today's weather, we would have brought an umbrella. (→ had known)
③ Ben talks as if he watched the movie already. (→ had watched)
④ I wish I don't tell a lie to my friends last week. (→ didn't tell)
⑤ If the shirt were cheap, I would have bought it. (→ had been)

Chapter 13

일치와 화법

주절과 종속절의 시제를 맞추는 것을 시제의 일치라고 한다.
화법은 말이나 생각을 전달하는 방식으로,
직접 화법과 간접 화법이 있다.

UNIT 01 시제의 일치

1 시제의 일치

❶ 주절이 현재시제인 경우 종속절에는 의미에 따라 모든 시제를 쓸 수 있다.

I *know* that the weather **is** sunny now.
I *know* that the weather **was** sunny yesterday.
I *know* that the weather **will be** sunny tomorrow.

❷ 주절이 과거시제인 경우 종속절에는 의미에 따라 과거시제나 과거완료시제를 쓴다.

I *thought* that Edward **did** his best.
I *thought* that Edward **had done** his best.
I *thought* that Edward **would do** his best.
→ 주절이 과거시제인 경우 종속절의 조동사도 과거형(would, could, might 등)을 쓴다.

2 시제 일치의 예외

❶ 다음과 같은 경우에는 주절의 시제와 상관없이 종속절에 항상 현재시제를 쓴다.

현재의 습관이나 반복되는 일을 나타낼 때	I *heard* that Monica **jogs** every morning.
일반적·과학적 사실을 나타낼 때	He *knew* that Stockholm **is** the capital city of Sweden. The students *learned* that Jupiter **has** 79 moons.
속담·격언을 말할 때	Aaron *said* that no news **is** good news. My mother *told* me that actions **speak** louder than words.

❷ 역사적 사실을 나타낼 때는 주절의 시제와 상관없이 종속절에 항상 과거시제를 쓴다.

He *doesn't know* that the Korean war **ended** in 1953.
I *taught* them that Edison **invented** the light bulb.

Smart Check 다음 빈칸에 들어갈 알맞은 것을 고르시오.

1 Hans thought that his brother ________ the chocolate.
① eats ② will eat ③ had eaten

2 I didn't know that oil ________ lighter than water.
① is ② was ③ has been

3 The teacher said that the French Revolution ________ out in 1789.
① breaks ② broke ③ will break

Practice

Answers p.19

A 괄호 안에서 알맞은 것을 고르시오.

1 I thought that I (lose / lost) my wallet at the bank.

2 The kids learned that water (boils / boiled) at 100°C.

3 The guide said that the festival (ends / had ended).

4 My sister promised that she (will / would) wake up early.

5 David knows that the Industrial Revolution (starts / started) in the 1760s.

boil 동 끓다
promise 동 약속하다
Industrial Revolution 산업혁명

B 다음 문장을 과거시제로 바꿀 때 빈칸에 알맞은 말을 쓰시오.

1 Linda tells me that she doesn't feel well.
→ Linda told me that she ________ ________ well.

2 I believe that the final exam will be easy.
→ I believed that the final exam ________ ________ easy.

3 Everyone knows that Seoul is the capital of Korea.
→ Everyone knew that Seoul ________ the capital of Korea.

4 I hear that haste makes waste.
→ I heard that haste ________ waste.

5 Mark says that he wants to be a soccer player.
→ Mark said that he ________ to be a soccer player.

6 Anna tells me that she stayed up late last night.
→ Anna told me that she ________ ________ up late last night.

capital 명 수도
haste 명 서두름
waste 명 낭비

C 우리말과 같도록 괄호 안의 말을 활용하여 빈칸에 쓰시오.

1 Angela는 태양계에서 수성이 태양에 가장 가깝다는 것을 들었다. (Mercury, be)
= Angela heard that ________ ________ closest to the Sun in the solar system.

2 선생님은 그의 강의가 지루했었다는 것을 깨달았다. (his lecture, be)
= The teacher realized that ________ ________ ________ ________ boring.

3 나는 베트남 전쟁이 1975년에 끝났다는 것을 안다. (the Vietnam War, end)
= I know that ________ ________ ________ ________ in 1975.

4 Eric은 그가 제시간에 숙제를 끝낼 수 있다고 생각했다. (can, finish)
= Eric thought that ________ ________ ________ the homework on time.

close 형 가까운
solar system 태양계
lecture 명 강의
realize 동 깨닫다, 알아차리다

UNIT 02 화법

다른 사람이 말한 내용을 큰따옴표(" ")를 사용하여 그대로 전달하는 것을 직접 화법이라고 하고, 큰따옴표 없이 전달하는 사람의 입장에서 말하는 것을 간접 화법이라고 한다.

1 평서문의 직접 화법 → 간접 화법 전환

Ted said, "I will fix my computer."
→ Ted said (that) he would fix his computer.
ⓐ ⓑ ⓒ ⓓ ⓒ

ⓐ 전달동사가 say인 경우 그대로 쓰고, say to인 경우 tell로 바꾼다.
ⓑ 콤마(,)와 큰따옴표(" ")를 없애고 접속사 that으로 두 절을 연결한다. 이때 that은 생략할 수 있다.
ⓒ that절의 인칭대명사를 전달하는 사람의 입장에 맞게 바꾼다.
ⓓ 전달동사가 현재시제인 경우 that절의 시제를 바꾸지 않고, 과거시제인 경우 과거시제나 과거완료시제로 바꾼다.

2 의문문의 직접 화법 → 간접 화법 전환

❶ 의문사가 있는 의문문

He said to me, "Where are you going?"
→ He asked me where I was going.
ⓐ ⓑ ⓒ, ⓓ

❷ 의문사가 없는 의문문

My sister said, "Did you solve the puzzle?"
→ My sister asked if[whether] I had solved the puzzle.
ⓐ ⓑ ⓒ, ⓓ

ⓐ 전달동사 say나 say to를 ask로 바꾼다.
ⓑ 콤마(,)와 큰따옴표(" ")를 없앤다. 의문사가 있으면 의문사로 두 절을 연결하고, 의문사가 없으면 if나 whether로 연결한다.
ⓒ 인칭대명사와 시제를 평서문의 화법 전환과 같은 방식으로 바꾼다.
ⓓ 의문사가 있으면 「의문사 + 주어 + 동사」의 어순으로 쓰고, 의문사가 없으면 「if[whether] + 주어 + 동사」의 어순으로 쓴다.

TIP 의문사가 주어인 경우 「의문사 + 동사」의 어순을 그대로 쓴다.
Sophia said, "**What made** him laugh?"
→ Sophia asked **what had made** him laugh.

Smart Check 다음 문장을 간접 화법으로 바꿀 때 빈칸에 들어갈 알맞은 것을 고르시오.

1 Carol said to me, "I picked up a coin on the street."
→ Carol told me that ________ a coin on the street.
① I had picked up ② I picked up ③ she had picked up

2 He said to me, "Are you 15 years old?"
→ He asked me ________ 15 years old.
① if I was ② whether he was ③ if was I

Practice

Answers p.19

A 괄호 안에서 알맞은 것을 고르시오.

1 He (said / told) that he was looking for a bus station.

2 Hailey asked me (who had left / had left who) the classroom first.

3 I asked Lucy (that / if) she could help me to carry the boxes.

4 A woman asked me where (I had gotten / had I gotten) the free coupon.

station 명 정류장, 역
free 형 무료의
coupon 명 쿠폰

B 다음 문장을 간접 화법으로 바꿀 때 빈칸에 알맞은 말을 쓰시오.

1 Noah said to me, "Your shoes look fancy."
→ Noah ________ me that ________ ________ ________ fancy.

2 She said, "I want to have some water."
→ She ________ that ________ ________ to have some water.

3 My father said to me, "When will you finish your homework?"
→ My father ________ me ________ ________ ________ finish ________ homework.

4 The girl said, "Can you give me a hand?"
→ The girl ________ ________ ________ ________ give ________ a hand.

5 Nina said to me, "I was pleased to meet you."
→ Nina ________ me that ________ ________ ________ pleased to meet ________.

6 I said to Jason, "Why are you so upset?"
→ I ________ Jason ________ ________ ________ so upset.

7 My friend said to me, "Do you have a red pen?"
→ My friend ________ me ________ ________ ________ a red pen.

fancy 형 화려한
give a hand 도와주다
pleased 형 기쁜
upset 형 속상한, 마음이 상한

C 우리말과 같도록 괄호 안의 말을 활용하여 빈칸에 쓰시오.

1 그는 나에게 그가 나의 주소를 알지 못한다고 말했다. (know)
= He ________ me that ________ ________ ________ my address.

2 Rachel은 나에게 내가 기타를 잘 치는지 물었다. (be good at)
= Rachel ________ me ________ ________ ________ ________ ________ playing the guitar.

3 나는 요리사에게 무엇이 가장 인기 있는 요리인지 물었다. (popular, dish)
= I ________ the chef ________ ________ ________ ________ ________ ________.

address 명 주소
dish 명 요리, 음식

Writing Exercise

A 다음 문장의 밑줄 친 부분을 과거시제로 바꿔 완전한 문장을 쓰시오.

1 I hear that the new shopping mall will open in July.
→ ______________________________.

2 William thinks that he saw someone enter the house.
→ ______________________________.

3 They know that Beethoven died in 1827.
→ ______________________________.

4 Lisa says that she may move to another school.
→ ______________________________.

5 Ms. Harrison teaches us that an elephant lives up to 70 years.
→ ______________________________.

6 He tells me that he can't stay underwater so long.
→ ______________________________.

B 다음 직접 화법을 간접 화법으로 바꾼 문장에서 어법상 어색한 부분을 찾아 바르게 고쳐 완전한 문장을 쓰시오.

1 Daniel said to me, "Why do you need more blankets?"
→ Daniel asked me why I need more blankets.
→ ______________________________.

2 Mom said to me, "It's too late for you to play computer games."
→ Mom said me that it was too late for me to play computer games.
→ ______________________________.

3 Sandra said, "Who drank all the milk in the fridge?"
→ Sandra asked who drank all the milk in the fridge.
→ ______________________________.

4 He said to me, "Where can I get the information about the contest?"
→ He asked me where could he get the information about the contest.
→ ______________________________.

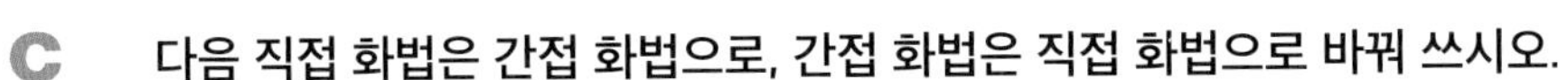

C 다음 직접 화법은 간접 화법으로, 간접 화법은 직접 화법으로 바꿔 쓰시오.

1 Jessica told me that she wanted me to help her.
→ Jessica ______________________________

2 The boy said, "I made the strawberry cake by myself."
→ The boy ______________________________.

3 Paul told me that he would join the soccer team.
→ Paul ______________________________

4 Charles said to me, "Have you been to New York?"
→ Charles ______________________________.

5 I asked how they could swim so fast in the river.
→ I ______________________________

6 My friend said to me, "Are you familiar with the rules of chess?"
→ My friend ______________________________.

D 다음은 Jake가 친구들과 나눈 문자 메시지이다. 문자 메시지의 내용을 간접 화법으로 바꿔 쓰시오.

1
Emily: I'm going to go to the library in 30 minutes.
Jake: OK. See you then.

2
Timothy: Where did you buy the blue shirt?
Jake: I bought it at the flea market.

3
Christine: Can I borrow your history notes?
Jake: Sure. I'll bring them tomorrow.

1 Emily told Jake that ______________________________.

2 Timothy asked Jake ______________________________.

3 Christine asked Jake ______________________________.

Chapter Test

[1-4] 다음 빈칸에 들어갈 알맞은 것을 고르시오.

1

I thought that James ________ well.

① don't feel ② doesn't feel
③ didn't feel ④ haven't felt
⑤ hasn't felt

2

We learned that water ________ at 0°C.

① froze ② freezes
③ was freezing ④ has frozen
⑤ had frozen

3

The students were taught that Columbus ________ America in 1492.

① discover ② discovers
③ discovered ④ has discovered
⑤ had discovered

4

Patrick asked me ________ I could lend him a pen.

① that ② as
③ what ④ unless
⑤ whether

[5-6] 다음 중 어법상 어색한 것을 고르시오.

5 ① Richard told me that he bought a new bag.
② People know that the earth is round.
③ Karen said that she studies Chinese every day.
④ I thought that we will pass the exam.
⑤ The teacher taught us that light travels faster than sound.

6 ① Mr. Jenkins asked us if were we hungry.
② My sister said that she would go to the mall.
③ Mark asked me where his cell phone was.
④ Hazel told us that her family had moved to a new neighborhood.
⑤ I asked my friends when they could come to my house.

서술형

[7-8] 다음 문장을 간접 화법으로 바꿀 때 빈칸에 알맞은 말을 쓰시오.

7

My mom said, "Why is your room so dirty?" → My mom ________ ________ ________ ________ ________ so dirty.

8

Matthew said, "My laptop was broken." → Matthew said that ________ ________ ________ ________ ________.

Answers p.20

9 다음 문장을 간접 화법으로 바르게 바꾼 것은?

Ashley said, "I need some cold water."

① Ashley said that I need some cold water.
② Ashley told that she needs some cold water.
③ Ashley said that she needs some cold water.
④ Ashley told that she needed some cold water.
⑤ Ashley said that she needed some cold water.

10 다음 빈칸에 들어갈 알맞은 것을 모두 고르시오.

We thought that Ms. Davis ________ a poet.

① is ② was ③ were
④ has been ⑤ had been

[11-12] 다음 대화의 빈칸에 들어갈 말이 순서대로 짝지어진 것을 고르시오.

11

A: I can't find my book. Did you see it?
B: You ________ me that you ________ your book at home.

① said - left ② said - will leave
③ said - had left ④ told - will leave
⑤ told - had left

12

A: When can Kate come to the party?
B: Kate ________ that she ________ come at 6 P.M.

① said - can ② said - could
③ said to - can ④ told - could
⑤ told - can

서술형

[13-14] 다음 직접 화법을 간접 화법으로 바꾼 문장에서 어법상 어색한 부분을 찾아 쓰고 바르게 고쳐 쓰시오.

13

Mia said to me, "What is your favorite song?"
→ Mia asked me what your favorite song was.

________________ → ________________

14

Kevin said, "I am going to the market."
→ Kevin said that he is going to the market.

________________ → ________________

15 다음 중 직접 화법을 간접 화법으로 잘못 바꾼 것은?

① Mike said, "You're my best friend."
→ Mike said that I was his best friend.
② Olivia said, "I finished my homework."
→ Olivia said that she had finished her homework.
③ They said, "We are having fun."
→ They said that we were having fun.
④ My sister said to me, "Did you see my jacket?"
→ My sister asked me if I had seen her jacket.
⑤ Mr. Smith said to us, "Why are you so noisy?"
→ Mr. Smith asked us why we were so noisy.

서술형

16 다음 문장을 과거시제로 바꿀 때 빈칸에 알맞은 말을 쓰시오.

Linda believes that she can become a professor.
→ Linda believed that she ________ ________ a professor.

서술형 고난도

[17-18] 우리말과 같도록 괄호 안의 말을 활용하여 문장을 완성하시오.

17 Alice는 나에게 내가 언제 미술관에 갈 것인지 물었다. (go to the art museum)

= Alice asked me ________________
________________________.

18 우리는 코끼리가 뛸 수 없다는 것을 알아냈다. (elephants, jump)

= We found out that ________________.

[19-20] 다음 빈칸에 들어갈 말이 순서대로 짝지어진 것을 고르시오.

19
- Jenny realized that her train ticket ________ missing.
- The news reported that the victim ________ no injuries.

① is - has ② is - had
③ was - has ④ was - had
⑤ was - has had

20
- Sam knows that J.K. Rowling ________ the first Harry Potter book in 1994.
- I learned that about 75 percent of the human brain ________ made of water.

① writes - is ② writes - was
③ wrote - is ④ wrote - was
⑤ had written - has been

서술형 고난도

[21-22] 다음 문장을 직접 화법으로 바꿔 쓰시오.

21 Mary said that she would bake cookies for her friends.

→ ________________________
____

22 Thomas asked me what I wanted for my birthday.

→ ________________________
____

23 다음 문장을 과거시제로 바꿀 때 밑줄 친 부분이 어법상 어색한 것은?

Few people know that sharks don't have any bones.

→ Few people knew(①) that(②) sharks(③) didn't(④) have(⑤) any bones.

고난도

24 다음 중 어법상 바른 것을 모두 고르시오.

① He said that he goes to the gym every week.
② The history teacher taught us that the First World War had started in 1914.
③ She asked me whether had I completed the essay.
④ We didn't expect that Jeff could come.
⑤ Rosy told me that she will send an invitation.

불규칙 동사 변화표

1. A-A-A형 원형-과거형-과거분사형이 모두 같은 경우

원형	과거형	과거분사형
cost 비용이 들다	cost	cost
hit 치다, 때리다	hit	hit
hurt 다치게 하다	hurt	hurt
let ~하게 하다	let	let

원형	과거형	과거분사형
put 놓다	put	put
read[ri:d] 읽다	read[red]	read[red]
shut 닫다	shut	shut
spread 펼치다	spread	spread

2. A-B-A형 원형-과거분사형이 같은 경우

원형	과거형	과거분사형
become ~이 되다	became	become
come 오다	came	come

원형	과거형	과거분사형
overcome 극복하다	overcame	overcome
run 달리다	ran	run

3. A-B-B형 과거형-과거분사형이 같은 경우

원형	과거형	과거분사형
bring 가져오다	brought	brought
build 짓다, 만들다	built	built
feed 먹이를 주다	fed	fed
feel 느끼다	felt	felt
find 찾다	found	found
get 얻다	got	got(ten)
have 가지다	had	had
hear 듣다	heard	heard
keep 유지하다	kept	kept
lay 놓다, 낳다	laid	laid
lead 이끌다	led	led

원형	과거형	과거분사형
leave 떠나다	left	left
lose 잃다, 지다	lost	lost
make 만들다	made	made
meet 만나다	met	met
send 보내다	sent	sent
sleep 자다	slept	slept
spend 쓰다	spent	spent
tell 말하다	told	told
think 생각하다	thought	thought
understand 이해하다	understood	understood
win 이기다	won	won

4. A-B-C형 원형-과거형-과거분사형이 모두 다른 경우

원형	과거형	과거분사형
be ~이다, ~하다	was/were	been
bear 낳다	bore	born
begin 시작하다	began	begun
bite 물다	bit	bitten
blow 불다	blew	blown
break 깨다	broke	broken
choose 선택하다	chose	chosen
do 하다	did	done
draw 그리다	drew	drawn
drink 마시다	drank	drunk
drive 운전하다	drove	driven
eat 먹다	ate	eaten
fall 떨어지다, 넘어지다	fell	fallen
fly 날다	flew	flown
forbid 금지하다	forbade	forbidden
forget 잊다	forgot	forgotten
forgive 용서하다	forgave	forgiven
freeze 얼다	froze	frozen
give 주다	gave	given
go 가다	went	gone
grow 자라다	grew	grown

원형	과거형	과거분사형
hide 숨다	hid	hidden
know 알다	knew	known
lie 눕다	lay	lain
mistake 실수하다	mistook	mistaken
ride 타다	rode	ridden
ring 울리다	rang	rung
rise 오르다	rose	risen
see 보다	saw	seen
shake 흔들다	shook	shaken
show 보여주다	showed	showed shown
sing 노래하다	sang	sung
sink 가라앉다	sank	sunk sunken
sow (씨를) 뿌리다	sowed	sowed sown
speak 말하다	spoke	spoken
steal 훔치다	stole	stolen
swell 붓다, 부풀다	swelled	swelled swollen
swim 수영하다	swam	swum
take 가지고 가다	took	taken
throw 던지다	threw	thrown
wear 입고 있다	wore	worn
write 쓰다	wrote	written

Hackers Grammar Smart

문법 인덱스

문법 사항	세부 내용	Starter	Level 1	Level 2	Level 3
be동사	be동사	O	O		
	There + be동사	O	O		
일반동사	일반동사	O	O		
시제	현재시제	O	O	p.14	
	과거시제	O	O	p.14	
	미래시제	O	O	p.14	
	현재진행시제	O	O	p.14	
	과거진행시제		O	p.14	
	현재완료시제			p.16	O
	과거완료시제				O
	미래완료시제				O
조동사	can	O	O	p.24	O
	may	O	O	p.24	O
	will	O	O	p.24	
	must	O	O	p.26	O
	have to	O	O	p.26	O
	should		O	p.26	O
	would like to			p.28	
	had better			p.28	O
	used to			p.28	O
	would rather				O
	may as well				O
	조동사 + have + p.p.				O
수동태	수동태			p.46	O
	수동태의 다양한 형태			p.48	O
	4형식/5형식 문장의 수동태			p.50	O
	by 이외의 전치사를 쓰는 수동태			p.50	O
	목적어가 that절인 문장의 수동태				O
	구동사의 수동태				O
부정사	to부정사		O	p.58, 60, 62	O
	부정사를 목적격 보어로 쓰는 동사		O		O
	to부정사의 의미상 주어			p.64	O
	to부정사의 시제, 태				O
	to부정사 구문		O	p.64	O
	독립 부정사				O
동명사	동명사		O	p.72	O
분사	현재분사, 과거분사			p.82	O
	분사구문			p.84	O
	주의해야 할 분사구문				O
동사의 종류	주격 보어가 필요한 동사		O		
	감각동사	O	O	p.36	
	두 개의 목적어가 필요한 동사(수여동사)	O	O	p.36	
	목적격 보어가 필요한 동사		O	p.38	

문법 사항	세부 내용	Starter	Level 1	Level 2	Level 3
문장의 종류	명령문, 청유문, 감탄문	O	O		
	의문사 의문문	O	O		
	부정의문문, 선택의문문, 부가의문문		O		
명사와 관사	셀 수 있는 명사, 셀 수 없는 명사	O	O		
	관사		O		
대명사	인칭대명사	O	O		
	재귀대명사		O	p.96	
	지시대명사	O	O		
	비인칭 주어 it	O	O		
	부정대명사		O	p.92, 94	
형용사와 부사	형용사, 부사	O	O		
비교구문	원급/비교급/최상급 비교		O	p.128	O
	비교구문을 이용한 표현			p.130	O
전치사	장소 전치사	O	O		
	시간 전치사	O	O		
	기타 전치사		O		
접속사	등위접속사	O	O		
	시간 접속사	O	O	p.116	O
	이유 접속사	O	O	p.116	O
	결과 접속사			p.116	O
	조건 접속사		O	p.118	O
	양보 접속사			p.118	O
	that		O	p.118	
	명령문 + and/or		O	p.120	
	상관접속사		O	p.120	O
	간접의문문				O
관계사	관계대명사			p.104	O
	관계부사			p.108	O
	주의해야 할 관계사의 쓰임			p.106	O
	관계사의 계속적 용법				O
	복합관계사				O
가정법	가정법 과거, 가정법 과거완료			p.138	O
	혼합 가정법				O
	I wish 가정법			p.140	O
	as if 가정법			p.140	O
	It's time 가정법				O
	Without[But for] 가정법				O
	if를 생략한 가정법				O
일치와 화법	시제의 일치			p.148	O
	수의 일치				O
	화법			p.150	O
특수구문	강조, 도치, 병렬, 부정, 동격, 생략				O

MEMO

MEMO

MEMO

Smart, Useful, and Essential Grammar

HACKERS GRAMMAR SMART

LEVEL 2

초판 5쇄 발행 2024년 7월 1일
초판 1쇄 발행 2022년 1월 3일

지은이	해커스 어학연구소
펴낸곳	㈜해커스 어학연구소
펴낸이	해커스 어학연구소 출판팀
주소	서울특별시 서초구 강남대로61길 23 ㈜해커스 어학연구소
고객센터	02-537-5000
교재 관련 문의	publishing@hackers.com 해커스북 사이트(HackersBook.com) 고객센터 Q&A 게시판
동영상강의	star.Hackers.com
ISBN	978-89-6542-456-7 (53740)
Serial Number	01-05-01

HACKERS GRAMMAR SMART

LEVEL 2

WORKBOOK

HACKERS GRAMMAR SMART LEVEL 2

WORKBOOK

Chapter 01 시제

UNIT 01 현재/과거/미래/진행시제

Answers p.22

A 괄호 안에서 알맞은 것을 고르시오.

1 I (lose / lost) my glasses last weekend.

2 Bats usually (sleep / slept) during the day.

3 My brother (teaches / will teach) me math tomorrow.

4 Ice in the Arctic (is melting / will melt) fast these days.

B 밑줄 친 부분이 어법상 맞으면 O를 쓰고, 틀리면 바르게 고쳐 쓰시오.

1 Water freezes at 0°C. → ____________

2 Luke is having a lovely smile. → ____________

3 He spends too much money last month. → ____________

4 Angela learned Spanish next year. → ____________

5 The phone was ringing when I entered the room. → ____________

C <보기>의 동사를 활용하여 빈칸에 알맞은 말을 쓰시오.

<보기>	complete	publish	wear	feed

1 I ________ ________ a new coat right now.

2 Lena ________ her goldfish 30 minutes ago.

3 The author ________ his first novel in 2008.

4 The students ________ ________ their homework soon.

D 우리말과 같도록 괄호 안의 말을 알맞게 배열하시오.

1 나의 친구는 어제 상하이로 이사했다. (Shanghai, moved, yesterday, to)
= My friend ______________________.

2 그 이탈리아 식당은 다음 달에 문을 열 예정이다. (to, next, is, going, open, month)
= The Italian restaurant ______________________.

3 많은 사람들은 월요일 아침을 싫어한다. (mornings, Monday, hate)
= Many people ______________________.

4 Jimmy는 지금 그의 여동생과 함께 점심을 먹고 있다. (with, eating, his, is, sister, lunch)
= Jimmy ______________________ now.

UNIT 02 현재완료시제

Answers p.22

A 밑줄 친 부분이 어법상 맞으면 O를 쓰고, 틀리면 바르게 고쳐 쓰시오.

1 I haven't slept well since a week. → ____________

2 He has fixed the broken TV yesterday. → ____________

3 They do volunteer work since last year. → ____________

4 Ben has participated in a speech contest before. → ____________

B 괄호 안의 말을 활용하여 대화를 완성하시오.

1 *A*: I haven't seen Hannah lately.
B: She ________________ to Peru last week. (go)

2 *A*: ________________ to Dokdo? (ever, be)
B: No, I haven't.

3 *A*: How long have they lived in this neighborhood?
B: They ________________ here for two years. (live)

C 현재완료시제를 이용하여 다음 두 문장을 한 문장으로 연결하시오.

1 I lost my pencil case. I can't find it now.
→ I ________________________________.

2 Mr. Brown taught history five years ago. He still teaches it.
→ Mr. Brown ________________________________.

3 My friend went abroad to study. She isn't here now.
→ My friend ________________________________.

4 Megan took piano lessons in January. She still takes them.
→ Megan ________________________________.

D 우리말과 같도록 괄호 안의 말을 알맞게 배열하시오.

1 너는 전에 이 애플리케이션을 사용해본 적이 있니? (this, you, application, have, used)
= ________________________________ before?

2 나는 방금 공항에 도착했다. (at, the, have, airport, just, arrived)
= I ________________________________.

3 그 회사는 2017년 이후로 많은 돈을 기부해왔다. (has, money, donated, much)
= The company ________________________________ since 2017.

Chapter Test+

Answers p.22

[1-2] 다음 빈칸에 들어갈 알맞은 것을 고르시오.

1

It ________ sunny since this morning.

① is ② being
③ has been ④ will be
⑤ was being

2

I ________ with my cat when my mom came home.

① play ② will play
③ have played ④ am playing
⑤ was playing

서술형

[3-4] 다음 문장에서 어법상 어색한 부분을 찾아 쓰고 바르게 고쳐 쓰시오.

3

Serena has downloaded the file an hour ago.

________ → ________

4

The Earth moved around the Sun.

________ → ________

5 다음 글의 빈칸에 들어갈 말이 순서대로 짝지어진 것은?

I ________ my watch for three years. Now, I don't need it anymore because I bought a new one. I ________ it to my younger brother tomorrow.

① used - give
② will use - have given
③ will use - will give
④ have used - give
⑤ have used - will give

[6-7] 다음 중 어법상 어색한 것을 고르시오.

6 ① Josh visited my house a few days ago.
② We are going to buy groceries next week.
③ I brush my teeth three times a day.
④ My father is liking classical music.
⑤ I have been to England once.

7 ① There is no oxygen in space.
② It snows heavily since last night.
③ Maria will clean her bedroom soon.
④ I am looking for my bag now.
⑤ Our English teacher has taught us for two years.

8 다음 빈칸에 들어갈 말이 순서대로 짝지어진 것은?

- Jake ________ his birthday party last Saturday.
- We ________ pizza for dinner tomorrow.

① throws - will have
② threw - has had
③ threw - will have
④ has thrown - had
⑤ has thrown - will have

서술형

[9-10] 괄호 안의 동사를 활용하여 문장을 완성하시오.

9

He ________________ these sneakers since he was 14. (wear)

10

I ________________ a soldier someday in the future. (be)

서술형

[11-12] 다음 두 문장을 한 문장으로 연결하시오.

11

Cathy lost her umbrella. She doesn't have it now.
→ Cathy ________________.

12

Dave liked Jessica two years ago. He still likes her.
→ Dave ________________ two years.

[13-14] 다음 대화의 빈칸에 들어갈 알맞은 것을 고르시오.

13

A: I haven't seen Claire lately.
B: Didn't you know? She ________ to America to see her family.

① goes ② will go
③ is going ④ has gone
⑤ was going

14

A: I heard you and Tom had a fight.
B: That is not true. We ________ a great time yesterday.

① have ② had
③ are having ④ will have
⑤ have had

15 다음 중 밑줄 친 부분이 어법상 바른 것은?

① A giraffe is having a long neck.
② She takes tennis lessons since 2002.
③ He has worked on the project tomorrow.
④ My mother will make sandwiches yesterday.
⑤ The scientists developed a new theory last month.

고난도

16 다음 중 어법상 바른 것의 개수는?

ⓐ My father has sold his car last week.
ⓑ I am meeting my cousin this afternoon.
ⓒ The baby was crying at that time.
ⓓ He visited his grandmother next month.
ⓔ Tim sees the musical *Cats* three times.

① 1개 ② 2개 ③ 3개
④ 4개 ⑤ 5개

[17-18] 주어진 문장의 밑줄 친 부분과 용법이 같은 것을 고르시오.

17 The dog has already eaten all of the food.

① Have you ever played hockey?
② She has climbed this mountain before.
③ It has been cloudy for a week.
④ I haven't read today's newspaper yet.
⑤ Ms. Jenkins has left for Spain.

18 The train has left the platform.

① I have known Jim since elementary school.
② We have just arrived at the station.
③ Chris has gone to his hometown.
④ I have been to Fiji island once.
⑤ The singer's fans have waited outside for hours.

서술형 고난도

19 다음 글의 밑줄 친 ⓐ~ⓔ 중 어법상 어색한 것을 찾아 기호를 쓰고 바르게 고쳐 쓰시오.

My aunt's wedding was last Sunday. My aunt ⓐlooked very beautiful in her dress. That day, she ⓑhas been happy to see her friends and relatives. After the wedding, she ⓒwent to Hawaii for her honeymoon. I ⓓam knowing the scenery in Hawaii is beautiful, so I also ⓔwant to go there for a trip.

*honeymoon 신혼여행

(1) ______ → ______________

(2) ______ → ______________

20 다음 우리말을 알맞게 영작한 것은?

나는 다음 주에 치과에 갈 예정이다.

① I have gone to the dentist next week.
② I went to the dentist next week.
③ I was going to the dentist next week.
④ I will going to the dentist next week.
⑤ I am going to go to the dentist next week.

서술형

[21-22] 우리말과 같도록 괄호 안의 말을 활용하여 문장을 완성하시오.

21 그들은 영어를 공부하기 위해 해외로 가버렸다. (go, abroad)

= They ______________ to study English.

22 나는 이틀 전에 새 축구공을 샀다. (buy, new, soccer ball)

= I ______________ two days ago.

서술형

[23-24] 우리말과 같도록 괄호 안의 말을 알맞게 배열하시오.

23 내가 Steve에게 전화했을 때, 그는 목욕을 하고 있었다. (a, taking, bath, was)

= When I called Steve, he ______________ ______________.

24 나의 친구는 수족관에 가본 적이 없다. (aquarium, been, the, has, to, never)

= My friend ______________.

Chapter 02

조동사

UNIT 01 can, may, will

Answers p.23

A 다음 문장의 밑줄 친 부분을 바르게 고쳐 쓰시오.

1 You may went home early today. → ____________

2 Will I see your notes, please? → ____________

3 He can getting to the terminal by nine. → ____________

4 Ellie is able jump really high. → ____________

B 밑줄 친 부분의 의미를 <보기>에서 골라 그 기호를 쓰시오.

<보기>	ⓐ 능력·가능	ⓑ 허가·요청	ⓒ 추측

1 May I sit here for a minute? [ ]

2 Mr. Anderson can drive a truck. [ ]

3 Sienna might be upset with me. [ ]

4 The news can't be wrong. [ ]

5 Can you pass me the ball? [ ]

C 다음 두 문장의 의미가 같도록 문장을 완성하시오.

1 I could not find my earrings.
→ I ____________ my earrings.

2 Teddy will watch the musical tomorrow.
→ Teddy ____________ the musical tomorrow.

3 Is it OK if I look at this photo album?
→ ____________ at this photo album?

4 My sister can cook a steak very well.
→ My sister ____________ a steak very well.

D 우리말과 같도록 괄호 안의 말을 알맞게 배열하시오.

1 물고기는 물속에서 숨을 쉴 수 있다. (breathe, fish, can)
= ____________ in water.

2 당신의 이름을 저에게 말해주시겠어요? (tell, would, you)
= ____________ me your name?

3 Gabriel은 판타지 소설을 좋아하지 않을지도 모른다. (may, Gabriel, not, like)
= ____________ fantasy novels.

UNIT 02 must, have to, should

Answers p.23

A 괄호 안에서 알맞은 것을 고르시오.

1 You should (water / to water) this plant twice a month.

2 These boots (have to / can't) be mine. They are too small for me.

3 Erica (must / must not) be a genius. She solved the difficult problem.

4 My mother (must not / doesn't have to) wash the dishes. I already did it.

B 다음 빈칸에 알맞은 말을 <보기>에서 한 번씩만 골라 쓰시오.

<보기>	must	have to	don't have to	should not

1 You ______________ go to bed too late. Tomorrow is Monday.

2 We ______________ worry. Everything will be okay.

3 The players ______________ be nervous before the game.

4 People ______________ wear helmets when they ride bicycles.

C 다음 두 문장의 의미가 같도록 빈칸에 알맞은 말을 쓰시오.

1 I'm sure she is the leader of the band.
→ She ________ ________ the leader of the band.

2 It will be good for you to be quiet in the library.
→ You ________ ________ quiet in the library.

3 You don't have to print out the report.
→ You ________ ________ ________ ________ out the report.

4 I'm sure this is not Ms. Logan's car. She sold her car last week.
→ This ________ ________ Ms. Logan's car.

D 우리말과 같도록 괄호 안의 말을 알맞게 배열하시오.

1 우리는 매일 아침을 먹어야 한다. (breakfast, we, eat, should)
= ________________________________ every day.

2 너는 TV를 너무 오래 보면 안 된다. (not, TV, must, watch, you)
= ________________________________ too long.

3 Jake는 곧 결정을 해야 할 것이다. (make, to, a, have, Jake, decision, will)
= ________________________________ soon.

UNIT 03 would like to, had better, used to

Answers p.23

A 괄호 안에서 알맞은 것을 고르시오.

1 Rachel used to (walk / walking) to school.

2 Would you like (decorate / to decorate) the room with me?

3 The boys are used to (stretch / stretching) before swimming.

B 다음 두 문장의 의미가 같도록 문장을 완성하시오.

1 Angela had a long hair, but she cut her hair.
→ Angela ________________ have a long hair.

2 I think Patrick should feed his dog three times a day.
→ Patrick ________________ feed his dog three times a day.

3 We want to join the skateboard club.
→ We ________________ join the skateboard club.

4 I think you should not tell her the bad news.
→ You ________________ tell her the bad news.

C <보기 1>의 말과 <보기 2>의 동사를 한 번씩만 활용하여 문장을 완성하시오.

<보기 1>	would like to	had better	used to

<보기 2>	be	invite	sleep

1 You look very tired. You ________________ now.

2 There ________________ a theater next to the hotel. I watched some movies there.

3 I ________________ you to my birthday party next Friday. Can you come?

D 우리말과 같도록 괄호 안의 말을 알맞게 배열하시오.

1 그들은 매년 함께 여행을 가곤 했다. (would, together, travel, they)
= ________________________ every year.

2 우리는 휴일 동안 집에 머무는 것이 좋겠다. (had, stay, we, better, home)
= ________________________ during the holiday.

3 너는 버스에서 내 옆에 앉고 싶니? (to, you, would, sit, like)
= ________________________ next to me on the bus?

4 Ronald는 그의 무거운 배낭을 가지고 다니는 데 익숙하다. (is, carrying, to, used, Ronald)
= ________________________ his heavy backpack.

Chapter Test

Answers p.23

[1-2] 다음 빈칸에 들어갈 알맞은 것을 고르시오.

1

> If you want to pass the exam, you ________ study harder.

① should ② might
③ had to ④ would
⑤ used to

2

> You ________ translate the word into Korean. I understand it.

① would ② may
③ don't have to ④ must
⑤ had better

[3-4] 다음 밑줄 친 부분과 바꿔 쓸 수 있는 것을 고르시오.

3

> She would play basketball with her classmates when she was 12.

① should ② could
③ had to ④ used to
⑤ might

4

> The customer wants to get a refund on the broken cup.

① can ② should
③ used to ④ has to
⑤ would like to

5 다음 우리말을 영작할 때 빈칸에 들어갈 알맞은 것은?

> Jenny는 미술 수업을 위해 새 붓을 사야 할 것이다.
> = Jenny ________ buy a new brush for the art class.

① is able to ② is going to
③ will have to ④ is used to
⑤ would like to

[6-7] 다음 중 밑줄 친 조동사의 의미가 나머지 넷과 다른 것을 고르시오.

6 ① She must be at the museum now.
② They must be your favorite band.
③ You must be careful when you walk on ice.
④ Serena must be excited about the concert.
⑤ He must be disappointed after the tennis match.

7 ① Julie can fix the coffee machine.
② You can bring food to the classroom.
③ Cameron can write poems very well.
④ Can they finish the work by tomorrow?
⑤ I can get to the theater on time.

8 다음 우리말을 영작한 것 중 어색한 것은?

① 나는 어제 병원에 가야 했다.
= I had to go to the hospital yesterday.

② 그 유치한 소문은 사실일 리가 없다.
= The silly rumor can't be true.

③ 너는 너의 선생님을 존중해야 한다.
= You should respect your teacher.

④ Wood씨는 그의 결혼식을 위해 정장을 살 것이다.
= Mr. Wood will buy a suit for his wedding.

⑤ 그녀는 그녀의 여동생을 돌보곤 했다.
= She is used to taking care of her sister.

서술형

[9-10] 다음 문장에서 틀린 부분을 바르게 고쳐 완전한 문장을 쓰시오.

9

Clara can baking delicious cookies.

→ ______________________________.

10

There would be an old church in my town.

→ ______________________________.

서술형

[11-12] 다음 두 문장의 의미가 같도록 빈칸에 알맞은 말을 쓰시오.

11

I'm sure she is a nice person.
→ She ________ ________ a nice person.

12

There was a middle school across from my apartment, but not anymore.
→ There ________ ________ ________ a middle school across from my apartment.

서술형 고난도

[13-14] 다음 빈칸에 공통으로 들어갈 알맞은 말을 쓰시오.

13

• I ________ believe the news. It's too terrible.
• That person ________ be Robert. He has already gone back to his country.
• You ________ take the map. That's not free.

14

• I ________ like to be friends with her.
• We ________ go to the movies together last year, but we don't anymore.
• ________ you pass me the sauce?

[15-16] 다음 중 어법상 어색한 것을 고르시오.

15 ① Could you turn off the light?
② I'd like to buy the shirts on display.
③ She may go with us to the park.
④ He wasn't able to affording the car.
⑤ Sarah is used to climbing mountains.

16 ① Would you wait for a minute?
② I am going to call you tonight.
③ Josh had to spend the day alone.
④ Can I borrow your black pen?
⑤ We should to add some salt to the soup.

17 다음 중 어법상 바른 것을 모두 고르시오.

① The tall and skinny boy must be Peter.
② Would you like have a cup of tea?
③ It might to rain heavily in the evening.
④ Ms. Brown doesn't have to prepare dinner.
⑤ You not should press this button.

고난도

18 다음 중 짝지어진 두 문장의 의미가 다른 것은?

① My younger sister can count to ten.
→ My younger sister is able to count to ten.
② You must not forget the password.
→ You don't have to forget the password.
③ Would you help me find the key?
→ Could you help me find the key?
④ They don't need to bring their own bag.
→ They need not bring their own bag.
⑤ We will show our foreign friends around Seoul.
→ We are going to show our foreign friends around Seoul.

서술형

[19-20] 우리말과 같도록 괄호 안의 말을 알맞게 배열하시오.

19

Ella는 다음 달에 프랑스어를 배울 것이다. (learn, is, to, month, going, French, next)

= Ella ______________________.

20

너는 패스트푸드를 먹지 않는 것이 좋겠다. (eat, food, had, fast, not, better)

= You ______________________.

[21-22] 다음 글의 빈칸에 들어갈 말이 순서대로 짝지어진 것을 고르시오.

21

Alan ________ watch a horror movie with me tomorrow. I'm worried because I get scared too easily. I ________ ask Alan to change the plan and see a comedy movie instead.

① will - used to
② would - would like to
③ would - am going to
④ would like to - used to
⑤ would like to - am going to

22

This essay contest is only for middle school students. We will not accept any essays after the deadline, so students ________ apply before July 2. The students should only choose a real-life topic, and they ________ write a fictional story. *fictional: 지어낸, 허구의

① cannot - have to
② cannot - would
③ must - cannot
④ must - have to
⑤ would - must not

서술형

[23-24] 우리말과 같도록 괄호 안의 말을 활용하여 문장을 완성하시오.

23

Paul은 안경을 쓸 필요가 없다. (wear, glasses)

= Paul ______________________.

24

Jessie는 그 콘서트에 갈지도 모른다. (go, the concert)

= Jessie ______________________.

동사의 종류

UNIT 01 감각동사와 수여동사

Answers p.24

A 밑줄 친 부분이 어법상 맞으면 O를 쓰고, 틀리면 바르게 고쳐 쓰시오.

1 This mango ice cream tastes greatly. → ________

2 Your plan sounds like interesting. → ________

3 She passed a notebook to her friend. → ________

4 Dad will cook dinner us tonight. → ________

B 다음 빈칸에 알맞은 전치사를 쓰시오. (단, 전치사가 필요하지 않으면 X를 쓰시오.)

1 The artist showed his paintings ______ the public.

2 A man asked a favor ______ me on the street.

3 I write my friend ______ a letter twice a month.

4 Ms. Brown found a cute hat ______ her child.

C 다음 두 문장의 의미가 같도록 문장을 완성하시오.

1 I will buy Jacob new shoes.
→ I ____________________.

2 Mr. Johnson read a book to his son.
→ Mr. Johnson ____________________.

3 I built a sandcastle for my little sister.
→ I ____________________.

4 She passed the reporter a camera.
→ She ____________________.

D 우리말과 같도록 괄호 안의 말을 알맞게 배열하시오.

1 나에게 수건을 가져다줄 수 있니? (a, me, get, towel)
= Can you ____________________?

2 Kelly는 매우 외로워 보인다. (very, looks, lonely)
= Kelly ____________________.

3 Paul은 나에게 그의 주소를 줬다. (to, his, gave, me, address)
= Paul ____________________.

4 그녀의 향수는 장미 같은 냄새가 난다. (like, rose, smells, a)
= Her perfume ____________________.

UNIT 02 목적격 보어가 필요한 동사

Answers p.24

A 괄호 안에서 알맞은 것을 고르시오.

1 I saw you (dance / to dance) on the stage.
2 The song keeps the baby (calm / calmly).
3 My teacher expects me (get / to get) a better grade.
4 Sophia didn't let him (know / knows) the secret.
5 What made Vincent so (sad / sadly)?

B 괄호 안의 동사를 알맞은 형태로 바꿔 문장을 완성하시오.

1 The map helps us ______________ the way. (find)
2 I felt something ______________ under the chair. (move)
3 The comedy movie made me ______________. (laugh)
4 The police ordered everyone ______________ in the house. (stay)

C <보기>의 말을 활용하여 문장을 완성하시오.

<보기>	bring	fix	a great leader	comfortable

1 She asked me ______________ her a gift after the trip.
2 Lucas found his new bed ______________.
3 Her team members call her ______________.
4 I had the repairman ______________ the computer monitor.

D 우리말과 같도록 괄호 안의 말을 알맞게 배열하시오.

1 나는 항상 Olivia에게 조심하라고 말한다. (to, tell, be, Olivia, careful)
= I always ______________________________.

2 그녀는 그녀의 고양이를 Simba라고 이름 지었다. (her, Simba, cat, named)
= She ______________________________.

3 나의 어머니는 내가 야채를 먹게 하셨다. (me, eat, to, got, vegetables)
= My mother ______________________________.

4 우리는 그가 기타를 연주하는 것을 들었다. (the, him, playing, guitar, to, listened)
= We ______________________________.

Chapter Test+

Answers p.24

[1-2] 다음 빈칸에 들어갈 알맞은 것을 고르시오.

1 We asked our parents ________ us to the theme park.

① take ② took
③ to take ④ taking
⑤ is taking

2 Phil told a touching story ________ us.

① to ② in
③ of ④ on
⑤ from

[3-4] 다음 중 어법상 어색한 것을 고르시오.

3 ① Jimmy asked many questions of his teacher.
② The black shirt makes you to look thinner.
③ The firefighter told us to hold our breath.
④ The child saw a frog jump into the pond.
⑤ She named her doll Happy.

4 ① Her uncle gave an allowance to her.
② My sister asked me to spread jam on her bread.
③ Does the new blanket feel rough?
④ I don't want you tell a lie to me.
⑤ Jennifer smelled something burning in the kitchen.

[5-6] 다음 빈칸에 들어갈 말로 어색한 것을 모두 고르시오.

5 Mr. Davis ________ me read the science magazine.

① made ② got
③ helped ④ let
⑤ told

6 The cotton candy tastes ________.

① well ② sweet
③ amazing ④ like soft
⑤ like sugar

서술형

[7-8] 다음 두 문장의 의미가 같도록 문장을 완성하시오.

7 Tim's grandmother cooked him fried chicken.
→ Tim's grandmother ________________
________________.

8 The policeman asked the citizens some questions.
→ The policeman ________________
________________.

[9-10] 다음 중 어법상 바른 것을 고르시오.

9 ① The doctor advised him taking less salty food.
② Janice helped me finding my wallet.
③ Did he allow you use his computer?
④ I had my friend take my picture.
⑤ Her fantastic speech made her to win the contest.

10 ① Jane's backpack looks like new.
② She found the dress too expensively.
③ This soup doesn't taste nicely.
④ My dad bought a cell phone of me.
⑤ He heard someone knocking on the door.

11 다음 중 밑줄 친 부분의 쓰임이 나머지 넷과 다른 것은?

① The tailor made him a nice suit.
② The actor made the audience cry.
③ Please make me some fruit juice.
④ She makes her kids mittens every winter.
⑤ Patrick made his friends their favorite food.

12 다음 빈칸에 들어갈 말이 순서대로 짝지어진 것은?

- I expected Mark ________ the bags with me.
- She heard someone ________ her name far away.

① carry - call ② carry - calling
③ to carry - calling ④ to carry - to call
⑤ carrying - to call

서술형

[13-14] 괄호 안의 동사를 활용하여 문장을 완성하시오.

13 The pilot had the technician ________ the plane. (fix)

14 He advised me ________ enough water. (drink)

서술형

[15-16] 다음 두 문장을 한 문장으로 연결하시오.

15 He waited beside the gate. His mom told him to do it.
→ His mom told him ________
________.

16 Linda watched the pianist. He was playing Mozart's music.
→ Linda watched the pianist ________
________.

17 다음 빈칸에 들어갈 수 있는 것을 모두 고르시오.

Last night, I helped my younger brother ________ his school bag.

① pack ② packed
③ to pack ④ is packing
⑤ was packing

고난도

18 다음 중 밑줄 친 부분의 문장 성분이 나머지 넷과 다른 것은?

① The guard let him enter the building.
② She found the TV show interesting.
③ The light kept the room bright at night.
④ His voice sounded strange on the phone.
⑤ Why do you call him a fool?

19 다음 대화의 빈칸에 공통으로 들어갈 알맞은 것은?

> *A*: Are you going to Jim's place today?
> *B*: My mom won't let me go. She wants me ________ my homework first.
> *A*: That's too bad.
> *B*: Can you help me ________ the homework today? It's too difficult for me.

① finish ② finished
③ to finish ④ finishing
⑤ is finishing

서술형

[20-21] 우리말과 같도록 괄호 안의 말을 활용하여 영작하시오.

20

> 그녀의 어머니는 그녀가 그 콘서트에 가지 못하게 하셨다. (let, go, to the concert)

= ____.

21

> Cindy는 나에게 그 사진 앨범을 만들어줬다. (make, photo album, for)

= ____.

서술형 고난도

22 다음 글의 밑줄 친 ⓐ~ⓔ 중 어법상 어색한 것을 찾아 기호를 쓰고 바르게 고쳐 쓰시오.

> During class, the teacher got me ⓐ to solve a math problem on the board. I found the problem ⓑ easily. The answer was 'two'! However, my friend Steve whispered, "The answer is three." This made me ⓒ to write 'three' on the board. The answer was wrong, and the teacher had me ⓓ solve two more problems. I got upset, so my other friends asked Steve ⓔ to apologize to me.

(1) ______ → ______________
(2) ______ → ______________

서술형

23 우리말과 같도록 주어진 <조건>에 맞게 영작하시오.

> 나는 그가 방을 꾸미는 것을 도왔다.

> <조건>
> 1. help, decorate, the room을 활용하시오.
> 2. 6단어로 쓰시오.

= ____.

서술형

24 우리말과 같도록 괄호 안의 말을 알맞게 배열하시오.

> 그녀는 강아지 세 마리가 들판에서 뛰는 것을 봤다.
> (in, three, field, run, saw, the, puppies)

= She ____
____.

Chapter 03 동사의 종류

Hackers Grammar Smart Level 2

Chapter 04 수동태

UNIT 01 수동태의 쓰임

Answers p.25

A 다음 문장의 밑줄 친 부분을 바르게 고쳐 쓰시오.

1 I was invited many friends to my birthday party. → ____________

2 Melissa was bite by a dog when she was seven. → ____________

3 The novel purchases by high school students. → ____________

4 The actress was appeared on the stage. → ____________

B <보기>의 동사를 활용하여 문장을 완성하시오.

<보기>	happen	paint	teach	serve

1 Dinner ____________ soon.

2 The accident ____________ last night.

3 The class ____________ by Ms. Garcia these days.

4 *Mona Lisa* ____________ by Leonardo da Vinci in 1503.

C 다음 능동태 문장을 수동태로 바꿔 쓰시오.

1 He drives the tour bus.
→ ____________________________.

2 The soldiers guarded the gate.
→ ____________________________.

3 Justin heated the chicken in the microwave.
→ ____________________________ in the microwave.

4 I will return the library books tomorrow.
→ ____________________________ tomorrow.

D 우리말과 같도록 괄호 안의 말을 활용하여 빈칸에 쓰시오.

1 그 서류는 캐비닛에 보관될 것이다. (keep)
= The document ______ ______ ______ in the cabinet.

2 도둑은 경찰관에 의해 잡혔다. (catch, the police officer)
= The thief ______ ______ ______ ______ ______ ______.

3 이 스마트폰 모델은 많은 사람들에 의해 사용된다. (use, many people)
= This smartphone model ______ ______ ______ ______ ______ ______.

4 그 어려운 퍼즐은 어린 소녀에 의해 해결되었다. (solve, a young girl)
= The difficult puzzle ______ ______ ______ ______ ______ ______.

UNIT 02 수동태의 다양한 형태

Answers p.25

A 괄호 안의 말을 활용하여 빈칸에 쓰시오.

1 ________ mangoes ________ in Thailand? (grow)

2 This medicine ________ ________ ________ by the patient. (must, take)

3 ________ your hat ________ yesterday? (buy)

4 The issues ________ ________ in the meeting last week. (not, discuss)

B 밑줄 친 부분이 어법상 맞으면 O를 쓰고, 틀리면 바르게 고쳐 쓰시오.

1 Did the photo posted on a website? → ________

2 The environment should protected. → ________

3 When was the first computer invented? → ________

4 The paint colors were selected not by Mr. Kane. → ________

C 다음 능동태 문장을 수동태로 바꿔 쓰시오.

1 He can plan the activities.
→ ________________________________.

2 Who watered the plants?
→ ________________________________?

3 Most students didn't attend the lecture.
→ ________________________________.

4 Did Linda bring an umbrella?
→ ________________________________?

D 우리말과 같도록 괄호 안의 말을 알맞게 배열하시오.

1 그 행사는 어디에서 열렸니? (was, held, the, where, event)
= ________________________________?

2 숙제는 베껴지면 안 된다. (should, copied, homework, be, not)
= ________________________________.

3 이 새우들은 어부들에 의해 잡혔니? (were, caught, shrimps, these)
= ________________________________ by the fishermen?

4 규칙은 제대로 설명되지 않았다. (not, the, explained, were, rules)
= ________________________________ properly.

UNIT 03 주의해야 할 수동태

Answers p.25

A 괄호 안에서 알맞은 것을 고르시오.

1 The file was sent (to / of) her by Michael.

2 I was advised (rest / to rest) by the doctor.

3 A cup of coffee was gotten (for / of) me by Anna.

4 A boy was heard (shout / shouting) in the hallway.

B 다음 빈칸에 with, to, at 중 알맞은 것을 쓰시오.

1 The room was filled ________ smoke.

2 Luke was surprised ________ the news.

3 Customers are satisfied ________ the service of the shop.

4 The love story of Romeo and Juliet is known ________ everyone.

C 다음 능동태 문장을 수동태로 바꿔 쓰시오.

1 We asked the police officer a favor.
→ The police officer ________________________ by us.
→ A favor ________________________ by us.

2 Jonathan gave the little girl a cookie.
→ The little girl ________________________ by Jonathan.
→ A cookie ________________________ by Jonathan.

3 The teacher allowed the students to leave early.
→ The students ________________________ by the teacher.

D 우리말과 같도록 괄호 안의 말을 알맞게 배열하시오.

1 이 셔츠는 면으로 만들어진다. (shirt, of, made, this, cotton, is)
= ________________________.

2 그들은 과제를 위해 협력하게 되었다. (work, to, they, made, together, were)
= ________________________ for the assignment.

3 Scott은 나에 의해 쇼핑몰로 가는 것이 보였다. (going, was, Scott, the, mall, to, seen)
= ________________________ by me.

4 꽃들은 Kelly에 의해 그녀의 엄마에게 사주어 졌다. (for, bought, flowers, her, mother, were)
= ________________________ by Kelly.

Chapter Test+

Answers p.25

[1-2] 다음 빈칸에 들어갈 알맞은 것을 고르시오.

1

The thief ________ by a brave man yesterday.

① catches ② caught
③ is caught ④ was caught
⑤ was catching

2

Kitchen knives should ________ by young children.

① not touched ② not be touch
③ be not touching ④ be not touch
⑤ not be touched

서술형

3 다음 문장에서 틀린 부분을 바르게 고쳐 완전한 문장을 쓰시오.

Can the light bulb be replacing?

→ ________________________________?

4 다음 우리말을 수동태 문장으로 알맞게 영작한 것은?

아이는 그 인형을 Sally라고 부른다.

① Sally is called to the doll by the child.
② Sally is called the doll by the child.
③ The doll is calling Sally by the child.
④ The doll is called Sally by the child.
⑤ The doll is called to Sally by the child.

[5-6] 다음 빈칸에 공통으로 들어갈 알맞은 것을 고르시오.

5

• The bag is made ________ leather.
• Any questions can be asked ________ the guide.

① in ② of ③ by
④ for ⑤ to

6

• He was heard ________ sing on the street.
• This popular brand is known ________ everyone.

① in ② of ③ to
④ for ⑤ by

서술형

[7-8] 다음 문장을 수동태로 바꿔 쓰시오.

7

The coach advised the players to keep calm.

→ ________________________________
________________________________.

8

She didn't put the dishes in the sink.

→ ________________________________
________________________________.

9 다음 문장을 능동태로 바르게 바꾼 것은?

Was the car accident caused by Ms. Nolan?

① Did Ms. Nolan cause the car accident?
② Did Ms. Nolan caused the car accident?
③ Was Ms. Nolan caused by the car accident?
④ Was Ms. Nolan cause the car accident?
⑤ Was Ms. Nolan caused the car accident?

10 다음 중 어법상 어색한 것은?

① Alice was hit by a bicycle.
② Will the presentation prepared by you?
③ This heavy desk can't be moved.
④ The battery must be charged right now.
⑤ How is the machine turned on?

11 다음 중 밑줄 친 부분을 생략할 수 없는 것은?

① Some orange juice was spilled by Jake.
② The windows were closed by somebody.
③ The dolphins can be seen here by people.
④ Elderly people should be respected by everyone.
⑤ English is spoken in the United States by citizens.

12 다음 글의 빈칸에 들어갈 말이 순서대로 짝지어진 것은?

When I entered the kitchen, I was surprised ________ some noise. A cup ________ by my baby sister! Fortunately, my sister was not hurt.

① at - broke ② at - was broken
③ of - broke ④ to - was broke
⑤ to - was broken

13 다음 문장을 수동태로 바르게 바꾼 것을 모두 고르시오.

Mr. Wilson teaches them science.

① They are teaching science by Mr. Wilson.
② They are taught to science by Mr. Wilson.
③ They are taught science by Mr. Wilson.
④ Science is taught to them by Mr. Wilson.
⑤ Science is taught them by Mr. Wilson.

서술형

[14-15] 괄호 안의 말을 활용하여 문장을 완성하시오.

14

He was seen ______________ in front of the audience. (speak)

15

Ice cream ______________ after dinner. (will, serve)

고난도

16 다음 중 문장의 태를 바르게 바꾼 것은?

① Many people were saved by the hero.
→ The hero was save many people.
② The doctor treated my disease.
→ My disease treated by the doctor.
③ The cows can be seen in the field by us.
→ We can see the cows in the field.
④ The fans made the singer sing one more song.
→ The singer was made sing one more song by the fans.
⑤ The storm broke the fence last night.
→ The fence was breaking by the storm last night.

서술형

17 우리말과 같도록 주어진 <조건>에 맞게 문장을 완성하시오.

멋진 경치가 그 관광객들에게 보여졌다.

<조건>
1. a nice view, show, the tourists를 활용하시오.
2. 8단어로 쓰시오.

= ____________________.

서술형

[18-19] 우리말과 같도록 괄호 안의 말을 활용하여 문장을 완성하시오.

18 그 집은 우리 아빠에 의해 우리에게 지어졌다. (build)

= The house ____________________.

19 나는 나의 친구에 의해 그 책을 읽게 되었다. (make, read, the book)

= I ____________________.

20 다음 중 어법상 바른 것은?

① Did the project finished by John?
② I was allowed playing computer games.
③ The sun was appeared behind the mountain.
④ Something was felt moving under the desk.
⑤ This copy machine is using by the teachers.

21 다음 중 수동태 문장으로 바꿀 수 있는 것은?

① Everyone likes the actor.
② I stayed calm during the emergency.
③ My aunt has a fancy sports car.
④ These black pants fit me perfectly.
⑤ A wonderful thing happened to us.

22 다음 중 어법상 어색한 것의 개수는?

ⓐ The child was told to brush her teeth.
ⓑ Tim was bitten by a mosquito.
ⓒ I was kept to warm by this blanket.
ⓓ When was the bread baked?
ⓔ The stars can seen at clear night.

① 1개 ② 2개 ③ 3개
④ 4개 ⑤ 5개

서술형 고난도

23 다음 글의 밑줄 친 ⓐ~ⓔ 중 어법상 어색한 것을 찾아 기호를 쓰고 바르게 고쳐 쓰시오.

When you visit the library for the first time, you will be told ⓐ<u>to write</u> your name and address on a form. They ⓑ<u>must be written</u> correctly if you want to get a library card. The card ⓒ<u>will send</u> to you in a week. If you have any questions, they can be asked ⓓ<u>to</u> the librarian. Also, the computers on the second floor ⓔ<u>may be used</u> if you want to find some information online.

(1) ______ → ____________
(2) ______ → ____________

서술형

24 다음 문장을 수동태로 바꾼 문장에서 어법상 어색한 부분을 찾아 쓰고 바르게 고쳐 쓰시오.

I asked Sam to go to the party together.
→ Sam was asked going to the party together by me.

____________ → ____________

Chapter 04 수동태 | Hackers Grammar Smart Level 2

Chapter 05

to부정사

UNIT 01 to부정사의 명사적 용법

Answers p.26

A <보기>의 동사를 활용하여 문장을 완성하시오.

<보기> win become ask

1 I want ______________ a favor of you.

2 Julia expects ______________ first prize in the contest.

3 Sandra's dream is ______________ a doctor.

B 다음 문장을 가주어 it을 사용한 문장으로 바꿔 쓰시오.

1 To protect our environment is important.
→ ____.

2 To watch the soccer game was exciting.
→ ____.

3 To master a language takes a long time.
→ ____.

C 다음 두 문장의 의미가 같도록 문장을 완성하시오.

1 Please let me know where to visit in Italy.
→ Please let me know ________________________________.

2 I haven't decided what I should buy for his birthday.
→ I haven't decided ________________________________.

3 Emily taught Daniel how he should use the software.
→ Emily taught Daniel ________________________________.

4 Olivia is not sure when to feed her hamster.
→ Olivia is not sure ________________________________.

D 우리말과 같도록 괄호 안의 말을 알맞게 배열하시오.

1 나의 계획은 오늘 숙제를 끝내는 것이다. (the, to, finish, is, homework)
= My plan ________________________________ today.

2 Parker씨는 그의 일을 그만두지 않기로 결심했다. (decided, his, to, not, quit, job)
= Mr. Parker ________________________________.

3 미래를 예측하는 것은 불가능하다. (the, is, impossible, predict, it, to, future)
= ________________________________.

UNIT 02 to부정사의 형용사적 용법

Answers p.26

A <보기>와 같이 to부정사를 이용하여 다음 두 문장을 한 문장으로 연결하시오.

<보기>	I will make my sister a sandwich. She will eat the sandwich. → I *will make my sister a sandwich to eat* .

1 I booked a hotel. I will visit the hotel.
→ I ______________________________.

2 A chameleon has the ability. It can change its color.
→ A chameleon ______________________________.

3 In the park, there are many benches. People can sit on the benches.
→ In the park, there ______________________________.

4 May I take a piece of paper? I need to write on the piece of paper.
→ May I ______________________________?

5 Can you get the dog a ball? It will play with the ball.
→ Can you ______________________________?

B 다음 두 문장의 의미가 같도록 빈칸에 알맞은 말을 쓰시오.

1 They were destined to achieve their goal.
→ They ________ ________ ________ their goal.

2 You have to turn in your essay on time.
→ You ________ ________ ________ in your essay on time.

3 If you intend to buy a new coat, you can go to the mall downtown.
→ If you ________ ________ ________ a new coat, you can go to the mall downtown.

C 우리말과 같도록 괄호 안의 말을 알맞게 배열하시오.

1 Charles는 그의 부모님께 보낼 편지를 쓸 것이다. (send, letter, his, a, to, parents)
= Charles will write ______________________________.

2 나는 오늘 그 뮤지컬을 볼 기회가 있었다. (musical, to, see, a, the, chance)
= I had ______________________________ today.

3 Ashley는 고기를 자를 날카로운 무언가가 필요하다. (sharp, meat, to, something, the, cut)
= Ashley needs ______________________________.

4 몇 분 동안 아무 소리도 들을 수 없었다. (no, was, heard, sound, be, to)
= ______________________________ for a few minutes.

UNIT 03 to부정사의 부사적 용법

Answers p.26

A <보기>에서 알맞은 말을 한 번씩만 골라 to부정사 형태로 문장을 완성하시오.

<보기>	eat	be a violinist	stay healthy	buy a new laptop

1 This chicken is still warm ________________.

2 You should exercise every day ________________.

3 The little girl grew up ________________.

4 Anthony is saving money ________________.

<보기>	play alone	tell you the bad news	catch the plane	stay awake

5 I drank coffee ________________.

6 I am sorry ________________.

7 Some sports are impossible ________________.

8 Lucas took a taxi to the airport ________________.

B to부정사를 이용하여 다음 두 문장을 한 문장으로 연결하시오.

1 I received your invitation. I was pleased.
→ I ________________.

2 My brother is shouting at me. He must be angry.
→ My brother ________________.

3 She completed the history project. She was relieved.
→ She ________________.

C 우리말과 같도록 괄호 안의 말을 알맞게 배열하시오.

1 나는 나의 고향을 떠나서 슬프다. (leave, my, to, hometown)
= I'm sad ________________.

2 그는 그의 차를 고쳤지만, 결국 다시 손상을 입혔다. (damage, to, it, again, only)
= He fixed his car, ________________.

3 Linda는 벽에 그림들을 그리기 위해 이 페인트를 사용했다. (draw, on, to, wall, pictures, the)
= Linda used this paint ________________.

UNIT 04 to부정사의 의미상 주어, to부정사 구문

Answers p.27

A 다음 빈칸에 for나 of 중 알맞은 것을 쓰시오.

1 It is fun ________ me to watch comedy movies.

2 It is nice ________ you to take care of your brother.

3 It is foolish ________ her to believe Ivan's story.

4 It is impossible ________ Eva to focus during science class.

B 밑줄 친 부분이 어법상 맞으면 O를 쓰고, 틀리면 바르게 고쳐 쓰시오.

1 The mountain is so high for me to climb. → ____________

2 The weather is enough warm for us to go out. → ____________

3 My sister is too short to reach the shelf. → ____________

4 It was careless for Joan to lose her cell phone. → ____________

C 다음 두 문장의 의미가 같도록 문장을 완성하시오.

1 Eric ran fast enough to win the race.
→ Eric ran ______________________.

2 Nancy was so sick that she couldn't leave the hospital.
→ Nancy was ______________________.

3 The camping tools are too expensive for me to buy.
→ The camping tools are ______________________.

4 Harry is so intelligent that he can solve the puzzle.
→ Harry is ______________________.

D 우리말과 같도록 괄호 안의 말을 알맞게 배열하시오.

1 내가 제시간에 거기에 도착하는 것은 가능하다. (get, for, is, me, to, possible, it)
= ______________________ there on time.

2 그 영화는 아이들이 보기에 너무 지루했다. (for, was, boring, watch, too, kids, to)
= The film ______________________.

3 저 방은 손님들이 사용할 만큼 충분히 깨끗하다. (enough, to, guests, clean, for, is, use)
= That room ______________________.

Chapter Test+

Answers p.27

[1-2] 다음 빈칸에 들어갈 알맞은 것을 고르시오.

1

Ken's goal is ________ Spanish this year.

① learn ② learned
③ to learning ④ to learn
⑤ to learned

2

I'm not sure what ________ when I feel sad.

① do ② doing
③ to do ④ to doing
⑤ should do

서술형

3 우리말과 같도록 주어진 <조건>에 맞게 영작하시오.

오토바이는 타기에 위험하다.

<조건> 1. A motorcycle을 주어로 하시오. 2. dangerous, ride를 사용하시오.

= ________________________________.

서술형

4 괄호 안의 말을 활용하여 문장을 완성하시오.

Jane promised ____________ to her family again. (not, lie)

서술형

[5-6] 다음 두 문장의 의미가 같도록 문장을 완성하시오.

5

Dogs are so sensitive that they can hear small noises. → Dogs are ____________________________ ____________________________.

6

The movie is too scary for us to watch. → The movie is ____________________________ ____________________________.

7 다음 중 어법상 바른 것을 고르시오.

① It's time to going to bed.
② Is there any chair to sit?
③ It takes many years to become a nurse.
④ The documentary is enough fun to watch.
⑤ This computer program is easy of us to use.

서술형

8 다음 빈칸에 공통으로 들어갈 알맞은 말을 쓰시오.

• It was hard ________ me to focus for two hours. • It is impossible ________ him to keep the secret.

[9-10] 다음 중 어법상 어색한 것을 고르시오.

9 ① We are searching for a house to live.
② They were excited to win the soccer game.
③ I like to play the piano in the morning.
④ Josh has a lot of things to do today.
⑤ It was foolish of her to trust the liar again.

10 ① Her wish is to see the aurora in Iceland.
② I need something to wear comfortable at home.
③ Sandy is to write an essay by tomorrow.
④ It is safe to cross the street now.
⑤ The turtle lived to be 120 years old.

고난도

[11-12] 다음 중 밑줄 친 to부정사의 용법이 나머지 넷과 다른 것을 고르시오.

11 ① To remember everything in class is difficult.
② Samantha watches many documentaries to become smart.
③ It is harmful to swim right after a meal.
④ Harry hopes to meet his grandmother soon.
⑤ Mr. Kane's plan is to find a new job.

12 ① I'm glad to be friends with you.
② David must be rude to point at a person.
③ She grew up to become a well-known scientist.
④ My uncle is looking for a hotel to stay in.
⑤ He bought the book to learn communication skills.

[13-14] 다음 우리말을 알맞게 영작한 것을 고르시오.

13 | 그 아기는 가지고 놀 또 다른 장난감을 원한다. |

① The baby wants another toy for play to.
② The baby wants another toy for play with.
③ The baby wants another toy to play.
④ The baby wants another toy to play with.
⑤ The baby wants another toy to playing.

14 | 그 길은 우리가 걷기에 너무 어두웠다. |

① The street was so dark to us for walk.
② The street was very dark to us for walk.
③ The street was very dark for us walk.
④ The street was too dark to us walking.
⑤ The street was too dark for us to walk.

서술형

[15-16] to부정사를 이용하여 다음 두 문장을 한 문장으로 연결하시오.

15
• Laura lost her scarf three times.
• She must be careless.

→ Laura ______________________
______________________.

16
• Jake heard the good news.
• He was very happy.

→ Jake ______________________
______________________.

17 다음 중 짝지어진 두 문장의 의미가 다른 것은?

① Let's decide when to meet.
→ Let's decide when we should meet.

② It is necessary to follow the school rules.
→ To follow the school rules is necessary.

③ We must leave now to catch the flight.
→ We must leave now so as to catch the flight.

④ Josh is going to go to high school next year.
→ Josh is to go to high school next year.

⑤ Wood is so light that it can float on water.
→ Wood is too light to float on water.

18 다음 중 밑줄 친 부분을 바르게 고친 것은?

① She expects to arriving home early.
→ arriving

② Her voice was so quiet for me to hear.
→ enough quiet

③ I bought nice something to give to my mom.
→ something nice

④ He made a new friend to talking.
→ to talk

⑤ It is nice for him to lend me his coat.
→ to

서술형 고난도

19 다음 대화의 밑줄 친 ⓐ~ⓔ 중 어법상 어색한 것을 찾아 기호를 쓰고 바르게 고쳐 쓰시오.

A: I have nothing ⓐto do today. Do you have any plans?
B: I was planning ⓑto meet my cousin, but she canceled.
A: Why don't you go to the movies with me?
B: Is there ⓒinteresting anything to watch?
A: Let's go to the theater ⓓto find out.
B: I'm excited ⓔto hanging out with you!

(1) ______ → ________________

(2) ______ → ________________

서술형

[20-22] 우리말과 같도록 괄호 안의 말을 활용하여 문장을 완성하시오.

20 나는 쓸 펜이 필요하다. (a pen, write)

= I need ________________.

21 과학자들은 그 프로젝트를 시작하지 않기로 결정했다. (decide, start)

= The scientists ________________ the project.

22 그녀는 자라서 경찰관이 되었다. (grow up, a police officer)

= She ________________.

서술형

[23-24] 우리말과 같도록 괄호 안의 말을 알맞게 배열하시오.

23 그 영어책은 우리가 읽기에 너무 어려웠다. (for, to, English, difficult, read, book, the, was, too, us)

= ________________
________________.

24 Thomas는 열심히 공부했지만 결국 그 시험에 떨어졌다. (only, fail, to, studied, Thomas, the, hard, test)

= ________________
________________.

Chapter 06 동명사

UNIT 01 동명사의 쓰임

Answers p.27

A 괄호 안의 동사를 알맞은 형태로 바꿔 문장을 완성하시오.

1 She is good at __________ computers. (use)

2 __________ a parking lot is difficult in this town. (find)

3 Patrick is busy __________ the house. (clean)

4 The most important thing is __________ happy. (be)

B 밑줄 친 부분이 어법상 맞으면 O를 쓰고, 틀리면 바르게 고쳐 쓰시오.

1 I suggest going out for dinner tonight. → __________

2 I'm sorry about to be late for the class. → __________

3 Studying online is convenient for students. → __________

4 His job is teach how to cook Korean food. → __________

5 Playing basketball with my friends are exciting. → __________

C 동명사를 이용하여 다음 두 문장을 한 문장으로 연결하시오.

1 I sang on the stage. It made me nervous.
→ __________ made me nervous.

2 Sophie listens to classical music. She enjoys it.
→ Sophie enjoys __________.

3 She grows plants in the garden. It is her favorite hobby.
→ Her favorite hobby is __________.

D 우리말과 같도록 괄호 안의 말을 알맞게 배열하시오.

1 그들은 운동 후에 피곤하다고 느끼지 않을 수 없었다. (help, tired, feeling, couldn't)
= They __________ after the workout.

2 나는 차가운 무언가를 마시고 싶다. (like, cold, something, feel, drinking)
= I __________.

3 James는 한 시간 동안 전화로 계속 이야기했다. (talking, phone, kept, the, on)
= James __________ for an hour.

UNIT 02 동명사와 to부정사를 목적어로 쓰는 동사

Answers p.28

A 괄호 안에서 알맞은 것을 모두 고르시오.

1 Mark avoided (telling / to tell) me his secret.

2 She decided (calling / to call) the teddy bear Cuddles.

3 The kids like (drawing / to draw) on the wall.

4 They hope (seeing / to see) many stars tonight.

5 I should remember (buying / to buy) some milk tomorrow.

6 Edward will continue (growing / to grow) his hair.

7 The tourists stopped (walking / to walk) because they were tired.

8 Don't forget (locking / to lock) the door when you go out.

B 괄호 안의 동사를 알맞은 형태로 바꿔 문장을 완성하시오.

1 We agreed ________________ at the mall. (meet)

2 Do you mind ________________ the window? (close)

3 The man denied ________________ trash away on the street. (throw)

4 She prefers ________________ a bath in the morning. (take)

5 They are planning ________________ to the beach next week. (go)

6 John loves ________________ a can of soda after a meal. (drink)

7 Charlotte needs ________________ dinner for her mother today. (cook)

8 My sister enjoys ________________ with her friends at the coffee shop. (talk)

C 우리말과 같도록 괄호 안의 말을 활용하여 문장을 완성하시오.

1 그녀는 너무 늦게까지 일하는 것을 싫어한다. (hate, work)
= ________________________________ too late.

2 나의 삼촌은 작년에 담배 피는 것을 그만뒀다. (uncle, quit, smoke)
= ________________________________ last year.

3 Brian은 잠시 동안 혼자 있기를 바란다. (wish, be, alone)
= ________________________________ for a while.

4 나는 나의 남동생에게 소리쳤던 것을 후회한다. (regret, yell at, younger brother)
= ________________________________.

Chapter Test+

Answers p.28

[1-3] 다음 빈칸에 들어갈 알맞은 것을 고르시오.

1

Mr. Diaz is busy ________ breakfast.

① make ② made
③ to make ④ making
⑤ to making

2

We stopped ________ when the problem was solved.

① argue ② arguing
③ to argue ④ to arguing
⑤ argued

3

Henry ________ taking pictures of flowers.

① wants ② plans
③ wishes ④ enjoys
⑤ promises

[4-5] 다음 글의 빈칸에 들어갈 말이 순서대로 짝지어진 것을 고르시오.

4

Chris is a nice friend. He always loves ________ people and avoids ________ negatively. I want to be more like him.

① help - thinking
② to help - thinking
③ to help - to think
④ helping - to think
⑤ helping - to thinking

5

My brother came into my room and hid one of my hats. When I asked him to give it back, he denied ________ it. So, I said, "You should quit ________ to me. I know everything."

① hide - to lie ② to hide - lying
③ to hide - to lie ④ hiding - to lie
⑤ hiding - lying

서술형

[6-7] 다음 문장에서 어법상 어색한 부분을 찾아 쓰고 바르게 고쳐 쓰시오.

6

Remember bringing your lunch to school tomorrow.

________ → ________

7

I hope making many new friends in the book club.

________ → ________

8 다음 중 짝지어진 두 문장의 의미가 다른 것은?

① Paula prefers staying home during summer.
→ Paula prefers to stay home during summer.
② We started working on our new project.
→ We started to work on our new project.
③ He doesn't like drinking soda.
→ He doesn't like to drink soda.
④ I stopped walking along the river.
→ I stopped to walk along the river.
⑤ Ice in the Arctic continues melting.
→ Ice in the Arctic continues to melt.

[9-10] 다음 중 어법상 어색한 것을 고르시오.

9 ① My grandfather needs to wear a hearing aid.
② People should avoid eating late at night.
③ Breaking a habit takes a lot of effort.
④ Ms. Thomson agreed to attend the meeting.
⑤ The baby kept to cry all night.

10 ① Did you finish sweeping the floor?
② I regret to say that Angela is sick.
③ My family is thinking of moving to Seoul.
④ He promised returning home early.
⑤ The kid hates going to the dentist.

서술형

[11-12] 동명사를 이용하여 다음 두 문장을 한 문장으로 연결하시오.

11
Sandra plays with her dog. She enjoys it.
→ Sandra enjoys ______________________.

12
Jason watched the amazing opera. He will never forget it.
→ Jason will never forget ______________
______________________.

서술형

[13-15] 우리말과 같도록 괄호 안의 말을 활용하여 문장을 완성하시오.

13
너는 이번 주말에 빵을 구워 보는 것이 좋겠다. (try, bake, bread)

= You'd better ______________________ this weekend.

14
그녀의 숙제를 끝내자마자, 그녀는 밖으로 나갔다. (finish, homework)

= ______________________, she went outside.

15
그녀는 기말 시험을 통과하지 못할 것을 두려워한다. (afraid of, pass)

= She ______________________ the final exam.

서술형

16 우리말과 같도록 주어진 <조건>에 맞게 영작하시오.

과거에 대해 불평해도 소용없다.

<조건> 1. use, complain, the past를 활용하시오.
2. 8단어로 쓰시오.

= ______________________.

고난도

17 주어진 문장의 밑줄 친 부분과 쓰임이 같은 것은?

My goal is getting a high score on the math test.

① His job is editing magazine articles.
② I love jogging in the early morning.
③ Learning good manners is necessary for kids.
④ She left the house without saying anything.
⑤ My sister practiced writing the alphabet.

서술형 고난도

18 다음 글의 밑줄 친 ⓐ~ⓔ 중 어법상 어색한 것을 찾아 기호를 쓰고 바르게 고쳐 쓰시오.

Yesterday was my brother's birthday. I forgot ⓐto buy his present, so I went ⓑshopping at the department store. I expected ⓒfinding a nice shirt for him, but I couldn't. So, I decided ⓓto search for other useful items. Finally, I bought the perfect backpack for my brother. I couldn't help ⓔto smile and felt happy for him.

(1) ______ → ____________________

(2) ______ → ____________________

[19-20] 다음 중 어법상 옳은 것을 고르시오.

19 ① She began taking tennis lessons.
② My sister gave up to become an actress.
③ Nate promised not eating too many chocolates.
④ He loves to hanging out with his friends.
⑤ Amy is good at remember names.

20 ① They agreed having ice cream together.
② He needs talking to someone about his problem.
③ I feel like to stay in my bed today.
④ Jessie doesn't mind to sitting next to Sam.
⑤ She regrets not studying harder last semester.

서술형

[21-22] 괄호 안의 동사를 활용하여 문장을 완성하시오.

21 The doctors tried ____________ the patient, and they succeeded. (save)

22 Ms. Carter stopped ____________ something to drink and bought a latte. (get)

23 다음 중 짝지어진 두 문장의 의미가 다른 것끼리 묶인 것은?

ⓐ Sophia prefers wearing wide pants.
→ Sophia prefers to wear wide pants.
ⓑ Mr. Hills stopped buying flowers.
→ Mr. Hills stopped to buy flowers.
ⓒ I started watching a new TV series.
→ I started to watch a new TV series.
ⓓ She remembered taking her phone.
→ She remembered to take her phone.

① ⓐ, ⓑ ② ⓐ, ⓒ ③ ⓑ, ⓒ
④ ⓑ, ⓓ ⑤ ⓒ, ⓓ

서술형

24 우리말과 같도록 괄호 안의 말을 알맞게 배열하시오.

그 레스토랑은 줄을 서서 기다릴 가치가 있었다.
(worth, the, in, was, line, restaurant, waiting)

= ________________________________.

Chapter 07

분사

UNIT 01 현재분사와 과거분사

Answers p.29

A 밑줄 친 부분이 어법상 맞으면 O를 쓰고, 틀리면 바르게 고쳐 쓰시오.

1 The computer fixing yesterday works well. → ________

2 The concert hall filled with people was too hot. → ________

3 The band's performance was disappointed. → ________

4 Frank found the hiding present in the box. → ________

B 다음 빈칸에 알맞은 말을 <보기>에서 한 번씩만 골라 알맞은 형태로 바꿔 쓰시오.

<보기>	stand	excite	cover	ring

1 The kids are ________ to go to the amusement park.

2 Can you turn off the ________ alarm, please?

3 They want the cake ________ with chocolate.

4 The girl ________ by the front door is Ella.

C 우리말과 같도록 괄호 안의 말을 활용하여 문장을 완성하시오.

1 Hannah는 나에게 흥미로운 이야기를 말해줬다. (interest, story)
= Hannah told me an ________________.

2 찢어진 종이는 나의 과학 보고서이다. (tear, paper)
= The ________________ is my science report.

3 부엌에 타고 있는 무언가가 있는 것이 틀림없다. (burn, something)
= There must be ________________ in the kitchen.

D 분사를 이용하여 다음 두 문장을 한 문장으로 연결하시오.

1 I like the boy. He is playing the violin.
→ I like the boy ________________________.

2 There is the building. It was damaged by the earthquake.
→ There is the building ________________________.

3 Diane saw a bird. It was flying into the forest.
→ Diane saw a bird ________________________.

4 I can't understand this sign. It is written in Chinese.
→ I can't understand this sign ________________________.

UNIT 02 분사구문

Answers p.29

A 밑줄 친 부분이 어법상 맞으면 O를 쓰고, 틀리면 바르게 고쳐 쓰시오.

1 Waved their hands, they said goodbye. → ____________

2 Being lost in the forest, Grace felt scared. → ____________

3 Take a walk, my parents and I talked a lot. → ____________

4 Seen a long snake in our yard, we screamed. → ____________

B 다음 두 문장의 의미가 같도록 분사구문을 이용하여 문장을 완성하시오. (단, 접속사를 생략하시오.)

1 As she is shy, she has few friends.
→ ______________________, she has few friends.

2 When I left home, I forgot to turn off the light.
→ ______________________, I forgot to turn off the light.

3 Since he doesn't want to waste time, he gets up early every day.
→ ______________________, he gets up early every day.

C <보기>에서 가장 알맞은 접속사를 한 번씩만 골라 다음 두 문장의 의미가 같도록 문장을 완성하시오.

<보기>	if	because	while

1 Having homework to do, she can't go to the party.
→ ______________________, she can't go to the party.

2 Lying on the ground, they counted stars.
→ ______________________, they counted stars.

3 Cutting your hair, you'll look much better.
→ ______________________, you'll look much better.

D 우리말과 같도록 괄호 안의 말을 활용하여 빈칸에 쓰시오.

1 그녀는 학교로 뛰어가면서, 그녀의 지갑을 잃어버렸다. (run, to the school)
= ______ ______ ______ ______, she lost her wallet.

2 그는 너무 많은 물을 먹었기 때문에, 화장실에 가고 싶었다. (drink, too much water)
= ______ ______ ______ ______, he wanted to go to the toilet.

3 비록 경찰은 도둑을 잡기 위해 노력했지만, 그를 찾을 수 없었다. (try, catch the thief)
= ______ ______ ______ ______ ______ ______, the police couldn't find him.

Chapter Test+

Answers p.29

[1-2] 다음 빈칸에 들어갈 알맞은 것을 고르시오.

1 The famous director's new movie was ________.

① disappoint ② disappoints
③ to disappoint ④ disappointing
⑤ disappointed

2 We are sitting on chairs ________ of wood.

① make ② makes
③ made ④ making
⑤ to make

서술형

[3-4] 괄호 안의 동사를 활용하여 빈칸에 알맞은 말을 쓰시오.

3 The ________ birds woke me up in the morning. (sing)

4 The dress ________ by my sister looked beautiful. (wear)

[5-6] 다음 빈칸에 들어갈 말이 순서대로 짝지어진 것을 고르시오.

5
- The cookies ________ in this bakery are popular.
- The man ________ the suits is a well-known designer.

① make - designing ② making - designing
③ making - designed ④ made - designing
⑤ made - designed

6
- The tower ________ in the 1960s still looks new.
- The kid was given a box ________ with toys.

① build - fill ② built - filled
③ built - filling ④ building - filling
⑤ building - filled

서술형

7 다음 문장에서 어법상 어색한 부분을 찾아 쓰고 바르게 고쳐 쓰시오.

This is the town visiting by many tourists.

________ → ________

8 다음 중 어법상 옳은 것은?

① Swimming in the river, he lost his watch.
② Are you interesting in playing tennis?
③ The car accident was shocked.
④ Jonathan sat read a magazine.
⑤ Studied for the test, you'd better concentrate.

서술형

[9-10] 다음 문장의 밑줄 친 부분을 분사구문으로 바꿔 쓰시오.

9

As he wrote in his diary, he thought about his day.

→ ________________________, he thought about his day.

10

If you don't leave now, you will miss the bus.

→ ________________________, you will miss the bus.

11 다음 중 어법상 어색한 것은?

① The boring class made us sleepy.
② I'm worried about the weather tomorrow.
③ A baby cat is covering with a blanket.
④ The singer has an amazing voice.
⑤ Look at the girl skating beautifully.

고난도

12 다음 밑줄 친 부분과 바꿔 쓸 수 있는 것은?

Watching the comedy show, I laughed a lot.

① Because I watch the comedy show
② And I watched the comedy show
③ Although I watched the comedy show
④ While I watched the comedy show
⑤ If I watch the comedy show

서술형

[13-14] 우리말과 같도록 괄호 안의 말을 활용하여 분사구문을 완성하시오.

13

그는 그 벤치 위에 앉아서, 그의 친구를 기다렸다. (sit, on the bench)

= ________________________, he waited for his friend.

14

나는 아팠기 때문에, 침대 안에 머물렀다 (be, ill)

= ________________________, I stayed in my bed.

15 다음 중 어법상 바른 것의 개수는?

ⓐ There are children played outside.
ⓑ He will replace the broken windows tomorrow.
ⓒ Had nothing to do, she decided to go for a walk.
ⓓ Ms. Snow wants to purchase a using car.
ⓔ Resting on the sofa, he felt comfortable.

① 1개 ② 2개 ③ 3개
④ 4개 ⑤ 5개

고난도

16 다음 중 밑줄 친 부분의 쓰임이 나머지 넷과 다른 것은?

① My plan is going to Busan for holiday.
② He loves playing computer games.
③ Her job is writing children's books.
④ I don't like putting off my homework.
⑤ The girl listening to music is Sally.

서술형

[17-18] 우리말과 같도록 괄호 안의 말을 활용하여 빈칸에 쓰시오.

17 그는 저녁을 먹으면서, TV를 봤다. (have, dinner)

= ________ ________ ________ ________, he watched TV.

= ________ ________, he watched TV.

18 만약 네가 너무 많은 탄산음료를 마신다면, 너는 건강해지지 않을 것이다. (drink, too much soda)

= ________ ________ ________ ________ ________ ________, you won't get healthy.

= ________ ________ ________ ________, you won't get healthy.

서술형 고난도

19 다음 글의 밑줄 친 ⓐ~ⓔ 중 어법상 어색한 것을 찾아 기호를 쓰고 바르게 고쳐 쓰시오.

Today was the first day of middle school. ⓐEntering the class, I noticed many people ⓑlooked at me. I was ⓒembarrassed, so I tried to find my seat quickly. ⓓSitting on my seat, I saw someone familiar next to me. It was Jane! ⓔFelt excited, we started to talk about our new school.

(1) ______ → ______________________

(2) ______ → ______________________

서술형

[20-22] 분사를 이용하여 다음 두 문장을 한 문장으로 연결하시오.

20 I watched the sun. It was rising over the mountains.

→ I watched ______________________ ______________________.

21 Sarah can use the dishes. They were washed ten minutes ago.

→ Sarah can use ______________________ ______________________.

22 The car is my uncle's. It is parked in front of my house.

→ ______________________ is my uncle's.

고난도

23 다음 밑줄 친 부분을 부사절로 바꾼 것 중 어색한 것은?

① Taking a walk, we talked to each other.
→ While we took a walk

② Speaking English, you can make foreign friends.
→ If you speak English

③ Being tall, I can reach the ceiling.
→ Though I am tall

④ Going into the theater, she turned off her phone.
→ When she went into the theater

⑤ Not having an umbrella, he got wet.
→ Since he didn't have an umbrella

대명사

UNIT 01 부정대명사 I

Answers p.30

A 다음 빈칸에 알맞은 말을 <보기>에서 골라 대화를 완성하시오.

<보기>	ones	it	them

1 *A*: Where did you hear the rumor?
B: I heard ________ from Emma.

2 *A*: Are there only large bowls in the cupboard?
B: The small ________ are on the top shelf.

3 *A*: Scott sent me lots of packages.
B: Were there many interesting things in ________?

B 다음 빈칸에 알맞은 말을 <보기>에서 한 번씩만 골라 쓰시오.

<보기>	another	others	some	any

1 She is selfish, so she doesn't think about ________.

2 Do not give ________ food to the animals in the wild.

3 They are looking for ________ chairs to sit on.

4 I don't like this jacket. Can you recommend ________ for me?

<보기>	some	the other	the others

5 ________ like spring, and others like summer.

6 Ten bottles are on the table. Some are empty, and ________ are full.

7 I have two brothers. One lives in New York, and ________ lives in Texas.

C 우리말과 같도록 괄호 안의 말을 활용하여 빈칸에 쓰시오.

1 Betty는 지난 주말에 어떤 숙제도 하지 않았다. (do, homework)
= Betty didn't ________ ________ ________ last weekend.

2 이 노트북은 비싸요. 더 싼 것이 있나요? (cheaper)
= This laptop is expensive. Is there a ________ ________?

3 운동장에서, 몇몇의 학생들은 공을 던지고 있고, 나머지 전부는 공을 치고 있다. (student)
= In the playground, ________ ________ are throwing balls, and ________ ________ are hitting balls.

UNIT 02 부정대명사 II

Answers p.30

A 괄호 안의 동사를 알맞은 형태로 바꿔 빈칸에 쓰시오. (단, 현재시제로 쓰시오.)

1 Each of the pancakes ________ 15 dollars. (cost)

2 Both of my friends ________ to be a doctor. (want)

3 In summer, all the hotels in this city ________ booked. (be)

4 All of the furniture in this shop ________ modern. (look)

5 Each person ________ a different hobby. (have)

6 Every playground in the park ________ crowded with kids. (be)

7 Both of us ________ watching funny videos in our free time. (like)

B 다음 빈칸에 알맞은 말을 <보기>에서 한 번씩만 골라 쓰시오.

<보기>	all	both	each	one another	every

1 Since the concert was good, __________ the people were satisfied.

2 __________ of the workers has their own computer on the desk.

3 The participants of the game will compete with __________.

4 __________ movie looks interesting. I can't decide what to watch.

5 Melissa and Laura plan to go to the zoo. __________ of them are excited.

C 다음 문장에서 어법상 틀린 부분을 찾아 바르게 고쳐 완전한 문장을 쓰시오.

1 Both of the cameras was made in Korea.

→ ______________________________.

2 Each plates in the kitchen has a different pattern.

→ ______________________________.

3 All of the crops was destroyed by the storm.

→ ______________________________.

4 Every passengers is waiting in line to get on the plane.

→ ______________________________.

UNIT 03 재귀대명사

Answers p.30

A 밑줄 친 부분을 생략할 수 있으면 O를 쓰고, 생략할 수 없으면 X를 쓰시오.

1 Mr. Smith calls himself a hero. → ________

2 I myself answered the difficult questions. → ________

3 My sister is too young to cook a meal herself. → ________

4 We should protect ourselves from the disease. → ________

B 괄호 안의 말과 재귀대명사를 활용하여 빈칸에 알맞은 말을 쓰시오.

1 We ________ ________ at the front of the class. (seat)

2 She should be careful not to ________ ________ with that knife. (cut)

3 It might rain soon. You had better ________ ________ an umbrella. (buy)

4 Because I lost the game, I was ________ ________ ________. (disappointed in)

C <보기>의 말을 활용하여 대화를 완성하시오.

<보기> for oneself	beside oneself	help oneself to

1 *A*: The pasta smells good. Did you make it?
B: Yes. ____________________ it.

2 *A*: Jamie can do everything ____________________.
B: He must be really independent.

3 *A*: Sandra is ____________________ with fear.
B: What scared her so much?

D 우리말과 같도록 괄호 안의 말을 활용하여 빈칸에 쓰시오.

1 나는 항상 나 자신을 믿는다. (believe in)
= I always ________ ________ ________.

2 우리끼리 이야기지만, 그녀는 종종 그녀의 친구들에게 거짓말을 한다. (between)
= ________ ________, she often tells a lie to her friends.

3 그 여자는 그 집을 직접 설계했다. (the house)
= The woman designed ________ ________ ________.

4 Steven은 어렸을 때 혼잣말을 하곤 했다. (used to)
= Steven ________ ________ ________ ________ ________ when he was young.

Chapter Test+

Answers p.30

[1-2] 다음 빈칸에 들어갈 알맞은 것을 고르시오.

1

Where is my bag? I can't find ________ anywhere.

① one ② each ③ it
④ some ⑤ both

2

________ of the students has a student card.

① All ② Every ③ Some
④ Any ⑤ Each

3 다음 중 밑줄 친 부분을 생략할 수 없는 것은?

① Why don't you try baking a cake yourself?
② We made ourselves at home on the hotel bed.
③ I can deal with the problem myself.
④ They saw the famous actor himself.
⑤ Joy herself found the way to the restaurant.

서술형

4 우리말과 같도록 주어진 <조건>에 맞게 영작하시오.

방들 각각은 침대 두 개가 있다.

<조건>
1. 부정대명사를 사용하시오.
2. have, the room, bed를 활용하시오.
3. 7단어로 쓰시오.

= ________________________________.

서술형

[5-6] 우리말과 같도록 재귀대명사를 이용하여 빈칸에 쓰시오.

5

Ted는 요리하는 중에 종종 불에 덴다.

= Ted often ________ ________ while cooking.

6

우리는 한 벤치에 같이 앉았다.

= We ________ ________ on a bench together.

7 다음 (A)~(C)에 들어갈 말이 바르게 짝지어진 것은?

• Both of the books ___(A)___ novels.
• Every person ___(B)___ a different appearance.
• All of the smoke ___(C)___ coming from the factory.

	(A)	(B)	(C)
①	is	has	is
②	is	have	are
③	are	has	is
④	are	has	are
⑤	are	have	is

서술형

8 우리말과 같도록 빈칸에 알맞은 말을 쓰시오.

나의 친구 둘 다 등산을 잘 한다.

= ________ ________ ________ ________ are good at hiking.

서술형

[9-11] 다음 빈칸에 공통으로 들어갈 알맞은 부정대명사를 쓰시오.

9

- Jim and I helped each ________ when we did volunteer work at the community center.
- One of the two doors is locked. We have to use the ________.

10

- I loved the vanilla cupcake. May I have ________?
- The soccer team's members supported one ________ to win the game.

11

- You should respect ________ if you want to be respected.
- While some students played outside, the ________ stayed inside.

12 다음 중 어법상 바른 것은?

① Every boys was sitting on a chair quietly.
② All of my money are kept in the bank.
③ Jenna decided to make dinner by her.
④ There isn't some problem with your idea.
⑤ Let's keep this secret between ourselves.

[13-15] 다음 글의 빈칸에 들어갈 말이 순서대로 짝지어진 것을 고르시오.

13

Ms. Smith has three sons. ________ is a firefighter, and ________ are policemen.

① One - other ② One - the others
③ Another - others ④ Another - the others
⑤ Some - others

14

In the mall, Charles found two different coats. ________ of them suited him nicely. However, he had to pick ________ in the end because the two coats were too expensive for him to buy.

① Every - another ② Every - any
③ Both - other ④ Both - another
⑤ All - any

15

I lost my glasses, so I had to buy new ________. When I went to the store, the clerk recommended that I try contact lenses. But, I was afraid of wearing ________.

① ones - other ② ones - them
③ them - other ④ them - ones
⑤ one - them

서술형

16 다음 빈칸에 알맞은 말을 <보기>에서 한 번씩만 골라 쓰시오.

<보기> any all every

(1) ________ my friends in class are kind.

(2) Do you have ________ questions about this chapter?

(3) The singer shook hands with ________ fan at his concert.

[17-18] 다음 글을 읽고 주어진 질문에 답하시오.

> My parents went abroad for the holidays, but I couldn't go with them. So, (A) I stayed home alone for a week. At first, I thought I would be lonely. However, I was busy taking care of ⓐ myself.

서술형

17 위 글의 밑줄 친 (A)와 의미가 같도록 빈칸에 알맞은 말을 쓰시오.

→ I stayed home ________ ________ for a week.

고난도

18 위 글의 밑줄 친 ⓐ의 용법과 다른 것은?

① The author himself wrote the whole story.
② We saw ourselves in the mirror.
③ Amelia always calls herself a genius.
④ I hurt myself while playing tennis.
⑤ You should believe in yourself.

[19-20] 다음 중 어법상 어색한 것을 고르시오.

19 ① Each class lasts about 50 minutes.
② The problem in itself is not difficult.
③ He lost his wallet, so he will buy it.
④ Every painting looks beautiful to me.
⑤ All of the plates are on sale.

20 ① Both swimmers are diving into the pool.
② Be careful not to hurt you during P.E. class.
③ All people have the right to live.
④ Some of the apples are green.
⑤ Are there any parks near your apartment?

서술형 고난도

21 다음 글에서 어법상 어색한 부분을 모두 찾아 쓰고 바르게 고쳐 쓰시오.

> Jack took a math test yesterday. Every questions was difficult, but two of them were especially hard. However, Jack concentrated, and he finally solved both problem.

(1) ________ → ________
(2) ________ → ________

22 다음 대화의 빈칸에 들어갈 말이 순서대로 짝지어진 것은?

> *A*: I have two kinds of tea bags.
> *B*: Both of them ________ really nice!
> *A*: You can take one. Would you like this jasmine tea?
> *B*: Can I pick ________? I prefer green tea.

① smell - every
② smell - the other
③ smells - every
④ smells - the other
⑤ smelling - another

서술형

[23-24] 다음 문장에서 어법상 어색한 부분을 찾아 쓰고 바르게 고쳐 쓰시오.

23

> I think both choices has strengths.

________ → ________

24

> Jay doesn't have some suggestions on the group project.

________ → ________

Chapter 09 관계사

UNIT 01 관계대명사

Answers p.31

A 밑줄 친 부분이 어법상 맞으면 O를 쓰고, 틀리면 바르게 고쳐 쓰시오.

1 The boy whom is playing soccer is my brother. → ________

2 The wall who they painted yesterday is still wet. → ________

3 Sophia wrote a poem which is about her family. → ________

4 Crocodiles are animals whom teeth are very sharp. → ________

B 다음 빈칸에 who, which, whose 중 알맞은 것을 쓰시오.

1 The clock ________ is on the desk is not working.

2 Grace lives in the house ________ front yard is large.

3 I bought the laptop ________ Erica recommended.

4 The team needs players ________ are good at hitting balls.

C 관계대명사를 이용하여 다음 두 문장을 한 문장으로 연결하시오.

1 I know a man. His son is a guitarist.
→ I know a man ________________.

2 Emily couldn't find the book. She bought it last weekend.
→ Emily couldn't find the book ________________.

3 Mr. Ross is the history teacher. I respect him.
→ Mr. Ross is the history teacher ________________.

4 I want to go to the museum. It has modern artworks.
→ I want to go to the museum ________________.

D 우리말과 같도록 괄호 안의 말을 알맞게 배열하시오.

1 유명한 요리사가 만든 그 요리는 맛있었다. (famous, made, a, dish, the, which, chef)
= ________________ was delicious.

2 나는 아름다운 호수가 있는 그 도시에서 산다. (has, a, lake, which, city, beautiful, the)
= I live in ________________.

3 Johnson씨는 브레이크가 고장 난 그녀의 차를 고쳐야 한다. (broken, car, whose, her, brakes, are)
= Ms. Johnson has to repair ________________.

4 Andrew는 다른 학교로 전학을 간 그의 친구를 그리워했다. (who, friend, to, his, school, moved, another)
= Andrew missed ________________.

UNIT 02 관계대명사 that/what, 주의해야 할 관계대명사의 쓰임 Answers p.31

A 다음 빈칸에 that이나 what 중 알맞은 것을 쓰시오.

1 Would you like to have the pasta ________ I made?

2 This is the last train ________ goes to Busan.

3 ________ I want for Christmas is a new sweater.

4 Jason asked me ________ I planned for summer vacation.

5 The thing ________ we heard from the news was very surprising.

B 밑줄 친 부분을 생략할 수 있으면 O를 쓰고, 생략할 수 없으면 X를 쓰시오.

1 She is the girl whom I saw on the TV show. → ________

2 I would like to try that jacket whose color is black. → ________

3 Math is the subject which makes me bored. → ________

4 Ms. Watson collects plates that are from other countries. → ________

C 관계대명사를 이용하여 다음 두 문장을 한 문장으로 연결하시오. (단, 관계대명사는 생략하지 마시오.)

1 I know the woman. You were speaking to her.
→ I know the woman ______________________________.
→ I know the woman to ______________________________.

2 There are many chairs. People can sit on them.
→ There are many chairs ______________________________.
→ There are many chairs on ______________________________.

3 Martin is my friend. I can depend on him.
→ Martin is my friend ______________________________.
→ Martin is my friend on ______________________________.

D 우리말과 같도록 괄호 안의 말을 알맞게 배열하시오.

1 길거리에서 책을 팔고 있던 그 남자는 매우 착했다. (selling, man, the, books)
= ______________________________ on the street was very kind.

2 Ryan은 내가 이탈리아에서 샀던 것과 같은 지갑을 가지고 있다. (same, that, the, bought, wallet, I)
= Ryan has ______________________________ in Italy.

3 내가 사랑에 빠진 소녀는 Jane이다. (fell, with, love, I, the, whom, girl, in)
= ______________________________ is Jane.

UNIT 03 관계부사

Answers p.31

A 다음 빈칸에 알맞은 관계부사를 쓰시오.

1 Could you teach me ________ I can ride a bicycle?

2 8 o'clock was the time ________ all of the guests arrived.

3 Tell me the reason ________ you were late today.

4 Do you know the place ________ the festival will be held?

B 다음 두 문장의 의미가 같도록 빈칸에 알맞은 관계부사를 쓰시오.

1 Seoul is the city in which I was born.
→ Seoul is the city ________ I was born.

2 1980 is the year in which Mr. Williams first met his wife.
→ 1980 is the year ________ Mr. Williams first met his wife.

3 Victoria taught me the way in which Italians greet each other.
→ Victoria taught me ________ Italians greet each other.

4 This video shows you the reason for which you should wear a helmet.
→ This video shows you the reason ________ you should wear a helmet.

C 관계부사를 이용하여 다음 두 문장을 한 문장으로 연결하시오.

1 I remember the day. I introduced myself to my classmates on that day.
→ ____.

2 They're looking for the place. They can see the city's view from that place.
→ ____.

3 Natalie didn't tell us the reason. She cried yesterday for that reason.
→ ____.

D 우리말과 같도록 괄호 안의 말을 알맞게 배열하시오.

1 나는 나의 쿠키가 타버린 이유를 이해할 수 없다. (cookies, why, burned, my)
= I can't understand the reason ______________________________.

2 이곳은 그 커플이 그들의 사진을 찍었던 정원이다. (took, where, the, photos, couple, their)
= This is the garden ______________________________.

3 여름은 대부분의 사람들이 휴가를 가는 계절이다. (most, when, vacation, go, people, on, a)
= Summer is the season ______________________________.

Chapter Test+

Answers p.31

[1-3] 다음 빈칸에 들어갈 알맞은 것을 고르시오.

1

This is the problem ________ no one could solve.

① which ② whose ③ what
④ who ⑤ whom

2

________ she needed to buy was sold out.

① Who ② Whose ③ What
④ Which ⑤ That

3

The repairman will fix the house ________ walls have cracks.

① whom ② what ③ who
④ which ⑤ whose

4 다음 우리말을 알맞게 영작한 것은?

우리는 그가 과학자가 된 방법을 알기를 원한다.

① We want to know in how he became a scientist.
② We want to know the way he became a scientist.
③ We want to know the way which he became a scientist.
④ We want to know the way for which he became a scientist.
⑤ We want to know the way how he became a scientist.

5 다음 중 어법상 어색한 것은?

① This is the painting about that our art teacher talked.
② I ate the cake bought from the bakery.
③ The bag that Jenna was holding was heavy.
④ We had lunch with a girl who lives next door.
⑤ The man I met today looked happy.

6 다음 빈칸에 공통으로 들어갈 알맞은 것은?

• Claude Monet is the artist ________ my brother likes the most. • I finally met the actor to ________ I sent many fan letters.

① what ② that ③ whose
④ who ⑤ whom

7 다음 중 밑줄 친 부분을 생략할 수 없는 것은?

① Let's go to the restaurant that the famous blogger wrote about.
② Jenny is the person whom I asked to join our club.
③ My uncle couldn't find his car which was parked in the parking lot.
④ What do you think about the desk which Jack made?
⑤ Someone heard the issue about which we were talking.

서술형

[8-9] 알맞은 관계사를 이용하여 다음 두 문장을 한 문장으로 연결하시오.

8

Fred has a puppy. Its favorite food is sweet potato.
→ Fred has a puppy ______________________
______________________.

9

The movie was fantastic. A famous director made it.
→ The movie ______________________
______________ was fantastic.

서술형

10 주어진 <조건>에 맞게 다음 두 문장을 한 문장으로 연결하시오.

Do you know the reason? Ted moved to another city for that reason.

<조건> 1. 관계부사를 사용하시오.
2. the reason을 사용하시오.

= ______________________________
______________________________?

서술형

11 다음 빈칸에 알맞은 관계사를 <보기>에서 한 번씩만 골라 쓰시오.

<보기> who whom when

(1) Amy is my classmate __________ everybody likes.

(2) We are waiting for the day __________ our parents will come back from the trip.

(3) Dennis wants to make a friend with __________ he can go shopping.

12 다음 중 어법상 바른 것은?

① She read a book which story is touching.
② Students will go to the museum whom has many sculptures.
③ I gave the wallet that was on the street to a policeman.
④ The person which won the award is Thomas.
⑤ Anne was the girl whose I was arguing with.

서술형

[13-14] 다음 두 문장의 의미가 같도록 빈칸에 알맞은 말을 쓰시오.

13

The thing which Betty likes the most is watching old movies.
→ __________ Betty likes the most is watching old movies.

14

Frank will show you the way in which he plays the guitar.
→ Frank will show you __________ he plays the guitar.

고난도

15 다음 중 밑줄 친 <u>that</u>의 쓰임이 나머지 넷과 <u>다른</u> 것은?

① This shop has everything <u>that</u> we want.
② I have the same sneakers <u>that</u> Sam is wearing.
③ Ellen gave a speech <u>that</u> everyone praised.
④ I think <u>that</u> the event will be delayed.
⑤ The koala is an animal <u>that</u> sleeps a lot.

서술형

[16-17] 우리말과 같도록 관계사와 괄호 안의 말을 활용하여 빈칸에 쓰시오.

16 나는 선수들이 열심히 연습한 팀을 응원한다. (player, practice, hard)

= I support the team ________ ________ ________ ________.

17 그녀가 스마트폰을 산 가게는 저기 있다. (buy, the smartphone)

= The store ________ ________ ________ ________ ________ is over there.

[18-19] 다음 빈칸에 들어갈 말이 순서대로 짝지어진 것을 고르시오.

18
- I went to an art center about ________ I had read in the magazine.
- Do you remember the time ________ our parents took us to Disneyland?

① what - when ② which - when
③ what - that ④ which - what
⑤ that - what

19
- I love to see photos of kids and animals ________ are playing together.
- Can you tell me ________ you climbed to the top of the mountain?

① which - how ② who - the way how
③ that - how ④ that - who
⑤ which - who

고난도

20 다음 빈칸에 들어갈 관계사가 나머지 넷과 다른 것은?

① School is a place at ________ students learn.
② This is the path ________ leads to our destination.
③ Ron found the pen ________ he lost last night.
④ The day ________ a thief broke into my house was horrible.
⑤ I love the park ________ has a huge fountain.

서술형

[21-23] 다음 문장에서 어법상 어색한 부분을 찾아 쓰고 바르게 고쳐 쓰시오.

21 Sarah forgot the person to who she lent her laptop.

________ → ________

22 People didn't like the way how Owen behaved.

________ → ________

23 The city that have Gyeongbokgung Palace is Seoul.

________ → ________

Chapter 10 접속사

UNIT 01 시간/이유/결과를 나타내는 접속사

Answers p.32

A 괄호 안에서 알맞은 것을 고르시오.

1 Jack took some pictures (while / so) he was walking down the street.

2 The little girl was frightened (when / that) she heard the scary story.

3 (As soon as / Until) the door opens, please wait outside of the building.

4 There were many car accidents on the road (because / because of) the snow.

B 다음 두 문장의 의미가 같도록 <보기>에서 알맞은 접속사를 골라 쓰시오.

<보기>	before	because	so

1 As this smartphone is too expensive, I can't buy it.
→ This smartphone is too expensive, __________ I can't buy it.

2 After she washed her hands, she ate lunch.
→ __________ she ate lunch, she washed her hands.

3 Since there was a loud noise, everyone was surprised.
→ __________ there was a loud noise, everyone was surprised.

C 다음 빈칸에 가장 알맞은 말을 <보기>에서 골라 쓰시오.

<보기>	so his classmates like him	because she was thirsty
	when she was ten years old	since his best friend moved away

1 Ron has been lonely ______________________________.

2 Emily drank two cups of water ______________________________.

3 Aaron is kind and humorous, ______________________________.

4 Nancy could already speak two languages ______________________________.

D 우리말과 같도록 괄호 안의 말을 알맞게 배열하시오.

1 전화가 울리자마자, 그녀는 그것을 받았다. (the, soon, as, rang, as, phone)
= ______________________________, she answered it.

2 나는 잠시 쉰 후에 다시 뛰기 시작했다. (a, break, took, after, I, short)
= I started to run again ______________________________.

3 Tim은 꽃병을 탁자 위에 놓으면서 그것을 깨뜨렸다. (table, was, on, putting, as, the, it, he)
= Tim broke the vase ______________________________.

UNIT 02 조건/양보를 나타내는 접속사, 접속사 that

Answers p.32

A 다음 빈칸에 if, unless, though, that 중 알맞은 것을 한 번씩만 쓰시오.

1 ________ the ballerina hurt her toe, she didn't stop practicing.

2 ________ you don't hurry, you won't be able to catch the train.

3 My brother said ________ he saw someone strange at the park.

4 ________ you hand in your essay today, you should stay after school and finish it.

B <보기>의 접속사를 한 번씩만 활용하여 다음 두 문장을 한 문장으로 연결하시오. (단, 접속사를 문장 맨 앞에 쓰시오.)

<보기>	if	unless	although

1 Take this medicine. You'll feel better.
→ ________________________________.

2 The opera itself was great. It was boring to me.
→ ________________________________.

3 Sophia keeps her promise. Her friends won't trust her.
→ ________________________________.

C 다음 두 문장의 의미가 같도록 문장을 완성하시오.

1 Unless you take a taxi, you will miss the movie.
→ If ________________________________.

2 Brad was worried about the speech, but he tried to be confident.
→ Though ________________________________.

3 If Kelly doesn't focus during the class, she will get a poor grade.
→ Unless ________________________________.

D 우리말과 같도록 괄호 안의 말을 알맞게 배열하시오.

1 만약 네가 조심하지 않는다면, 너는 컵을 떨어뜨릴지도 모른다. (you, unless, are, careful)
= ________________________, you might drop the cup.

2 Jason이 어려운 퍼즐을 풀었다는 것은 놀랍다. (solved, puzzle, that, difficult, Jason, the)
= It is amazing ________________________.

3 비록 그 선수들은 최선을 다했지만 그 경기를 졌다. (tried, they, although, best, their)
= The players lost the game ________________________.

UNIT 03 명령문 + and/or, 상관접속사

Answers p.33

A 다음 빈칸에 알맞은 말을 <보기>에서 한 번씩만 골라 알맞은 형태로 바꿔 쓰시오.

<보기>	work	contain	play	watch

1 Either Julie or Hannah ________ tennis well.

2 Neither Walter nor I ________ scary movies.

3 Both my father and my mother ________ at the hospital.

4 Not only lemons but also oranges ________ lots of vitamin C.

B 밑줄 친 부분이 어법상 맞으면 O를 쓰고, 틀리면 바르게 고쳐 쓰시오.

1 I wanted to buy both pants or a t-shirt. → ________

2 Turn left at the corner, and you'll see the shopping mall. → ________

3 Do your homework, and you won't be allowed to play computer games. → ________

C 다음 두 문장의 의미가 같도록 문장을 완성하시오.

1 George doesn't enjoy swimming and Frank doesn't enjoy it, either.
→ ________________ enjoys swimming.

2 If you keep your promises, other people will trust you.
→ Keep your promises, ________________.

3 I need not only a pencil but also an eraser.
→ I need an eraser ________________.

4 If you talk loudly at night, your neighbors will get angry.
→ Do not talk loudly at night, ________________.

D 우리말과 같도록 괄호 안의 말을 알맞게 배열하시오.

1 Joan이나 Alice 둘 중 한 명이 노래 대회에서 우승할 것이다. (will, either, Joan, win, Alice, or)
= ________________ the singing contest.

2 너의 신발을 벗어라, 그렇지 않으면 바닥이 더러워질 것이다. (floor, get, or, the, dirty, will)
= Take off your shoes, ________________.

3 너의 주소를 나에게 말해라, 그러면 나는 너에게 선물을 보낼 것이다. (a, you, I, present, will, and, send)
= Tell me your address, ________________.

4 어른과 아이들 둘 다 이 행사에 참가할 수 있다. (children, can, participate, both, and, adults)
= ________________ in this event.

Chapter Test+

Answers p.33

[1-3] 다음 빈칸에 들어갈 가장 알맞은 것을 고르시오.

1

I've studied Spanish ________ I was a child.

① if ② since ③ as
④ after ⑤ unless

2

Kelly bought sunglasses ________ the sunlight was too strong.

① or ② so ③ unless
④ until ⑤ because

3

________ we make a reservation, we can't eat at that popular restaurant.

① Unless ② If ③ As
④ That ⑤ While

4 다음 중 밑줄 친 as의 의미가 나머지 넷과 다른 것은?

① As Jessie broke her arm, she went to the hospital.
② As he didn't eat anything, he was hungry.
③ As the mall was too crowded, Chloe couldn't find her friend.
④ As it snowed, the children went out to make a snowman.
⑤ As I was going home, I ran into my dad.

서술형

[5-6] 알맞은 접속사를 이용하여 다음 두 문장을 한 문장으로 연결하시오.

5

I took care of my younger sister by myself.
At that time, I felt worried.
→ ________ I took care of my younger sister by myself, I felt worried.

6

Rosie took the medicine. And then, she went to bed.
→ Rosie went to bed ________ she took the medicine.

서술형

[7-8] 다음 문장에서 어법상 어색한 부분을 찾아 쓰고 바르게 고쳐 쓰시오.

7

He is very busy that he cannot answer the phone.

________ → ________

8

Either green tea or coffee are fine with me.

________ → ________

서술형

[9-11] 우리말과 같도록 괄호 안의 말을 활용하여 문장을 완성하시오.

9

이 셔츠는 저렴할 뿐만 아니라 멋지기도 하다. (cheap, stylish)

= This shirt is ______________________.

10

Anne이 오늘 제시간에 온 것은 놀랍다. (come, on time)

= It is surprising ______________________ today.

11

만약 시험이 일찍 끝난다면, 나는 쇼핑하러 갈 것이다. (the test, finish, early)

= ______________________, I'll go shopping.

12 다음 빈칸에 들어갈 말이 순서대로 짝지어진 것은?

- Please close all the windows ________ you go out.
- Watch out for the slippery floor, ________ you'll fall down.

① before - and ② before - or
③ after - and ④ after - or
⑤ when - and

13 다음 중 어법상 바른 것은?

① The class was so that interesting we all enjoyed it.
② Read a lot of books, or you will get smarter.
③ The problem is that she didn't come to school.
④ Jeff as well as Carl like comic books.
⑤ If you will visit my house, I will cook your favorite food.

14 다음 중 밑줄 친 that의 쓰임이 나머지 넷과 다른 것은?

① Timothy believes that his friends are honest.
② We hope that we can go to Thailand for a trip.
③ The issue is that we need a new school president.
④ Some people think that they are better than others.
⑤ I guess that I need more wood for the campfire.

서술형

[15-16] 다음 두 문장의 의미가 같도록 빈칸에 알맞은 말을 쓰시오.

15

If you don't follow the rules, you can't join the game.
→ ________ ________ ________, ________ you can't join the game.

16

He brushed his teeth after he had dinner.
→ ________ ________ ________ ________ ________, he had dinner.

Chapter 10 접속사 Hackers Grammar Smart Level 2

17 다음 중 어법상 어색한 것은?

① I'm tired because of I couldn't sleep well.
② Either my mom or dad picks me up every day.
③ He'll be back after he finishes his work.
④ The K-pop singer is so famous that everyone knows her.
⑤ When Ms. Brown was a child, she wanted to be a doctor.

18 다음 중 밑줄 친 부분의 쓰임이 어색한 것을 고르시오.

① I missed the flight because I was late.
② Let's chat together until the bus comes.
③ When I get older, I will travel to New York.
④ If it rains tomorrow, we will play outside.
⑤ While Janice was playing the piano, Owen sang a song.

19 다음 우리말을 알맞게 영작한 것은?

비록 그가 사과했지만, 나는 여전히 화났다.

① If he apologized, I'm still angry.
② Although he apologized, I'm still angry.
③ Because he apologized, I'm still angry.
④ Unless he apologized, I'm still angry.
⑤ Before he apologized, I'm still angry.

서술형 고난도

20 다음 빈칸에 알맞은 접속사를 <보기>에서 한 번씩만 골라 쓰시오.

<보기> as soon as because unless

(1) Ron woke up ______________ the alarm rang.
(2) I'll see you on Saturday, ______________ I have other appointments.
(3) Ben envies Monica ______________ she achieved her dream.

고난도

21 다음 빈칸에 들어갈 접속사가 나머지 넷과 다른 것은?

① ______ I wake up early, I'll go jogging.
② ______ you don't exercise, you'll get weaker.
③ ______ we want to save the animals, we should protect the environment.
④ ______ he finishes his homework, he won't be allowed to play computer games.
⑤ ______ you want to get a refund, you must bring the receipt.

22 다음 밑줄 친 as와 의미가 같은 것은?

As his racket is broken, he can't play tennis.

① That ② So ③ Because
④ Until ⑤ After

[23-24] 다음 빈칸에 공통으로 들어갈 알맞은 것을 고르시오.

23

• These boxes are ________ heavy that even Mr. Hills can't lift them. • I was too sleepy, ________ I couldn't focus on the class.

① and ② so ③ after
④ or ⑤ that

24

• I made a wish ________ I blew out the candles. • ________ he is clever, he remembers everything.

① unless ② although ③ before
④ till ⑤ as

비교구문

UNIT 01 원급/비교급/최상급 비교

Answers p.34

A 밑줄 친 부분이 어법상 맞으면 O를 쓰고, 틀리면 바르게 고쳐 쓰시오.

1 Nancy is as taller as her mother. → __________
2 The black car is cheap than the white one. → __________
3 This painting is the largest artwork in the museum. → __________
4 The flu is very more dangerous than the common cold. → __________

B 다음 빈칸에 알맞은 말을 <보기>에서 한 번씩만 골라 알맞은 형태로 바꿔 쓰시오.

<보기>	good	early	cold	difficult

1 Joshua comes to school __________ than his classmates.
2 The math test was __________ as the science test.
3 Your English skills are __________ than mine.
4 Antarctica is __________ area in the world.

C 괄호 안의 말을 활용하여 다음 문장을 한 문장으로 바꿔 쓰시오.

1 Susan exercises five times a week. Carol also exercises five times a week. (often)
→ Carol exercises __________ Susan.

2 I can run 50 meters in eight seconds. My brother can run 50 meters in seven seconds. (fast)
→ My brother can run __________ me.

3 A tennis ball is 60 grams. A soccer ball is 450 grams. A basketball is 600 grams. (heavy)
→ A basketball is __________ of the three balls.

4 George has three hats. Edward has five hats. (many)
→ Edward has ________ hats ________ George does.

D 우리말과 같도록 괄호 안의 말을 알맞게 배열하시오.

1 그것은 나의 동네에서 가장 오래된 식당이다. (oldest, the, restaurant)
= It is ______________________ in my town.

2 이 새 셔츠는 예전 것보다 훨씬 더 크다. (the, than, one, far, bigger, old)
= This new shirt is ______________________.

3 몇몇 동물들은 인간만큼 똑똑하다. (as, humans, intelligent, as)
= Some animals are ______________________.

UNIT 02 비교구문을 이용한 표현

Answers p.34

A 괄호 안의 말을 활용하여 문장을 완성하시오.

1 You should wake up ____________________ possible not to miss the train. (early)

2 The ____________ my bag got, the ____________ it became. (empty, light)

3 Write down your address ____________________ you can. (clearly)

4 The soccer stadium is becoming more and ____________________. (crowded)

B 다음 두 문장의 의미가 같도록 문장을 완성하시오.

1 This box is three times as big as that one.
→ This box is ___________________________ that one.

2 Barbara used to clean her room as often as possible.
→ Barbara used to clean her room ___________________________.

3 A dog lives four times longer than a hamster.
→ A dog lives ___________________________ a hamster.

C <보기>와 같이 다음 문장을 「the + 비교급, the + 비교급」을 이용하여 바꿔 쓰시오.

<보기>	As I exercised more regularly, I became stronger. → *The more regularly I exercised, the stronger I became*.

1 When it got sunnier, we felt more active.
→ ____.

2 If the test is more difficult, students will be more tired.
→ ____.

3 If you buy a plane ticket earlier, the tickets are cheaper.
→ ____.

D 우리말과 같도록 괄호 안의 말을 알맞게 배열하시오.

1 태블릿 PC는 점점 더 유용해지고 있다. (more, getting, useful, and, more, is)
= The tablet PC ___________________________________.

2 스티비 원더는 세계 최고의 가수들 중 한 명이었다. (the, singers, was, of, one, best)
= Stevie Wonder _____________________________________ in the world.

3 네가 더 많은 꽃을 키우면 키울수록 너의 정원은 더 다채로워질 것이다. (your, more, be, colorful, the, will, garden)
= The more flowers you grow, ___________________________________.

Chapter Test+

Answers p.34

[1-4] 다음 빈칸에 들어갈 알맞은 것을 고르시오.

1 This chocolate cookie is ________ of all the desserts.

① delicious ② more delicious
③ the delicious ④ the more delicious
⑤ the most delicious

2 The more you practice running, ________ you will become.

① fast ② faster
③ fastest ④ the faster
⑤ the fastest

3 The new washing machine is working ________ than the old one.

① good ② well
③ better ④ best
⑤ more well

4 My doll is ________ cuter than your teddy bear.

① far ② most
③ more ④ very
⑤ as

[5-6] 다음 중 어법상 어색한 것을 고르시오.

5 ① My bed is softer than my sister's.
② Mr. Hill's son is as lovely as his daughter.
③ This cave is the deepest in the world.
④ The pizza is more tasty than the pasta.
⑤ Charlie began to talk more and more loudly.

6 ① Summer is the hottest of the four seasons.
② I was as happy as my friend on her birthday.
③ You should study harder than you did last semester.
④ Please be as quiet as possible in the library.
⑤ The more we read, the most we learn.

서술형

[7-8] 괄호 안의 말을 활용하여 다음 문장을 한 문장으로 바꿔 쓰시오.

7
- The bracelet costs 20 dollars.
- The ring costs 30 dollars.

→ The ring is ____________________ the bracelet. (expensive)

8
- Jake's test score was 76.
- Jessica's test score was 80.
- Bill's test score was 98.

→ Bill's test score was ____________________ the three. (high)

서술형

[9-10] 우리말과 같도록 괄호 안의 말을 활용하여 문장을 완성하시오.

9

Tom은 나만큼 높게 뛰지 못한다. (high)

= Tom can't jump ______________________ I do.

10

Andrew는 우리 학교에서 가장 똑똑한 학생들 중 한 명이다. (smart, student)

= Andrew is ______________________ in our school.

서술형

11 우리말과 같도록 주어진 <조건>에 맞게 영작하시오.

그 화가는 점점 더 유명해졌다.

<조건>
1. painter, become, famous를 활용하시오.
2. 비교급 표현을 사용하시오.

= ______________________.

12 다음 빈칸에 공통으로 들어갈 알맞은 것은?

- The ________ you cry, the sadder you might feel.
- I think tulips are a lot ________ beautiful than roses.

① more ② much ③ most
④ many ⑤ very

서술형

[13-14] 다음 두 문장의 의미가 같도록 문장을 완성하시오.

13

I submitted my essay as early as possible.
→ I submitted my essay ______________________.

14

When the subway is more crowded, it gets hotter.
→ The more crowded the subway is, ______________________.

15 다음 빈칸에 들어갈 말이 순서대로 짝지어진 것은?

- His backpack is ________ bigger than mine.
- Katie's advice was far ________ helpful than yours.

① a lot - as ② a lot - more
③ even - so ④ even - as
⑤ very - more

16 다음은 세 명의 학생을 비교하는 표이다. 다음 표를 바르게 설명한 것을 모두 고르시오.

이름	Josh	Ken	Nate
나이	15	13	16
키	170 cm	160 cm	167 cm
몸무게	60 kg	50 kg	65 kg

① Nate is the youngest of all.
② Ken is older than Josh.
③ Nate is heavier than Josh.
④ Ken is not as light as Josh.
⑤ Josh is the tallest of the three.

서술형

[17-18] 다음 문장에서 틀린 부분을 바르게 고쳐 완전한 문장을 쓰시오.

17

I studied hard than Jess.

→ ________________________________.

18

Russia has the bigger land on earth.

→ ________________________________.

서술형

19 다음 대화에 나온 표현을 활용하여 빈칸에 알맞은 말을 쓰시오.

A: I didn't understand you before we talked, but I think I understand you deeply now.
B: I agree. As we talked more, we understood each other more deeply.

→ ________ ________ they talked, ________ ________ ________ they understood each other.

서술형 고난도

20 다음은 세 개의 과일을 비교하는 표이다. 괄호 안의 말을 활용하여 문장을 완성하시오.

과일	Apple	Mango	Pear
가격	$1	$3	$2
무게	200 g	100 g	200 g

(1) The apple is ________________ of the three. (cheap)

(2) The pear is ________________ the apple. (heavy)

(3) The mango is ________________ the pear. (light)

21 다음 중 어법상 바른 것은?

① Jane speaks English fluently than me.
② What is the most brightest star in the sky?
③ Thomas is one of the kindest students in our class.
④ This spring isn't as warm than the last one.
⑤ This shampoo smells as sweeter as honey.

22 다음 중 밑줄 친 부분을 바르게 고친 것은?

① Today was busiest day in my life. (→ the busier)
② My grandparents are as more healthy as my parents. (→ healthier)
③ I'm far good than her at swimming. (→ best)
④ The weather is getting more and more cold. (→ colder and colder)
⑤ The actor was the more attractive in the movie. (→ the attractivest)

고난도

23 다음 중 어법상 바른 것끼리 묶인 것은?

ⓐ The higher we climbed, the more tired we became.
ⓑ This building is the taller in the city.
ⓒ The Mississippi River is not as longest as the Nile River.
ⓓ The classroom is the dirtiest than yesterday.
ⓔ This book is much thicker than the other one.

① ⓐ, ⓒ ② ⓐ, ⓔ ③ ⓑ, ⓓ
④ ⓒ, ⓓ ⑤ ⓒ, ⓔ

Chapter 12

가정법

UNIT 01 가정법 과거, 가정법 과거완료

Answers p.35

A 밑줄 친 부분이 어법상 맞으면 O를 쓰고, 틀리면 바르게 고쳐 쓰시오.

1 If I <u>am</u> you, I would spend more time with your parents. → ______

2 If Brian knew Anna's phone number, he <u>could have called</u> her. → ______

3 If the concert <u>had been canceled</u>, I would have been disappointed. → ______

4 If Emily <u>exercised</u> regularly, she could have become healthier. → ______

B 다음 문장을 가정법 문장으로 바꿔 쓰시오.

1 As I'm not in Seoul, I can't meet you.
→ If I ______, I ______.

2 As she didn't wear her seat belt, she was hurt.
→ If she ______, she ______.

3 As the child isn't tall enough, he can't ride the roller coaster.
→ If the child ______, he ______.

4 As I am sick, I can't go to the party tonight.
→ If I ______, I ______.

5 As Helen didn't practice the piano hard, she couldn't become a good pianist.
→ If Helen ______, she ______.

6 As he forgot my birthday, he didn't send me presents.
→ If he ______, he ______.

C 우리말과 같도록 괄호 안의 말을 활용하여 문장을 완성하시오.

1 만약 그녀가 차를 가지고 있다면, 직장에 운전해서 갈 텐데. (have a car, drive)
= If she ______, she ______ to work.

2 만약 방학이 더 길다면, 나는 더 많은 관광지로 여행을 갈 수 있을 텐데. (be longer, travel)
= If the vacation ______, I ______ to more tourist sites.

3 만약 영화가 더 흥미로웠더라면, 그들은 그렇게 일찍 극장을 떠나지 않았을 텐데. (be more interesting, leave)
= If the movie ______, they ______ the theater so soon.

UNIT 02 I wish 가정법, as if 가정법

Answers p.35

A 괄호 안에서 알맞은 것을 고르시오.

1 Last Sunday was foggy. I wish it (were / had been) sunny that day.

2 Thomas acts as if he (is / were) a teacher. In fact, he is not.

3 I wish I (could go / could have gone) to Mars now. It sounds exciting.

4 They look as if they (knew / had known) each other for a long time.

B <보기>의 동사를 한 번씩만 활용하여 가정법 문장을 완성하시오.

<보기> be live know

1 I can't play the violin. I wish I ____________ how to play it.

2 Kyle talks as if he ____________ in London when he was younger.

3 I wish you ____________ more kind to your friends. You were so rude yesterday.

C 다음 문장을 가정법 문장으로 바꿔 쓰시오.

1 I'm sorry that I can't return these shoes.
→ I wish ________________________________.

2 In fact, Chloe didn't pass the science test.
→ Chloe talks as if ________________________________.

3 In fact, the little boy can't swim.
→ The little boy acts as if ________________________________.

4 I'm sorry that Joshua didn't tell me the truth.
→ I wish ________________________________.

D 우리말과 같도록 괄호 안의 말을 알맞게 배열하시오.

1 Henry는 마치 원어민인 것처럼 스페인어를 말한다. (he, native, a, if, speaker, as, were)
= Henry speaks Spanish ________________________________.

2 내가 아침으로 샌드위치를 먹었더라면 좋았을 텐데. (eaten, for, I, breakfast, had, sandwiches)
= I wish ________________________________.

3 Ellie는 마치 며칠 동안 아팠던 것처럼 보인다. (as, sick, if, she, had, been)
= Ellie looks ________________________________ for a few days.

4 그 감독이 판타지 영화를 만든다면 좋을 텐데. (make, the, movies, would, fantasy, director)
= I wish ________________________________.

Chapter Test +

Answers p.35

[1-3] 다음 빈칸에 들어갈 알맞은 것을 고르시오.

1

If I had purchased the plane ticket earlier, I ________ less for it.

① pay ② have paid
③ had paid ④ would pay
⑤ would have paid

2

He is sweating. He looks as if he ________ through the rain.

① walk ② walks
③ is walking ④ had walked
⑤ has walked

3

I wish I ________ to the concert with you tomorrow.

① go ② could go
③ will go ④ can go
⑤ had gone

서술형

4 다음 빈칸에 공통으로 들어갈 알맞은 말을 쓰시오.

• ________ you had heard the news, we could have talked about it.
• He sounds as ________ there were a big problem.

서술형

[5-7] 다음 문장을 가정법 문장으로 바꿔 쓰시오.

5

I'm sorry that you won't join our club.
→ I wish ________________.

6

As the math class was boring, I fell asleep.
→ If the math class ________________,
________________.

7

As they don't have an invitation, they can't enter the building.
→ If they ________________,
________________.

서술형

[8-9] 우리말과 같도록 괄호 안의 말을 활용하여 문장을 완성하시오.

8

Hills씨는 마치 스포츠카를 소유하고 있는 것처럼 말한다. (own, a sports car)

= Mr. Hills talks ________________.

9

내가 더 많은 돈을 저축했더라면 좋았을 텐데. (save, more money)

= I wish ________________.

[10-11] 다음 빈칸에 들어갈 말이 순서대로 짝지어진 것을 고르시오.

10

- He talks as if he ________ the food. In fact, he didn't.
- If the movie were interesting, I ________ it to the end.

① cooks – watch
② cooked – will watch
③ cooked – would watch
④ had cooked – would watch
⑤ had cooked – will watch

11

- I wish I ________ many books when I was young.
- If the train ________ on time, Laura wouldn't have been late.

① read – arrives
② have read – arrived
③ had read – had arrived
④ had read – arrived
⑤ have read – had arrived

고난도

12 다음 밑줄 친 부분을 바르게 고치지 못한 것은?

① She speaks as if she met the president before. (→ had met)
② If the air conditioner worked well, it wouldn't have been hot. (→ had worked)
③ Tim talks as if he has been friends with me. (→ had been)
④ I wish the store sells better products. (→ sold)
⑤ If Nathan had been honest, he would be forgiven. (→ is)

13 다음 대화의 빈칸에 들어갈 말이 순서대로 짝지어진 것은?

A: I wish everyone ________ to the party last month. I'm sorry that I couldn't meet Eric.
B: Me too. If Eric had not been in the hospital, we ________ him there.

① come – can see
② came – could see
③ came – could have seen
④ had come – could see
⑤ had come – could have seen

서술형

14 다음 두 문장의 의미가 비슷하도록 문장을 완성하시오.

He feels as if ____________ in the rain forest.
→ In fact, he wasn't in the rain forest.

[15-16] 다음 중 밑줄 친 부분이 어법상 어색한 것을 고르시오.

15 ① I wish the restaurant had not canceled our reservation.
② If she had not quit singing, she could have become a singer.
③ If there were more food, Sam will eat more.
④ He appears as if he had not made the mistake.
⑤ I wish my cat didn't hate being washed.

16 ① I wish I had a younger sister.
② Jeremy talks as if he had seen a UFO before.
③ If she knew the truth, she would be angry.
④ I wish you have gone to the movies with me last week.
⑤ If I had more flour, I could bake more muffins.

17 다음 우리말을 알맞게 영작한 것은?

아기가 지금 잠을 더 자면 좋을 텐데.

① I wish the baby sleeps more now.
② I wish the baby slept more now.
③ I wish the baby has slept more now.
④ I wish the baby had slept more now.
⑤ I wish the baby would have slept more now.

고난도

18 다음 문장을 가정법 문장으로 바르게 바꾸지 못한 것은?

① I'm sorry that I didn't focus in class.
→ I wish I had focused in class.
② As Larry didn't study hard, he failed the exam.
→ If Larry had studied hard, he wouldn't fail the exam.
③ As the bag isn't heavy, Kate can carry it.
→ If the bag were heavy, Kate couldn't carry it.
④ I'm sorry that I don't have more cookies for my nephew.
→ I wish I had more cookies for my nephew.
⑤ As the hat is sold out, Lisa is disappointed.
→ If the hat weren't sold out, Lisa wouldn't be disappointed.

서술형

[19-20] 괄호 안의 말을 활용하여 가정법 문장을 완성하시오.

19

Emily speaks as if she ________ a high grade last semester. (get)

20

If the question ________ difficult, we would have solved it. (not, be)

21 다음 중 밑줄 친 부분이 어법상 바른 것은?

① Brad talks as if he were a genius when he was a child.
② I wish I had had my own room now.
③ If I had woken up early, I would have had breakfast.
④ If Anna had been 19 years old now, she could get a driver's license.
⑤ She behaves as if she didn't break the cup yesterday.

22 다음 문장을 가정법 문장으로 바르게 바꾼 것은?

I'm sorry that I can't meet my favorite actor.

① I wish I can't meet my favorite actor.
② I wish I can meet my favorite actor.
③ I wish I couldn't meet my favorite actor.
④ I wish I could meet my favorite actor.
⑤ I wish I had met my favorite actor.

서술형

[23-24] 다음 글에서 어법상 어색한 부분을 찾아 쓰고 바르게 고쳐 쓰시오.

23

My glasses are broken. I wish I can fix them myself.

________ → ________

24

The man acts as if he is the owner of the laptop. In fact, that's my laptop.

________ → ________

Chapter 13

일치와 화법

UNIT 01 시제의 일치

Answers p.36

A 밑줄 친 부분이 어법상 맞으면 O를 쓰고, 틀리면 바르게 고쳐 쓰시오.

1 Betty believed that she makes a good decision. → ____________

2 I knew that 1000 kilograms is equal to 1 ton. → ____________

3 They promised that they will follow the safety rules. → ____________

4 Dan heard that the first Nobel Prizes have been awarded in 1901. → ____________

B <보기>의 말을 알맞은 형태로 바꿔 빈칸에 쓰시오.

<보기>	move	open	can	have

1 We know that chicken ________ a lot of protein.

2 My teacher told me that I ________ win in chess contest.

3 I thought that the bakery ________ at 10 A.M. every day.

4 Some people didn't believe that the Earth ________ around the Sun.

C 다음 문장을 과거시제로 바꿀 때 빈칸에 알맞은 말을 써서 문장을 완성하시오.

1 Mr. Hall teaches the kids that Wright brothers invented the airplane.
→ Mr. Hall taught the kids that ________________________.

2 My sister thinks that I am angry with her.
→ My sister thought that ________________________.

3 Lucas believes that his friends will arrive early.
→ Lucas believed that ________________________.

4 I remember that someone broke a window of the shop.
→ I remembered that ________________________.

D 우리말과 같도록 괄호 안의 말을 활용하여 문장을 완성하시오.

1 학생들은 교실이 너무 작다고 불평했다. (the classroom, be, too small)
= The students complained that ________________________.

2 Jonathan은 하루 종일 도서관에 있을 것이라고 말했다. (will be, at the library)
= Jonathan said that ________________________ all day.

3 나는 일찍 일어나는 새가 벌레를 잡는다고 생각했다. (the early bird, catch, the worm)
= I thought that ________________________.

UNIT 02 화법

Answers p.36

A 다음 직접 화법을 간접 화법으로 바꾼 문장에서 어법상 어색한 부분을 찾아 밑줄을 치고 바르게 고쳐 쓰시오.

1 Billy said to me, "What will you do during vacation?"
→ Billy asked me what I will do during vacation. → ____________

2 The teacher said to us, "You should come to school on time."
→ The teacher said us that we should come to school on time. → ____________

3 Julie said to me, "Do you know where the bank is?"
→ Julie asked me that I knew where the bank was. → ____________

B 다음 문장을 간접 화법으로 바꿔 쓰시오.

1 I said to the waiter, "Can I get a knife and a fork?"
→ I asked the waiter ______________________________.

2 Mom said to me, "When do you want to have lunch?"
→ Mom asked me ______________________________.

3 Steve said, "I took a walk at the park."
→ Steve said ______________________________.

C 다음 문장을 직접 화법으로 바꿔 쓰시오.

1 The police told him that he needed to drive more slowly.
→ The police said to him, "______________________________."

2 Kyle asked me where he could go to fix his laptop.
→ Kyle said to me, "______________________________?"

3 The girl asked if it would rain in the afternoon.
→ The girl said, "______________________________?"

D 우리말과 같도록 괄호 안의 말을 활용하여 문장을 완성하시오.

1 Victoria는 그녀가 뮤지컬 보는 것을 즐긴다고 말했다. (say, enjoy watching musicals)
= Victoria ______________________________.

2 은행원은 나에게 그가 나의 새로운 주소가 필요하다고 말했다. (tell, need my new address)
= The bank teller ______________________________.

3 Joseph은 나에게 내가 그 문제를 어떻게 풀었는지 물었다. (ask, solve the problem)
= Joseph ______________________________.

Chapter Test+

Answers p.36

[1-4] 다음 빈칸에 들어갈 알맞은 것을 고르시오.

1

I knew that Janice ________ the soccer team.

① join ② will join
③ would join ④ has joined
⑤ is going to join

2

My dad taught me that a friend in need ________ a friend indeed.

① is ② was
③ been ④ will be
⑤ had been

3

The science teacher said that light ________ in straight lines.

① will travel ② travels
③ traveled ④ has traveled
⑤ had traveled

4

Jason asked me ________ I had eaten lunch already.

① with ② what
③ though ④ that
⑤ if

서술형

[5-6] 다음 문장을 간접 화법으로 바꿀 때 빈칸에 알맞은 말을 쓰시오.

5

Angela said to me, "Do you need my help?"
→ Angela ________ ________ ________ ________ ________ ________ help.

6

Scott said, "I can go to the exhibition with you."
→ Scott said that ________ ________ ________ ________ ________ ________ ________ ________.

서술형

[7-8] 다음 직접 화법을 간접 화법으로 바꾼 문장에서 어법상 어색한 부분을 찾아 쓰고 바르게 고쳐 쓰시오.

7

Helen said to me, "Can you wait for me in the lobby?"
→ Helen asked me if I can wait for her in the lobby.

________ → ________

8

Kevin said to me, "I was worried about my grade."
→ Kevin told me that he was worried about his grade.

________ → ________

9 다음 문장을 간접 화법으로 바르게 바꾼 것은?

Mia said to me, "Did you watch the movie?"

① Mia asked me that I had watched the movie.
② Mia said to me if you had watch the movie.
③ Mia asked me if I had watched the movie.
④ Mia asked me whether I watch the movie.
⑤ Mia said whether I watched the movie.

10 다음 빈칸에 들어갈 알맞은 것을 모두 고르시오.

Ethan said that he ________________.

① had traveled to New York
② is tired after the marathon
③ has been a guitarist in the band
④ is going to the shopping mall
⑤ was absent from school

[11-12] 다음 대화의 빈칸에 들어갈 알맞은 것을 고르시오.

11

A: Why didn't you call me yesterday? *B*: I ____________ to bed early.

① said that I will go
② said that I would go
③ told that I will go
④ told that I would go
⑤ said to that I will go

12

A: What did she ask you? *B*: She ________________.

① told where the public restroom was
② told where is the public restroom
③ asked where was the public restroom
④ asked where the public restroom was
⑤ asked whether the public restroom is

[13-14] 다음 중 어법상 어색한 것을 고르시오.

13 ① The security guard said that we couldn't go inside the building.
② My friend asked me that I would join the orchestra.
③ We asked Sharon why she was crying.
④ Larry asked when the festival would start.
⑤ Amy told her friends that she had been to France.

14 ① My grandfather said that a bird in the hand is worth two in the bush.
② We knew that spiders were not insects.
③ They thought that they had done their best.
④ Emma told me that she would post the picture on the Internet.
⑤ The students learned that the first man in space was Yuri Gagarin.

15 다음 중 직접 화법을 간접 화법으로 잘못 바꾼 것은?

① He said to me, "Did you turn off the TV?"
→ He asked me if I had turned off the TV.
② We said to ourselves, "We will finish the project on time."
→ We told ourselves that we would finish the project on time.
③ The children said, "We can clean the house for our mom."
→ The children said that they can clean the house for their mom.
④ Anna said, "Who opened the door?"
→ Anna asked who had opened the door.
⑤ Frank said, "I was the class president in 2020."
→ Frank said that he had been the class president in 2020.

서술형

16 다음 문장을 과거시제로 바꿀 때 빈칸에 알맞은 말을 쓰시오.

> Brandon tells us that he will do the dishes.
> → Brandon told us that he ________ ________ the dishes.

서술형 고난도

17 우리말과 같도록 주어진 <조건>에 맞게 영작하시오.

> 나의 아버지는 내가 신문을 가져올 수 있는지 물으셨다.

> <조건> 1. 간접화법으로 쓰시오.
> 2. bring, the newspaper를 사용하시오.

= ______________________________
______________________________.

[18-19] 다음 빈칸에 들어갈 말이 순서대로 짝지어진 것을 고르시오.

18

> • I discovered that my cat ________ hungry.
> • Dad told us that he ________ home late.

① is - may come ② is - might come
③ was - may come ④ was - might come
⑤ had been - may come

19

> • Students learned that there ________ no oxygen in space.
> • We were taught that the Second World War ________ in 1939.

① is - had begun ② is - began
③ was - had begun ④ was - began
⑤ had been - began

서술형 고난도

[20-21] 다음 문장을 직접 화법으로 바꿔 쓰시오.

20

> Dennis told us that he could speak three languages.
> → ______________________________
> ______________________________

21

> She asked if I wanted more soup.
> → ______________________________
> ______________________________

22 다음 문장을 현재시제로 바꿀 때 밑줄 친 부분이 어법상 어색한 것은?

> We were taught that telephone was invented in 1876.
> → We ①are taught ②that ③telephone ④is invented ⑤in 1876.

23 다음 중 어법상 바른 것을 모두 고르시오.

① Peter asked whether the dinner is ready.
② Megan doesn't know that I ate her chocolate.
③ The tourists asked where was the Blue House.
④ We believed that Noah had not lied to us.
⑤ I already knew that Beijing was the capital of China.

MEMO

MEMO

MEMO

HACKERS

GRAMMAR SMART

LEVEL 2

WORKBOOK

해커스 그래머 스마트가 특별한 이유!

[Completely master English grammar]

1 누구나 쉽게 이해할 수 있는 **간결한 문법 설명**

2 실생활에서 그대로 사용할 수 있는 **유용한 표현과 예문**

3 **'개념 확인' → '연습 문제' → '작문 연습' → '단원 마무리'**로 이어지는 **4단계 문제풀이**

[Effectively prepare for middle school English exams]

1 학교 시험 기출경향을 완벽 반영한 문제로 **서술형 포함 내신 완벽 대비**

2 **풍부한 문제의 Workbook**과 **다양한 부가 학습 자료**로 **학습효과 Up Up!**

HACKERS GRAMMAR SMART

LEVEL 2

ANSWERS

HACKERS GRAMMAR SMART LEVEL 2

ANSWERS

Chapter 01 시제

UNIT 01 현재/과거/미래/진행시제

Smart Check p.14

1 ②

Practice p.15

A 1 visit 2 studied
3 is leaving 4 knows
5 are going to take 6 was watching

B 1 will be 2 began
3 bakes 4 is practicing

C 1 need 2 will finish
3 is listening 4 published

D 1 likes hot drinks
2 borrowed comic books
3 were playing board games
4 am going to meet my friends

UNIT 02 현재완료시제

Smart Check p.16

1 ③ 2 ①

Practice p.17

A 1 have been 2 had 3 has lived
4 hasn't 5 since

B 1 practiced 2 has rained
3 has stayed 4 Did you go

C 1 has left 2 have known
3 has worked 4 have lost

D 1 have liked Vernon
2 has already eaten lunch
3 have gone to their hometown
4 has won the gold medal

Writing Exercise p.18

A 1 have been 2 had 3 drink
4 tastes 5 ran
6 will[am going to] make

B 1 We go to the beach
2 Mark has learned scuba diving
3 I am going to visit my grandparents
4 A koala usually sleeps 20 hours
5 Nelson Mandela won the Nobel Peace Prize
6 He was sitting on the bench
7 Susan has written poems

C 1 is the capital of Germany
2 have read the book
3 is moving south
4 will[are going to] prepare dinner
5 was taking a shower
6 bought Christmas presents
7 is spending time

D 1 cut his hair 2 watered the plants
3 is going to the post office
4 will[is going to] clean the room

Chapter Test p.20

1 ③ 2 ⑤ 3 played
4 will[is going to] jog 5 ② 6 ④ 7 ①
8 ③ 9 have lived 10 has 11 ② 12 ⑤
13 ④ 14 has left
15 have been popular since 16 ③ 17 ①
18 ⑤ 19 has been sick
20 will[is going to] study history
21 (1) ⓑ → forgot (2) ⓔ → have 22 ⑤
23 is going to take a yoga lesson
24 has already arrived at the restaurant

1 last night이 있으므로 과거시제를 쓴다.

2 once가 있으므로 현재완료시제를 쓴다.

3 yesterday가 있으므로 과거시제를 쓴다. 현재완료시제는 특정한 과거 시점을 나타내는 표현과 함께 쓸 수 없다.

4 tomorrow morning이 있으므로 미래시제를 쓴다.

5 • next week가 있으므로 미래시제를 쓴다.
• before가 있으므로 현재완료시제를 쓴다.

6 ④ have gone → went

7 ① is doing → was doing

8 two years ago(2년 전에)가 있으므로 과거시제를 쓴다.

9 「for + 기간」이 있으므로 현재완료시제를 쓴다.

10 일반적 사실을 나타내고 있으므로 현재시제를 쓴다.

11 A가 어젯밤에 일어난 일에 대해 묻고 있으므로 과거시제로 답한다.

12 tomorrow가 있으므로 미래시제를 쓴다.

13 ① have → had
② tries → has tried[tried]
③ is tasting → tastes

⑤ is going to film → filmed

14 Amanda가 한국을 떠났고 그 결과 지금 여기에 없으므로 현재완료시제를 쓴다.

15 노래가 1990년대에 인기 있었고 여전히 인기 있으므로 현재완료시제를 쓴다. the 1990s는 일이 시작된 시점이므로 since(~ 이후로)를 쓴다.

16 ⓒ has bought → bought
ⓔ looked → is looking

17 주어진 문장과 ①: 경험
②⑤: 결과 ③: 계속 ④: 완료

18 주어진 문장과 ⑤: 계속
①: 결과 ②: 경험 ③④: 완료

19 과거부터 현재까지 계속되는 일을 나타내는 현재완료시제 문장이다. 현재완료시제는 「have/has + p.p.」의 형태이다.

20 앞으로 일어날 일을 나타내는 미래시제 문장이다. 미래시제는 「will + 동사원형」이나 「be going to + 동사원형」의 형태이다.

21 (1) yesterday가 있으므로 과거시제를 쓴다. 현재완료시제는 특정한 과거 시점을 나타내는 표현과 함께 쓸 수 없다.
(2) 소유의 의미를 나타내는 동사 have는 진행형으로 쓸 수 없다.

22 첫 번째 빈칸: 빈칸 뒤에 일이 지속된 기간(a long time)이 왔으므로 for를 쓴다.
두 번째 빈칸: 빈칸 뒤에 일이 시작된 시점(2014)이 왔으므로 since를 쓴다.

23 앞으로 일어날 일을 나타내는 미래시제 문장이다. 미래시제는 「be going to + 동사원형」의 형태이다.

24 과거에 일어난 일이 현재에 완료되었음을 나타내는 현재완료시제 문장이다. 현재완료시제는 「have/has + p.p.」의 형태이다.

Chapter 02 조동사

UNIT 01 can, may, will

Smart Check p.24

1 ② 2 ①

Practice p.25

A 1 open 2 Can
3 may 4 Would

B 1 can 2 Can[Could/May]
3 will 4 couldn't

C 1 can't 2 was able to
3 will 4 may

D 1 can play 2 will order
3 can[may] use 4 is going to jog

UNIT 02 must, have to, should

Smart Check p.26

1 ①, ② 2 ① 3 ②, ③

Practice p.27

A 1 must not 2 to feed
3 will have to 4 doesn't have to
5 should

B 1 respect 2 doesn't have to
3 not drink 4 had to

C 1 must be 2 don't have to buy
3 have to wear

D 1 must[should] finish 2 had to fix
3 must be 4 don't have[need] to go

UNIT 03 would like to, had better, used to

Smart Check p.28

1 ② 2 ③ 3 ①

Practice p.29

A 1 to go 2 had better
3 used to 4 visit

B 1 had better 2 would like to
3 used to

C 1 had better not believe
2 used to take
3 would like to make

D 1 Would you like to take
2 We had better change
3 Ella used to be
4 She is used to waiting

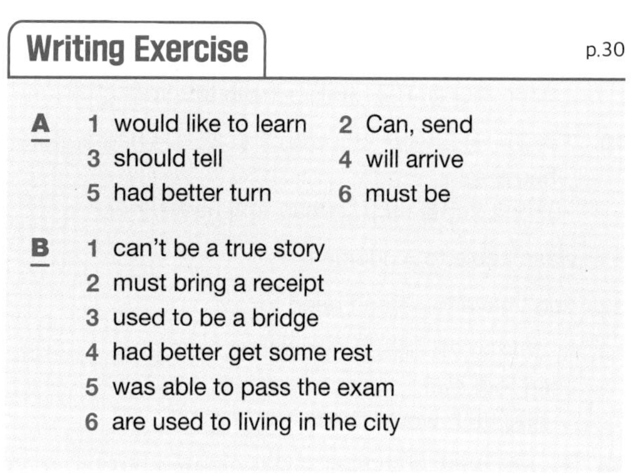

Writing Exercise p.30

A 1 would like to learn 2 Can, send
3 should tell 4 will arrive
5 had better turn 6 must be

B 1 can't be a true story
2 must bring a receipt
3 used to be a bridge
4 had better get some rest
5 was able to pass the exam
6 are used to living in the city

C
1 Can[Could] I see
2 Their house must be
3 We used to go
4 The boy had to come
5 Helen could meet
6 I would[I'd] like to ask
7 He doesn't have to wear

D
1 must not enter
2 can cross the street
3 have to drive slowly

Chapter Test

p.32

1 ③ 2 ⑤ 3 ③ 4 ② 5 ②
6 had better not make
7 don't need to go[need not go] 8 ⑤ 9 to
10 had 11 ② 12 ③ 13 ② 14 ①
15 have to save 16 is able to make
17 ②, ⑤ 18 ⑤
19 used to[would] sleep a lot
20 would like to eat a piece of cake 21 ⑤
22 ④ 23 is going to go for a walk
24 He will have to wait for his friends

1 과거의 상태(전에는 ~이었다)를 나타내는 used to를 쓴다.

2 충고·의무(~해야 한다)를 나타내는 should의 부정형인 should not을 쓴다.

3 ③: 약한 추측 주어진 문장과 ①②④⑤: 허가

4 ②: 강한 추측 주어진 문장과 ①③④⑤: 의무

5 약한 추측(~일지도 모른다)을 나타내는 might를 쓴다.

6 had better의 부정형은 had better not을 쓴다.

7 don't need to = need not '~할 필요가 없다'

8 ⑤ don't have to → must[should] not

9 • '~하고 싶다'라는 의미인 would like to의 to를 쓴다.
• 과거의 반복적인 습관(~하곤 했다)을 나타내는 used to의 to를 쓴다.
• 의무(~해야 한다)를 나타내는 have to의 to를 쓴다.

10 • 충고나 권고(~하는 것이 낫다)를 할 때 쓰는 had better의 had를 쓴다.
• 과거의 의무를 나타내는 had to의 had를 쓴다.

11 wasn't able to = couldn't

12 don't have to = don't need to

13 첫 번째 빈칸: 과거의 상태(전에는 ~이었다)를 나타내는 used to를 쓴다.
두 번째 빈칸: would like to '~하고 싶다'

14 첫 번째 빈칸: 불필요(~할 필요가 없다)를 나타내는 don't have to를 쓴다.
두 번째 빈칸: 충고·의무(~해야 한다)를 나타내는 should를 쓴다.

15 must = have to

16 can = be able to

17 ① to sell → sell
③ worry → to worry
④ to go → go

18 must not '~하면 안 된다'
don't have to '~할 필요가 없다'

19 과거의 반복적인 습관(~하곤 했다)을 나타내는 used to [would]를 쓴다.

20 '~하고 싶다'라는 의미의 would like to를 쓴다.

21 ⑤ is used to → used to

22 ④ sing → to sing

23 미래(~할 것이다)를 나타내는 be going to를 쓴다.

24 have to(~해야 한다)의 미래형은 will have to를 쓴다.

Chapter 03 동사의 종류

UNIT 01 감각동사와 수여동사

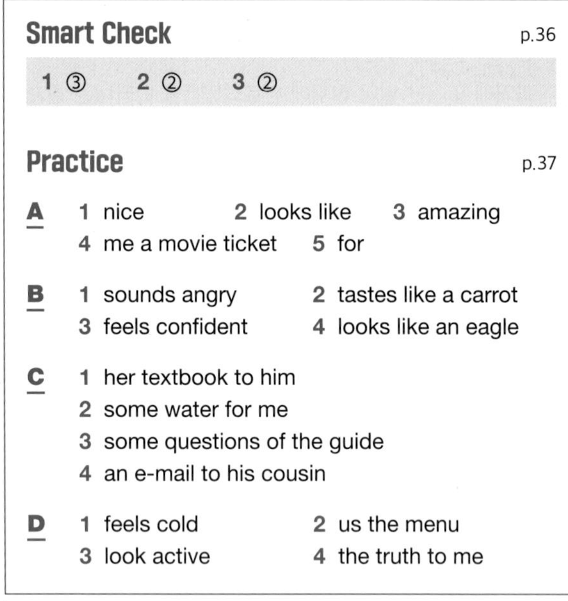

Smart Check

p.36

1 ③ 2 ② 3 ②

Practice

p.37

A 1 nice 2 looks like 3 amazing
4 me a movie ticket 5 for

B 1 sounds angry 2 tastes like a carrot
3 feels confident 4 looks like an eagle

C 1 her textbook to him
2 some water for me
3 some questions of the guide
4 an e-mail to his cousin

D 1 feels cold 2 us the menu
3 look active 4 the truth to me

UNIT 02 목적격 보어가 필요한 동사

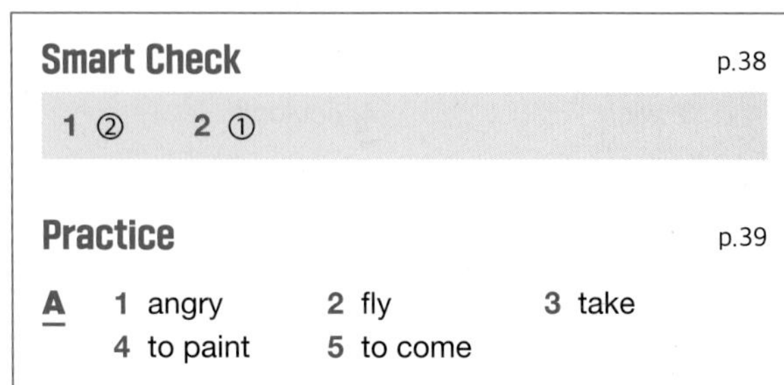

Smart Check

p.38

1 ② 2 ①

Practice

p.39

A 1 angry 2 fly 3 take
4 to paint 5 to come

B 1 to be 2 fresh 3 to put
4 use

C 1 ride[to ride] 2 selfish
3 to raise 4 sing[singing]

D 1 call him a genius
2 made me wash the car
3 advised her to exercise
4 watched them throw[throwing] coins

Writing Exercise

p.40

A 1 made the students move the desks
2 saw a strange man enter[entering] the building
3 allowed me to play outside in the afternoon
4 helped Alex find[to find] a useful book in the library
5 advised my brother to take vitamin C

B 1 This soap smells really nice
2 helped his friend carry the boxes
3 My friend sent some photos to me
4 got Eva to bring the mail
5 told us to wear seat belts
6 don't let her watch violent movies

C 1 tastes sweet
2 found the math test difficult
3 brought her sister a blanket[brought a blanket to her sister]
4 looks like a mouse
5 made Ryan a popular writer
6 cooks me breakfast[cooks breakfast for me]

D 1 watched people play[playing] badminton
2 helped her mother plant[to plant] a tree
3 made students read the textbook

Chapter Test

p.42

1 ② 2 ⑤ 3 to get 4 ③ 5 ②
6 ③ 7 ④ 8 ① 9 ③ 10 ③ 11 ④
12 ①, ④ 13 some Spanish words to me
14 a safe shelter for the cats
15 Thomas got his dog to bring the newspaper
16 ordered him to come home early
17 come[coming] inside the house
18 to write her diary every day
19 tastes like peaches
20 lent his friend a laptop[lent a laptop to his friend]
21 wanted me to keep the secret
22 (1) ⓑ → clean (2) ⓔ → to go 23 ③ 24 ②

1 「cook + 직접 목적어 + for + 간접 목적어」

2 감각동사의 주격 보어 자리에는 형용사만 온다.

3 「expect + 목적어 + to부정사」

4 첫 번째 빈칸: 「help + 목적어 + 동사원형/to부정사」
두 번째 빈칸: 「ask + 목적어 + to부정사」

5 ① beautifully → beautiful
③ sit → to sit
④ read → to read
⑤ safely → safe

6 ① bitterly → bitter
② to cross → cross[crossing]
④ feels like → feels
⑤ taking → to take

7 목적격 보어 자리에 to부정사(to go)가 왔으므로 목적격 보어 자리에 동사원형이 오는 사역동사 make는 쓸 수 없다.

8 간접 목적어 앞에 전치사 to가 왔으므로 for와 함께 쓰는 bought는 쓸 수 없다.

9 ③의 make는 간접 목적어와 직접 목적어를 필요로 하는 수여동사이고, ①②④⑤의 make는 목적어와 목적격 보어를 필요로 하는 동사이다.

10 • 「expect + 목적어 + to부정사」
• 「let + 목적어 + 동사원형」

11 ④: 직접 목적어 ①②③⑤: 목적격 보어

12 「see + 목적어 + 동사원형/V-ing형」

13 「teach + 간접 목적어 + 직접 목적어」
= 「teach + 직접 목적어 + to + 간접 목적어」

14 「build + 간접 목적어 + 직접 목적어」
= 「build + 직접 목적어 + for + 간접 목적어」

15 「get + 목적어 + to부정사」

16 「order + 목적어 + to부정사」

17 「hear + 목적어 + 동사원형/V-ing형」

18 「tell + 목적어 + to부정사」

19 「taste + like + 명사」

20 「lend + 간접 목적어 + 직접 목적어」 또는 「lend + 직접 목적어 + to + 간접 목적어」

21 「want + 목적어 + to부정사」

22 (1) 「keep + 목적어 + 형용사」
(2) 「allow + 목적어 + to부정사」

23 ③ sounds like → sounds

24 ② play → to play

Chapter 04 수동태

UNIT 01 수동태의 쓰임

Smart Check p.46

1 ③

Practice p.47

A 1 drawn 2 built
3 were planted 4 checked
5 fits

B 1 are loved 2 is cleaned
3 are spoken 4 are held

C 1 are baked 2 was stolen
3 was found 4 will be eaten

D 1 was sent 2 will be released
3 is locked 4 was written

UNIT 02 수동태의 다양한 형태

Smart Check p.48

1 ② 2 ① 3 ③ 4 ①

Practice p.49

A 1 Was 2 can be carried
3 built 4 wasn't
5 By whom

B 1 were 2 offered
3 wasn't 4 be remembered

C 1 Is, fed 2 By whom, published
3 must be followed 4 wasn't completed

D 1 can be stored 2 was, broken
3 aren't delivered 4 Was, changed

UNIT 03 주의해야 할 수동태

Smart Check p.50

1 ②

Practice p.51

A 1 shaking[to shake] 2 to
3 is called 4 with

B 1 for 2 to 3 to 4 of

C 1 was cooked for 2 was made to help
3 is kept sharp 4 are expected to come

D 1 am interested in 2 was made of
3 was heard playing 4 will be given to you

Writing Exercise p.52

A 1 Were many cities destroyed by the war
2 Your textbook should be opened by you
3 My text messages weren't read by my brother
4 English is spoken in Singapore (by people)
5 Was his key lost by him yesterday
6 This poem was written by a famous poet

B 1 I will be given Ben's address by her
2 Her son is called a prince by Ms. Evans
3 A family was seen relaxing[to relax] on the grass by me
4 I was told to be quiet by my mother
5 A postcard was sent to Austin by me
6 Her friends were asked to find the lost dog by Eva

C 1 must be cleaned
2 occurred in a huge building
3 Will the marathon be canceled
4 is satisfied with the result
5 can be done by him
6 is filled with cold water

D 1 my wallet was stolen (by someone)
2 Were many photos taken by you
3 You will be shown the photos by me[The photos will be shown to you by me]

Chapter Test p.54

1 ⑤ 2 ⑤ 3 ② 4 ①
5 The desk was covered with dust 6 ③
7 ④ 8 ① 9 ②
10 We were made to go to bed early by our parents
11 By whom was the valuable painting stolen
12 ④ 13 ①, ④ 14 was held
15 are invited 16 ⑤
17 wasn't written by the author
18 was shown to us by Harry
19 is known to many tourists
20 ⑤ 21 (1) ⓒ → be taken (2) ⓓ → not be used
22 ②, ③ 23 ③

1 시장이 존경하는 것이 아니라 존경받는 것이므로 수동태를 쓴다. 수동태의 동사는 「be동사 + p.p.」의 형태이므로 is respected를 쓴다.

2 나무가 심는 것이 아니라 심어져야 하는 것이므로 수동태를 쓴다. 조동사가 있는 수동태는 「조동사 + be + p.p.」의 형태이므로 be planted를 쓴다.

3 ②: 행위자가 일반인이거나 중요하지 않을 때는 「by + 행위자」를 생략할 수 있다.

4 ① will be leading → will be led

5 be covered with '~으로 덮여 있다'

6 '보내질 것이다'라는 미래의 의미이므로 미래시제의 수동태인 「will be + p.p.」를 쓴다.

7 • be satisfied with '~에 만족하다'
• be filled with '~으로 가득 차 있다'

8 • cook은 간접 목적어 앞에 전치사 for를 쓰는 동사이다.
• buy는 간접 목적어 앞에 전치사 for를 쓰는 동사이다.

9 행위자인 Josh를 능동태 문장의 주어로 쓰고 과거시제 수동태 동사 wasn't carried를 didn't carry로 바꾼다. 수동태 문장의 주어인 The bag를 능동태 문장의 목적어로 쓴다.

10 사역동사가 쓰인 5형식 문장을 수동태로 바꿀 때는 목적격 보어로 쓰인 동사원형을 to부정사로 바꾼다.

11 주어가 who인 능동태 의문문을 수동태 의문문으로 바꿀 때는 「By whom + be동사 + 주어 + p.p. ~?」의 형태로 쓴다.

12 ④: disappear는 목적어를 가지지 않는 동사이므로 수동태로 쓸 수 없다.

13 목적어가 두 개(us, a sad story)인 4형식 문장이므로 두 개의 수동태 문장을 만들 수 있다. 직접 목적어가 주어인 수동태 문장은 간접 목적어 앞에 전치사 to/for/of 중 하나를 쓰며, tell은 to를 쓰는 동사이다.

14 축구 경기가 여는 것이 아니라 열리는 것이므로 수동태를 쓴다. 주어 The soccer tournament는 3인칭 단수이고 yesterday는 과거를 나타내는 표현이므로 과거시제 was held를 쓴다.

15 외국인 친구들이 초대하는 것이 아니라 초대받는 것이므로 수동태를 쓴다. 주어 My foreign friends는 3인칭 복수이고 every year는 반복되는 일을 나타내는 표현이므로 현재시제 are invited를 쓴다.

16 첫 번째 빈칸: be interested in '~에 흥미가 있다'
두 번째 빈칸: 내가 티켓을 준 것이 아니라 주어진 것이므로 수동태를 쓴다. 수동태의 동사는 「be동사 + p.p.」의 형태이므로 was given을 쓴다.

17 '쓰이지 않았다'라는 과거의 의미이고 주어 The fantasy novel은 3인칭 단수이므로 wasn't written을 쓴다. 행위자는 「by + 행위자」의 형태로 쓴다.

18 '보여졌다'라는 과거의 의미이고 주어 A new invention은 3인칭 단수이므로 was shown을 쓴다. 4형식 문장을 직접 목적어가 주어인 수동태 문장으로 쓸 때 간접 목적어 앞에 전치사 to/for/of 중 하나를 쓰며, show는 to를 쓰는 동사이다. 행위자는 「by + 행위자」의 형태로 쓴다.

19 be known to '~에게 알려져 있다'

20 ⑤ → A laptop was bought for his brother by him.

21 (1) 조동사가 있는 수동태: 「조동사 + be + p.p.」
(2) 조동사가 있는 수동태의 부정문: 「주어 + 조동사 + not + be + p.p.」

22 지각동사가 쓰인 5형식 문장을 수동태로 바꿀 때는 목적격 보어로 쓰인 동사원형을 V-ing형이나 to부정사로 바꾼다.

23 ⓐ to flying → flying[to fly]
ⓑ in → at
ⓓ is resembled by → resembles

Chapter 05 to부정사

UNIT 01 to부정사의 명사적 용법

Smart Check p.58

1 ② 2 ③

Practice p.59

A 1 to help 2 is
3 not to be 4 It

B 1 It, to swim in the deep sea
2 It, to travel to different countries
3 It, to drink lots of water

C 1 where to hang 2 when to water
3 what to do 4 how to get

D 1 is to read 2 hopes to go
3 It, to ride

UNIT 02 to부정사의 형용사적 용법

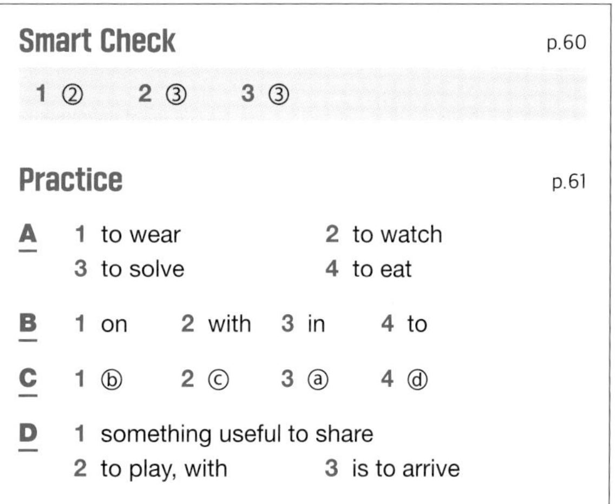

Smart Check p.60

1 ② 2 ③ 3 ③

Practice p.61

A 1 to wear 2 to watch
3 to solve 4 to eat

B 1 on 2 with 3 in 4 to

C 1 ⓑ 2 ⓒ 3 ⓐ 4 ⓓ

D 1 something useful to share
2 to play, with 3 is to arrive

UNIT 03 to부정사의 부사적 용법

Smart Check p.62

1 ① 2 ② 3 ③

Practice
p.63

A
1 to buy[in order[so as] to buy]
2 to tell 3 to touch 4 to find

B
1 모든 질문들은 답하기에 쉬웠다
2 나는 이 축제에서 너를 봐서 기쁘다
3 이 시를 이해하다니 그녀는 똑똑한 것이 틀림없다

C
1 to know you are well
2 to worry about everything
3 to meet each other in Paris

D
1 in[so] order[as] to prepare dinner
2 impossible to read
3 to be a singer

UNIT 04 to부정사의 의미상 주어, to부정사 구문

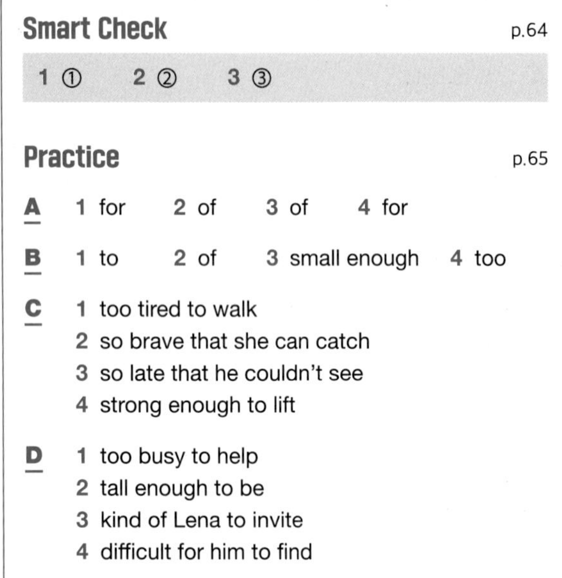

Smart Check
p.64

1 ① 2 ② 3 ③

Practice
p.65

A
1 for 2 of 3 of 4 for

B
1 to 2 of 3 small enough 4 too

C
1 too tired to walk
2 so brave that she can catch
3 so late that he couldn't see
4 strong enough to lift

D
1 too busy to help
2 tall enough to be
3 kind of Lena to invite
4 difficult for him to find

Writing Exercise
p.66

A
1 to see my cousins
2 to send a package
3 wide enough for cars to pass on
4 to take walks with her dog
5 to lose the game
6 not to get any presents

B
1 It, to eat ice cream
2 interesting to watch
3 how to use this machine
4 many friends to talk to
5 are to succeed
6 too old to repair

C
1 to read you this poem
2 to protect her skin
3 for him to adapt to change
4 a place to hold the event
5 where to park his car
6 must be rich to spend money

D
1 big enough to carry
2 too expensive for him to buy
3 warm enough for her to wear

Chapter Test
p.68

1 ④ 2 ⑤ 3 ③ 4 ⑤ 5 ③ 6 ④
7 how I should turn on 8 in[so] order[as] to give
9 ① 10 ② 11 ④ 12 to go
13 what to do[what we should do]
14 ② 15 (1) ⓑ → so (2) ⓒ → to gather
16 It was generous of you to forgive him
17 The soup is too hot for me to eat
18 kind to help
19 smart enough to speak[so smart that she can speak] 20 ④ 21 ③
22 a comic book to read 23 to get many presents

1 to부정사가 주어로 쓰일 때 주어 자리에 가주어 it을 쓰고 진주어 to부정사(구)를 뒤로 보낼 수 있다.

2 to부정사가 수식하는 명사 paper가 전치사의 목적어이므로 to부정사 뒤에 전치사 on을 쓴다.

3 ③ of → for

4 ⑤ to eat sweet → sweet to eat

5 사람의 성격·성질을 나타내는 형용사(kind, foolish) 뒤에 오는 to부정사의 의미상 주어는 「of + 목적격」의 형태로 쓴다.

6 ① of → for
② enough big → big enough
③ visit → to visit
⑤ are → is

7 「의문사 + to부정사」는 「의문사 + 주어 + should + 동사원형」으로 바꿔 쓸 수 있다.

8 목적의 의미를 강조하기 위해 to를 in order to나 so as to로 바꿔 쓸 수 있다.

9 '~하기 위해'라는 의미로 목적을 나타내는 to부정사이므로 '나는 샤워를 하기 위해 욕실로 갔다.'라고 해석한다.

10 '(…해서 결국) ~하다'라는 의미로 결과를 나타내는 to부정사이므로 'Thomas는 새 목도리를 샀지만, 결국 그것을 잃어버렸다.'라고 해석한다.

11 ① → to become
② → too

③ → to write with
⑤ → what

12 「too + 형용사/부사 + to부정사」 '…하기에 너무 ~한/하게'

13 '무엇을 ~할지'라는 의미의 「what + to부정사」를 쓴다. 「what + to부정사」는 「what + 주어 + should + 동사원형」으로 바꿔 쓸 수 있다.

14 「too + 형용사/부사 + to부정사」는 「so + 형용사/부사 + that + 주어 + can't + 동사원형」으로 바꿔 쓸 수 있다.

15 (1) '너무 피곤해서 거기에 갈 수 없었다'라는 의미이므로 「so + 형용사/부사 + that + 주어 + can't + 동사원형」의 so를 쓴다.
(2) decide는 to부정사를 목적어로 쓰는 동사이므로 to gather를 쓴다.

16 to부정사가 주어로 쓰일 때 주어 자리에 가주어 it을 쓰고 진주어 to부정사(구)를 뒤로 보낼 수 있다. 사람의 성격·성질을 나타내는 형용사 뒤에 오는 to부정사의 의미상 주어는 「of + 목적격」의 형태로 쓴다.

17 '…하기에 너무 ~한/하게'라는 의미인 「too + 형용사/부사 + to부정사」를 쓰고, 의미상 주어는 「for + 목적격」의 형태로 쓴다.

18 '~하다니'라는 의미로 판단의 근거를 나타내는 부사적 용법의 to부정사를 쓴다.

19 '…할 만큼 충분히 ~한/하게'라는 의미인 「형용사/부사 + enough + to부정사」나 「so + 형용사/부사 + that + 주어 + can + 동사원형」을 쓴다.

20 주어진 문장과 ④: 명사적 용법
①⑤: 형용사적 용법　②③: 부사적 용법

21 주어진 문장과 ③: 형용사적 용법
①④: 부사적 용법　②⑤: 명사적 용법

22 '읽을 만화책'이라는 의미로 명사 comic book을 수식하는 형용사적 용법의 to부정사를 쓴다.

23 '많은 선물을 받아서 기뻤다'라는 의미로 감정의 원인을 나타내는 부사적 용법의 to부정사를 쓴다.

Chapter 06 동명사

UNIT 01 동명사의 쓰임

Smart Check p.72

1 ②　2 ③

Practice p.73

A 1 Spending　2 fishing
3 traveling　4 losing

B 1 ⓑ　2 ⓓ　3 ⓐ　4 ⓒ

C 1 writing novels　2 speaking in public
3 Getting enough sleep

D 1 is worth visiting　2 buying a new car
3 On arriving home

UNIT 02 동명사와 to부정사를 목적어로 쓰는 동사

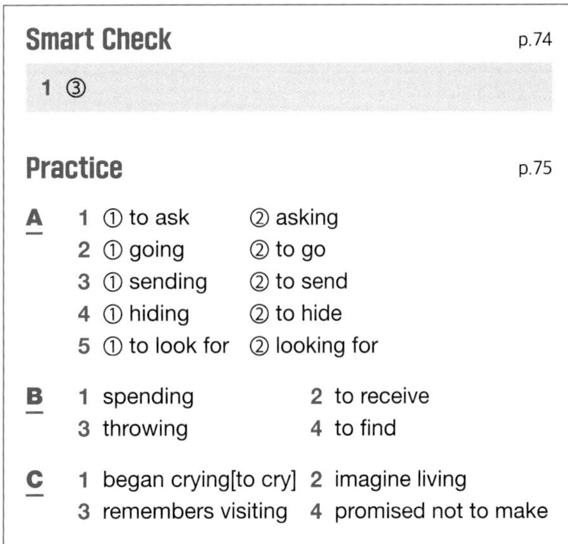

Smart Check p.74

1 ③

Practice p.75

A 1 ① to ask　② asking
2 ① going　② to go
3 ① sending　② to send
4 ① hiding　② to hide
5 ① to look for　② looking for

B 1 spending　2 to receive
3 throwing　4 to find

C 1 began crying[to cry]　2 imagine living
3 remembers visiting　4 promised not to make

Writing Exercise p.76

A 1 Becoming rich and famous
2 traveling by train
3 Brushing your teeth
4 replying to many e-mails
5 not turning off the oven

B 1 enjoy watching　2 wants to go
3 need to save　4 practices speaking
5 finish reading　6 decided to buy
7 kept standing

C 1 It is no use complaining
2 couldn't help laughing
3 like going to the zoo
4 forgot to bring her his notebook
5 is proud of being a firefighter
6 People in the office stopped working

D 1 playing with a ball　2 to run a marathon
3 staying[to stay] home
4 getting a shot

Chapter Test p.78

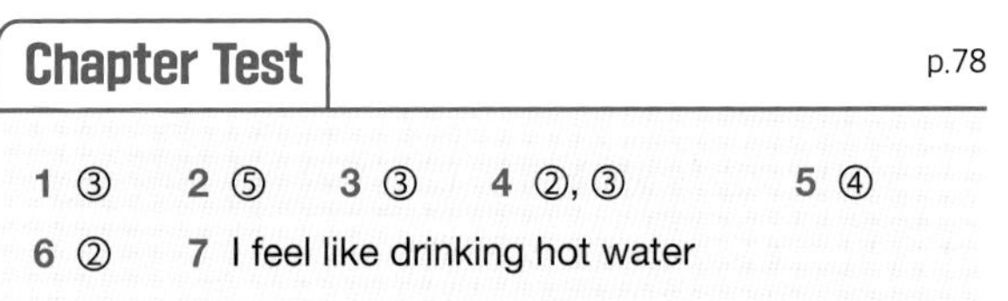

1 ③　2 ⑤　3 ③　4 ②, ③　5 ④
6 ②　7 I feel like drinking hot water

8 to go → going 9 to do 10 speaking
11 buying 12 ③ 13 ① 14 ① 15 ④
16 ⑤ 17 (1) ⓑ → to travel (2) ⓔ → getting
18 ② 19 not seeing his grandmother yesterday
20 Meeting my old friend 21 practiced dancing
22 is worth watching 23 ③
24 It is no use denying the facts

1 finish는 동명사를 목적어로 쓰는 동사이므로 writing을 쓴다.

2 「on + V-ing」 '~하자마자'

3 '(시험 삼아) ~해보다'라는 의미이므로 동사 try 뒤에 동명사 surfing을 쓴다.

4 continue는 동명사와 to부정사를 모두 목적어로 쓰는 동사이므로 walking이나 to walk를 쓴다.

5 ④ put off → putting off

6 ② to use → using

7 「feel like + V-ing」 '~하고 싶다'

8 '(과거에) ~한 것을 기억하다'라는 의미이므로 동사 remember 뒤에 동명사 going을 쓴다.

9 agree는 to부정사를 목적어로 쓰는 동사이므로 to do를 쓴다.

10 전치사의 목적어 자리이므로 동명사 speaking을 쓴다.

11 '(과거에) ~한 것을 잊다'라는 의미이므로 동사 forget 뒤에 동명사 buying을 쓴다.

12 ① study → studying
② to analyzing → analyzing[to analyze]
④ to steal → stealing
⑤ going → to go

13 ② buying → to buy
③ to eat → eating
④ to telling → telling
⑤ bringing → to bring

14 동명사 chatting이 목적어이므로 to부정사를 목적어로 쓰는 wish는 쓸 수 없다.

15 첫 번째 빈칸: '그는 운동을 너무 열심히 한 것을 후회했다.'라는 의미이므로 동사 regret 뒤에 동명사 exercising을 쓴다.
두 번째 빈칸: decide는 to부정사를 목적어로 쓰는 동사이므로 to go를 쓴다.

16 첫 번째 빈칸: enjoy는 동명사를 목적어로 쓰는 동사이므로 being을 쓴다.
두 번째 빈칸: expect는 to부정사를 목적어로 쓰는 동사이므로 to have를 쓴다.

17 (1) hope는 to부정사를 목적어로 쓰는 동사이므로 to travel을 쓴다.
(2) 전치사의 목적어 자리이므로 동명사 getting을 쓴다.

18 주어진 문장과 ②: 동사의 목적어
①④: 주어 ③⑤: 보어

19 'Aaron은 어제 그의 할머니를 보지 않은 것을 후회한다.'라는 의미이므로 동사 regret 뒤에 동명사 seeing을 쓴다. 동명사의 부정형은 동명사 앞에 not을 쓴다.

20 '나의 오랜 친구를 만나는 것은 나를 울게 했다.'라는 의미이므로 주어 자리에 동명사 Meeting을 쓴다.

21 practice는 동명사를 목적어로 쓰는 동사이므로 dancing을 쓴다.

22 「be worth + V-ing」 '~할 가치가 있다'

23 「try + 동명사」는 '(시험 삼아) ~해보다'라는 의미이고, 「try + to부정사」는 '~하려고 노력하다'라는 의미이다.

24 「It is no use + V-ing」 '~해도 소용없다'

Chapter 07 분사

UNIT 01 현재분사와 과거분사

Smart Check

p.82

1 ② 2 ①

Practice

p.83

A 1 broken 2 arguing 3 amazed
4 dancing

B 1 sitting 2 lost 3 cleaning
4 pleased 5 left

C 1 ⓐ 2 ⓑ 3 ⓑ 4 ⓐ

D 1 boiled eggs 2 smiling at us
3 running in the garden
4 made of gold

UNIT 02 분사구문

Smart Check

p.84

1 Seeing their favorite actor
2 Not feeling well
3 Sitting on the sofa

Practice

p.85

A 1 Listening 2 Being 3 Turning
4 Not knowing

B 1 Seeing 2 Not having 3 Cleaning
4 Being

C 1 If you take this bus
2 After he came home from school
3 Because I'm good at singing

D 1 Not eating lunch
2 Hearing the good news
3 Walking on the street
4 Having many friends

Writing Exercise

p.86

A 1 ① surprising ② surprised
2 ① interested ② interesting
3 ① excited ② exciting
4 ① bored ② boring
5 ① disappointed ② disappointing

B 1 posted on this board
2 boiling water
3 made in Germany
4 confusing puzzle
5 waiting for the actor

C 1 he saw a snake, Seeing a snake
2 he had homework to do, Having homework to do
3 I didn't have a swimsuit, Not having a swimsuit
4 she arrived home, Arriving home
5 we climb the mountain, Climbing the mountain

D 1 playing the guitar 2 dropped on the ground
3 filled with flowers 4 Listening to music

Chapter Test

p.88

1 ④ 2 ③ 3 ③ 4 ⑤
5 Seeing the flower 6 Having a toothache
7 ④ 8 Played → Playing
9 Standing near the table 10 broken 11 ①
12 ② 13 Not having a key 14 ②
15 While[As] she got off the bus, Getting off the bus
16 Because[As/Since] he realized his mistake, Realizing his mistake 17 ⑤ 18 ③
19 (1) ⓐ → satisfying (2) ⓓ → Comparing
20 a car coming toward me 21 barking dog
22 the doughnut filled with chocolate 23 ③

1 The trip to London은 감정을 일으키는 원인이므로 현재분사 exciting을 쓴다.

2 '집에 도착한 후에'라는 의미의 부사절을 분사구문으로 나타낸 것이므로 Arriving을 쓴다.

3 • Their love for each other는 감정을 일으키는 원인이므로 현재분사 touching을 쓴다.
• Dave는 감정을 느끼는 대상이므로 과거분사 bored를 쓴다.

4 • 명사 frog를 수식하고 명사와의 관계가 능동이므로 현재분사 jumping을 쓴다.
• 명사 people을 수식하고 명사와의 관계가 수동이므로 과거분사 invited를 쓴다.

5 접속사 When과 주어 she를 생략하고 동사 saw를 Seeing으로 바꾼다.

6 접속사 Because와 주어 he를 생략하고 동사 has를 Having으로 바꾼다.

7 ① interested → interesting
② Hear → Hearing
③ bored → boring
⑤ calling → called

8 '축구를 하는 동안'이라는 의미의 부사절을 분사구문으로 나타낸 것이므로 Playing을 쓴다.

9 '그 탁자 가까이에 서서'라는 의미의 부사절을 분사구문으로 나타낼 수 있으므로 Standing near the table을 쓴다.

10 명사 arm을 수식하고 명사와의 관계가 수동이므로 과거분사 broken을 쓴다.

11 ① amazed → amazing

12 ② Washing not → Not washing

13 이유를 나타내는 분사구문이고, 분사구문의 부정형은 분사 앞에 not을 붙여 만들므로 Not having a key를 쓴다.

14 ②: 동명사 주어진 문장과 ①③④⑤: 현재분사

15 첫 번째 문장: '~하면서'라는 의미의 접속사 While[As]를 쓰고, 문장의 시제가 과거이므로 got을 쓴다.
두 번째 문장: 접속사 While[As]와 주어 she를 생략하고 동사 got을 Getting으로 바꾼다.

16 첫 번째 문장: '~하기 때문에'라는 의미의 접속사 Because[As/Since]를 쓰고, 문장의 시제가 과거이므로 realized를 쓴다.
두 번째 문장: 접속사 Because[As/Since]와 주어 he를 생략하고 동사 realized를 Realizing으로 바꾼다.

17 '만약 네가 좌측으로 돌면, 도서관을 발견할 것이다.'라는 의미이므로 조건을 나타내는 If you turn to the left를 쓴다.

18 '그녀는 버스를 봤을 때, 버스 정류장으로 뛰어갔다.'라는 의미이므로 시간을 나타내는 When she saw the bus를 쓴다.

19 (1) score는 감정을 일으키는 원인이므로 현재분사 satisfying을 쓴다.
(2) '나의 친구들과 답을 비교해본 후에'라는 의미의 부사절을 분사구문으로 나타낸 것이므로 Comparing을 쓴다.

20 현재분사 coming이 전치사구(toward me)와 함께 구를 이루어 쓰였으므로 명사 car 뒤에서 명사를 수식한다.

21 현재분사 barking이 명사 dog 앞에서 명사를 수식한다.

22 과거분사 filled가 전치사구(with chocolate)와 함께 구를 이루어 쓰였으므로 명사 doughnut 뒤에서 명사를 수식한다.

23 ⓑ Traveled → Traveling
ⓒ pleasing → pleased

Chapter 08 대명사

UNIT 01 부정대명사 I

Smart Check
p.92

1 ②

Practice
p.93

A 1 one 2 the other 3 another
4 it 5 other

B 1 others 2 ones 3 other
4 another

C 1 any 2 some 3 any
4 some

D 1 one 2 others
3 Some, the others
4 One, another, the other

UNIT 02 부정대명사 II

Smart Check
p.94

1 ① 2 ①

Practice
p.95

A 1 All 2 Both 3 each
4 Every 5 are

B 1 Each 2 Both 3 All

C 1 question 2 are 3 has
4 O 5 opens

D 1 know each other 2 Both women are
3 Each of the bottles is
4 all the students were

UNIT 03 재귀대명사

Smart Check
p.96

1 ② 2 ① 3 ②

Practice
p.97

A 1 yourself 2 yourself 3 me
4 himself 5 themselves

B 1 X 2 O 3 O 4 X

C 1 in 2 talks to 3 by
4 enjoy

D 1 hurt himself 2 keep ourselves safe
3 were beside themselves
4 take care of myself

Writing Exercise
p.98

A 1 myself 2 Both 3 Each
4 any 5 all 6 one
7 herself 8 the other

B 1 is another scarf
2 disappointed in themselves
3 enjoyed ourselves
4 two small ones
5 Some are carrots, others are onions

C 1 You can make yourself at home
2 Both of the buses will take
3 He himself told me
4 Every store is closed
5 pass me some salt

D 1 each other 2 Some, the others
3 himself

Chapter Test
p.100

1 ② 2 ① 3 ③ 4 ③ 5 Each book
6 others 7 ② 8 ① 9 ⑤ 10 ④
11 Both of her sons are teachers 12 ③ 13 ②
14 ④ 15 ③ 16 talks to herself
17 hurt myself 18 ⑤ 19 enjoys herself
20 ④ 21 (1) ⓑ → gift (2) ⓔ → them
22 (1) one (2) Both (3) some 23 have → has

1 앞에서 언급된 명사(watch)와 같은 종류의 불특정한 사물을 가리키고 있으므로 부정대명사 one을 쓴다.

2 앞에서 언급된 특정한 대상(My smartphone)을 가리키고 있으므로 it을 쓴다.

3 '만약 네가 아직 목이 마르다면, 물 한 병을 더 마셔도 된다.'라는 의미이므로 another(하나 더)를 쓴다.

4 ③: 강조 용법(생략 가능)
①②④⑤: 재귀 용법(생략 불가능)

5 '각각의'라는 의미의 each 뒤에는 단수명사를 쓴다.

6 '다른 (사람들/것들)'이라는 의미의 others를 쓴다. 대명사로 쓰였으므로 복수형을 쓴다.

7 • 「some ~, the others -」 '(여럿 중) 몇몇은 ~, 나머지 전부는 -'

• 긍정문에서는 주로 some을 쓴다.

8 • 부정문에서는 주로 any를 쓴다.
• 의문문에서는 주로 any를 쓴다.

9 ⑤ need → needs

10 ④ any → some

11 「both of + 복수명사」 '둘 다'

12 「one ~, another -, the other …」 '(셋 중) 하나는 ~, 다른 하나는 -, 나머지 하나는 …'

13 「one ~, the other -」 '(둘 중) 하나는 ~, 나머지 하나는 -'

14 「some ~, the others -」 '(여럿 중) 몇몇은 ~, 나머지 전부는 -'

15 ① us → ourselves
② is → are
④ have → has
⑤ other → the others[others]

16 talk to oneself '혼잣말을 하다'

17 hurt oneself '다치다'

18 밑줄 친 부분과 ⑤: 재귀 용법
①②③④: 강조 용법

19 enjoy oneself '즐거운 시간을 보내다'

20 첫 번째 빈칸: 「each of + 복수명사」는 단수 취급하므로 costs를 쓴다.
두 번째 빈칸: 「the other + 복수명사」는 복수 취급하므로 are를 쓴다.

21 (1) every는 「every + 단수명사」의 형태로만 쓰이므로 gift를 쓴다.
(2) 앞에서 언급된 특정한 대상(a necklace, rings)을 가리키고 있으므로 them을 쓴다.

22 (1) 앞에서 언급된 명사(microwave)와 같은 종류의 불특정한 사물을 가리키고 있으므로 부정대명사 one을 쓴다.
(2) '(두 책들) 둘 다 그가 가장 좋아하는 작가에 의해 쓰였다.'라는 의미이므로 Both를 쓴다.
(3) 권유·요청을 나타내는 의문문에서는 주로 some을 쓴다.

23 「all (of) + 명사」의 형태로 쓸 때는 all (of) 뒤의 명사(milk)에 동사를 수일치시키므로 has를 쓴다.

Chapter 09 관계사

UNIT 01 관계대명사

Smart Check

p.104

1 ①

Practice

p.105

A
1 선행사: the man, 관계대명사: who
2 선행사: the designer, 관계대명사: whose
3 선행사: a watch, 관계대명사: which

B
1 who 2 whom 3 whose
4 which

C
1 which is going to Sydney
2 who(m) Stella introduced to me
3 who eat and exercise regularly
4 whose eyes are blue

D
1 someone who can help him
2 the person who(m) I respect
3 a smartphone whose color is unique

UNIT 02 관계대명사 that/what, 주의해야 할 관계대명사의 쓰임

Smart Check

p.106

1 ②

Practice

p.107

A
1 What 2 that 3 what
4 that

B
1 who is 2 which 3 that
4 which was

C
1 which[that], on 2 with whom
3 in which 4 which[that], to

D
1 What is important for me
2 the actor you talked about
3 the only sport that I enjoy
4 the boy who Eric plays with

UNIT 03 관계부사

Smart Check

p.108

1 ② 2 ① 3 ③

Practice

p.109

A
1 when 2 how 3 where
4 why

B
1 when 2 why 3 where
4 how

C
1 why she started to learn ballet
2 when Adam is going abroad to study
3 where the Great Wall is
4 how the CEO succeeded in business

D
1 the shop where I often buy clothes
2 the month when roses bloom
3 how she can get to the station

Writing Exercise

p.110

A
1 why 2 whose 3 that
4 what 5 which 6 where
7 when 8 who

B
1 The girl who is watering the plant is Sophia
2 Grace found the smartwatch which she lost last week
3 He read a novel which was written by Shakespeare
4 The police officer who(m) we saw on the news was brave
5 They are eating the sandwiches which are sold on the street
6 I miss the teacher who(m) I met in the second grade

C
1 an animal which lives really long
2 what you drew in your sketchbook
3 the day when the new year begins
4 The island where I went last summer
5 anything that you want in the market
6 the reason why he couldn't finish the homework

D
1 who likes to draw cartoons
2 who is good at playing the guitar
3 who(m) Katie met at the tennis club
4 whom Katie goes to school every day

Chapter Test

p.112

1 ① 2 ③ 3 ④ 4 ④ 5 where
6 why 7 ② 8 ⑤ 9 who[that] are honest
10 when Logan passed the exam 11 ③ 12 ①
13 (1) that (2) what (3) who 14 ⑤ 15 ③
16 ④ 17 ②
18 which[that] has a wonderful bridge
19 who(m)[that] I go to the gym with[with whom I go to the gym]
20 My mom still remembers the time when we went to her favorite singer's concert
21 whose → that 22 which → what
23 where → when 24 ⑤

1 선행사(the girl)가 사람이고 빈칸이 관계대명사절 안에서 주어 역할을 하고 있으므로 사람을 선행사로 하는 주격 관계대명사 who를 쓴다.

2 선행사(the year)가 시간을 나타내므로 관계부사 when을 쓴다.

3 선행사(the old man and his dog)에 사람과 동물이 포함되어 있으므로 관계대명사 that을 쓴다.

4 '그녀가 초대받았던 그 파티'라고 했으므로 선행사는 the party이고, 선행사가 사물이므로 관계대명사 which나 that을 쓴다. 전치사는 관계대명사절의 맨 뒤나 관계대명사 바로 앞에 오고, 관계대명사 바로 앞에 올 때는 that을 쓸 수 없다.

5 선행사(a hotel)가 장소를 나타내고 「전치사 + 관계대명사」는 관계부사로 바꿔 쓸 수 있으므로 관계부사 where를 쓴다.

6 선행사(the reason)가 이유를 나타내고 「전치사 + 관계대명사」는 관계부사로 바꿔 쓸 수 있으므로 관계부사 why를 쓴다.

7 ② the way how → how[the way]

8 ⑤ which → whose

9 선행사(people)가 사람이므로 관계대명사 who나 that을 쓰고, 선행사가 복수명사이므로 관계대명사절의 동사는 복수동사 are를 쓴다.

10 선행사(the day)가 시간을 나타내므로 관계부사 when을 쓴다.

11 • 선행사(The bird)가 동물이므로 관계대명사 which나 that을 쓴다.
• 선행사가 없으므로 선행사를 포함하는 관계대명사 what을 쓴다.

12 • 선행사(the only plant)에 the only가 포함되어 있으므로 관계대명사 that을 쓴다.
• 빈칸 뒤에 선행사(a tree)가 소유하는 대상인 명사(leaves)가 있으므로 소유격 관계대명사 whose를 쓴다.

13 (1) 선행사(anything)가 -thing으로 끝나는 대명사이므로 관계대명사 that을 쓴다.
(2) 선행사가 없으므로 선행사를 포함하는 관계대명사 what을 쓴다.
(3) 선행사(The lady)가 사람이므로 관계대명사 who를 쓴다.

14 ① who → which[that]
② that → which
③ when → where[in which]
④ which → what

15 • 선행사(a camera)가 사물이므로 관계대명사 which나 that을 쓴다.
• 선행사(the reason)가 이유를 나타내므로 관계부사 why 대신 쓸 수 있는 for which를 쓴다.

16 ④: 주격 관계대명사 (주격 관계대명사는 생략할 수 없다.)
①②⑤: 목적격 관계대명사
③: 「주격 관계대명사 + be동사」

17 ②: 의문사 ①③④⑤: 관계대명사

18 두 번째 문장은 첫 번째 문장의 a river에 대해 보충 설명하고 있고, 두 번째 문장의 It이 주어 역할을 하고 있으므로 사물을 선행사로 하는 주격 관계대명사 which나 that을 쓴다.

19 두 번째 문장은 첫 번째 문장의 the friend에 대해 보충 설명하고 있고, 두 번째 문장의 him이 목적어 역할을 하고 있으므로 사람을 선행사로 하는 목적격 관계대명사 who(m)이나 that을 쓴다. 전치사는 관계대명사절의 맨 뒤나 관계대명사 바로 앞에 오고, 관계대명사 바로 앞에 올 때는 관계대명사 who나 that을 쓸 수 없다.

20 두 번째 문장은 첫 번째 문장의 the time에 대해 보충 설명하고 있고, 선행사(the time)가 시간을 나타내므로 관계부사 when을 쓴다.

21 관계대명사가 관계대명사절 안에서 목적어 역할을 하고 있고, 선행사가 all이므로 관계대명사 that을 쓴다.

22 선행사가 없으므로 선행사를 포함하는 관계대명사 what을 쓴다.

23 선행사(the month)가 시간을 나타내므로 관계부사 when을 쓴다.

24 ⑤: whose ①②③④: what

Chapter 10 접속사

UNIT 01 시간/이유/결과를 나타내는 접속사

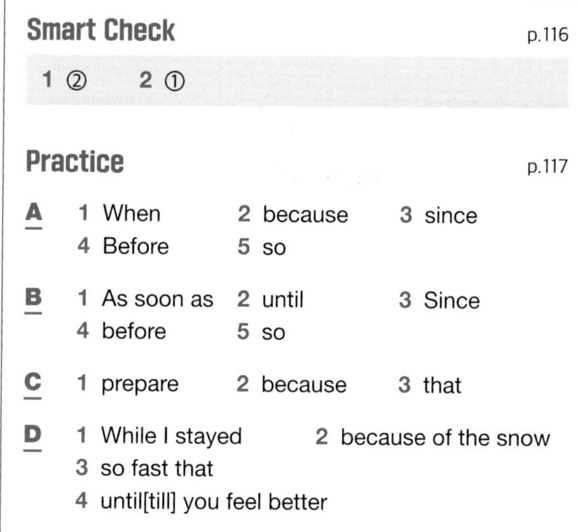

Smart Check p.116

1 ② 2 ①

Practice p.117

A 1 When 2 because 3 since
4 Before 5 so

B 1 As soon as 2 until 3 Since
4 before 5 so

C 1 prepare 2 because 3 that

D 1 While I stayed 2 because of the snow
3 so fast that
4 until[till] you feel better

UNIT 02 조건/양보를 나타내는 접속사, 접속사 that

Smart Check p.118

1 ② 2 ③ 3 ①

Practice p.119

A 1 If 2 Unless 3 Although
4 invite 5 send

B 1 unless we protect our environment
2 If you don't have a ticket
3 Unless Leah listens to the teacher's advice

C 1 ⓑ 2 ⓐ 3 ⓒ 4 ⓑ

D 1 If it snows
2 Although[Though] she doesn't live
3 It was interesting that

UNIT 03 명령문 + and/or, 상관접속사

Smart Check p.120

1 ③ 2 ① 3 ②

Practice p.121

A 1 or 2 and 3 Both 4 or

B 1 or 2 and
3 not only, but also 4 neither, nor

C 1 are 2 am 3 are 4 is

D 1 and you can save energy
2 not only diligent but (also) generous[generous as well as diligent]
3 or you'll slip on the ice
4 either a black pen or a blue pen

Writing Exercise p.122

A 1 When my dog sees a stranger
2 because he had a fever
3 Although I ate dinner
4 until her friends arrived
5 if you like reading books
6 as soon as I called him

B 1 after you drink hot tea
2 because of the rain
3 unless he changes his attitude
4 As people get older
5 since I was young
6 before I make a decision

C 1 so uncomfortable that I'll return it
2 or I won't be able to hear your voice
3 (that) Russia is the biggest country
4 and you won't make mistakes
5 so many people can't understand it
6 If you don't say sorry to him

D 1 Both Daniel and Matthew
2 Not only Matthew but (also) Nancy
3 Neither Jessica nor Nancy
4 Matthew as well as Nancy

Chapter Test p.124

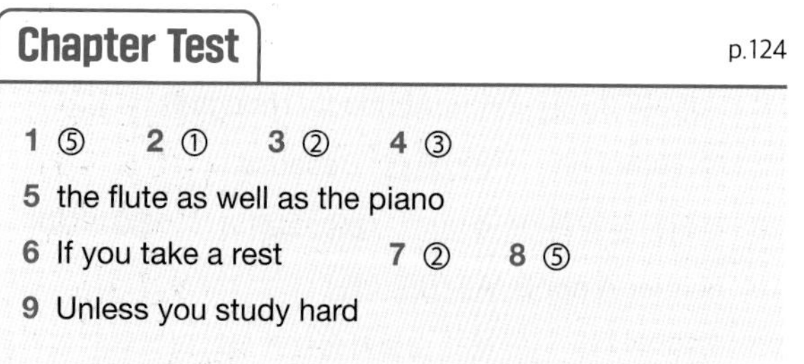

1 ⑤ 2 ① 3 ② 4 ③
5 the flute as well as the piano
6 If you take a rest 7 ② 8 ⑤
9 Unless you study hard

10 Both Lauren and her friend were late
11 before his mom comes 12 ② 13 ④
14 ⑤ 15 because[since/as]
16 Although[Though] 17 ③ 18 ①
19 and → nor 20 If, Unless 21 ① 22 ③
23 (1) because (2) though (3) if

1 '비록 나는 늦게 집을 나섰지만, 제시간에 도착했다.'라는 의미이므로 Although(비록 ~이지만)를 쓴다.

2 '지금 표를 사라, 그렇지 않으면 너는 나중에 그것을 위해 더 많이 지불해야 할 것이다.'라는 의미이므로 「명령문 + or ~」(…해라, 그렇지 않으면 ~)의 or를 쓴다.

3 '만약 네가 버스를 탈 것이 아니라면, 너는 줄에서 나와야 한다.'라는 의미이므로 If(만약 ~한다면)를 쓴다.

4 ③ Though → Because[Since/As]

5 not only A but also B(A뿐만 아니라 B도)는 B as well as A로 바꿔 쓸 수 있다.

6 「명령문 + and ~」(…해라, 그러면 ~)의 명령문은 조건을 나타내는 접속사 if를 이용하여 바꿔 쓸 수 있다.

7 ② like → likes

8 since/because는 '~하기 때문에'라는 의미로, 이유를 나타내는 부사절을 이끈다.

9 '만약 ~하지 않는다면'이라는 의미의 unless를 쓴다.

10 'A와 B 둘 다'라는 의미의 both A and B를 쓰며, both A and B 뒤에는 항상 복수동사를 쓴다.

11 '~하기 전에'라는 의미의 before를 쓰며, 시간을 나타내는 부사절에서는 미래시제 대신 현재시제를 쓴다.

12 • '만약 그가 사과하지 않는다면'이라는 의미이므로 if(만약 ~한다면)를 쓴다.
• '그 건물은 지진 때문에 피해를 입었다.'라는 의미이고, 빈칸 뒤에 명사(the earthquake)가 있으므로 because of(~ 때문에)를 쓴다.

13 ④: '~하고 있을 때, ~하면서' ①②③⑤: '~하기 때문에'

14 ① Unless Josh doesn't come → Unless Josh comes [If Josh doesn't come]
② and → or
③ will rain → rains
④ too → so

15 '그 소설은 훌륭해서'라는 의미는 '그 소설은 훌륭하기 때문에'라는 의미를 나타내므로 '~하기 때문에'라는 의미의 because/since/as를 쓴다.

16 'Alice는 나에게 거짓말을 했다. 하지만, 나는 여전히 그녀를 믿는다.'라는 의미는 '비록 Alice가 나에게 거짓말을 했지만, 나는 여전히 그녀를 믿는다.'라는 의미를 나타내므로 '비록 ~이지만'이라는 의미의 Although/Though를 쓴다.

17 ③: Although ①②④⑤: Because

18 주어진 문장과 ①: 주어 ②④: 목적어 ③⑤: 보어

19 neither A nor B 'A도 B도 아닌'

20 「명령문 + or ~」(…해라, 그렇지 않으면 ~)의 명령문은 조건을 나타내는 접속사 if나 unless를 이용하여 바꿔 쓸 수 있다.

21 • '그들에게 친절해라, 그러면 그들이 너를 좋아할 것이다.'라는 의미이므로 「명령문 + and ~」(…해라, 그러면 ~)의 and를 쓴다.
• '고양이와 개 둘 다 포유류이다.'라는 의미이므로 both A and B(A와 B 둘 다)의 and를 쓴다.

22 • '그는 아팠기 때문에 침대에 계속 있었다.'라는 의미이므로 since(~하기 때문에)를 쓴다.
• 'Sam과 나는 13살이었던 이후로 친구였다.'라는 의미이므로 since(~한 이후로)를 쓴다.

23 (1) '여름 방학이 시작했기 때문에 많은 여가 시간이 있다.'라는 의미이므로 because(~하기 때문에)를 쓴다.
(2) '비록 그의 그림은 훌륭했지만 아무도 그것을 사지 않았다.'라는 의미이므로 though(비록 ~이지만)를 쓴다.
(3) '만약 네가 원한다면 우리가 너에게 도움을 줄 수 있다.'라는 의미이므로 if(만약 ~한다면)를 쓴다.

Chapter 11 비교구문

UNIT 01 원급/비교급/최상급 비교

Smart Check p.128

1 ③

Practice p.129

A 1 newer 2 late
3 much 4 the highest

B 1 quickly 2 more comfortable
3 the smartest 4 less

C 1 younger than 2 as expensive as
3 stronger than 4 the hottest

D 1 not as[so] diligent as
2 more brightly than
3 the most famous building
4 much[even/far] more nervous than

UNIT 02 비교구문을 이용한 표현

Smart Check p.130

1 ① 2 ②

Practice p.131

A 1 twice as 2 as loudly as
3 days 4 longer, more
5 more and more

B 1 The more popular 2 older than
3 the fuller 4 larger and larger

C 1 as soon as I can
2 three times higher than
3 as hard as they could

D 1 brighter and brighter
2 30 times as fast as[30 times faster than]
3 as safely as possible[as safely as we can]
4 The more books, the wiser

Writing Exercise

p.132

A 1 longer 2 the smallest
3 more comfortable 4 as neatly as
5 as tall as 6 worse

B 1 the funniest boy
2 as high as possible[as high as I could]
3 one of the most popular tourist sites
4 getting worse and worse
5 not as[so] interesting as
6 The more friends, the more food

C 1 larger than 2 the biggest
3 warmer than 4 not as[so] cool as

D 1 as much as 2 The taller, the thinner
3 three times as thick as[three times thicker than]
4 the fastest

Chapter Test

p.134

1 ② 2 ③ 3 ④ 4 ②
5 more and more famous
6 as early as possible[as early as you can]
7 the brightest 8 ⑤ 9 ③ 10 ② 11 ①
12 as much as
13 three times as old as[three times older than]
14 longest → longer 15 actor → actors
16 This chair is not as[so] comfortable as the sofa
17 ③ 18 as often as you can
19 three times as big as 20 ②
21 (1) ⓑ → best (2) ⓒ → beautifully
22 ④ 23 ⑤ 24 ②

1 '이 액션 영화는 저 공포 영화보다 더 길다.'라는 의미이므로 비교급 longer를 쓴다.

2 '나의 남동생은 나의 가족 중에서 가장 키가 작다.'라는 의미이므로 최상급 the shortest를 쓴다.

3 「배수사 + as + 원급 + as」 '…보다 -배 더 ~한/하게'

4 ①: 책 C가 가장 무거우므로 '책 A는 모든 것들 중에서 가장 무거운 책이다.'는 적절하지 않다.
③: 책 B가 책 A보다 더 가벼우므로 '책 B는 책 A보다 더 무겁다.'는 적절하지 않다.
④: 책 C가 책 A보다 더 비싸므로 '책 C는 책 A만큼 싸다.'는 적절하지 않다.
⑤: 책 C가 책 B보다 더 무거우므로 '책 C는 책 B보다 더 가볍다.'는 적절하지 않다.

5 '점점 더 ~한/하게'라는 의미의 「비교급 + and + 비교급」을 쓴다.

6 '가능한 한 ~한/하게'라는 의미의 「as + 원급 + as + possible」 또는 「as + 원급 + as + 주어 + can[could]」를 쓴다.

7 '가장 ~한/하게'라는 의미의 「the + 최상급」을 쓴다.

8 빈칸 뒤에 비교급(more fluently)이 있으므로 '훨씬'이라는 의미로 비교급을 강조하는 much/even/a lot/far를 쓸 수 있다. very는 원급을 강조한다.

9 • '나의 아버지는 나의 어머니만큼 나를 사랑하신다.'라는 의미이므로 원급 much를 쓴다.
• 빈칸 뒤에 비교급(more perfectly)이 있으므로 비교급을 강조하는 much를 쓴다.

10 ② more cold → colder

11 ① smarter → smartest

12 파란색 가방과 빨간색 가방의 가격이 같으므로 원급 비교 as much as를 쓴다.

13 Tim의 아버지가 Tim보다 나이가 세 배 더 많으므로 three times as old as[three times older than]을 쓴다.

14 'Diana의 머리카락은 내 것보다 더 길다.'라는 의미이므로 비교급 longer를 쓴다.

15 「one of the + 최상급 + 복수명사」 '가장 ~한 것들 중 하나'

16 「not + as[so] + 원급 + as」 '…만큼 ~하지 않은/않게'

17 ① → better
② → much
④ → warmer
⑤ → less

18 「as + 원급 + as + possible」은 「as + 원급 + as + 주어 + can[could]」로 바꿔 쓸 수 있다.

19 「배수사 + 비교급 + than」은 「배수사 + as + 원급 + as」로 바꿔 쓸 수 있다.

20 • '나의 목소리는 너의 것만큼 크다.'라는 의미의 원급 비교이므로 as를 쓴다.
• '야채는 정크 푸드보다 훨씬 더 건강에 좋다.'라는 의미의 비교급 비교이므로 than을 쓴다.

21 (1) good의 최상급은 best이다.
(2) 「as + 원급 + as」의 형태로 쓰므로 원급 beautiful을 쓴다.

22 ① most → the most
② more hotter → hotter
③ low → lower
⑤ generous → more generous

23 '내가 공부를 더 많이 할수록 나의 점수는 높아졌다.'라는 의미의 문장이므로 '~하면 할수록 더 …하다'라는 의미의 「the + 비교급, the + 비교급」을 쓴다.

24 ⓑ → Cars are not as[so] safe as airplanes.
ⓔ → This desk is four times as heavy as that chair.

Chapter 12 가정법

UNIT 01 가정법 과거, 가정법 과거완료

Smart Check p.138

1 ③ 2 ③ 3 ②

Practice p.139

A 1 were 2 could
3 would have gone 4 knew

B 1 worked 2 wouldn't have run
3 weren't 4 could have lent

C 1 weren't hurt
2 would have been satisfied
3 could have gotten

D 1 were, would apologize
2 had arrived, would have missed
3 had not been, could have played
4 opened, would see

UNIT 02 I wish 가정법, as if 가정법

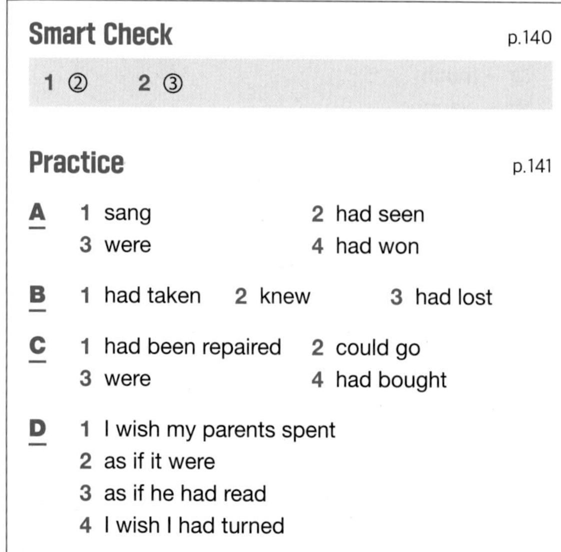

Smart Check p.140

1 ② 2 ③

Practice p.141

A 1 sang 2 had seen
3 were 4 had won

B 1 had taken 2 knew 3 had lost

C 1 had been repaired 2 could go
3 were 4 had bought

D 1 I wish my parents spent
2 as if it were
3 as if he had read
4 I wish I had turned

Writing Exercise p.142

A 1 the test had been easy, Robert could have gotten a perfect score
2 you were in Paris, you could meet Alexa
3 Daniel had had free time, he would have gone to the gym
4 I were a millionaire, I could buy a yacht
5 you didn't feel so disappointed
6 she had questions to ask

B 1 acts as if she were a child
2 I could run faster than my classmates
3 I had seen him, would have talked with him
4 it were Saturday, wouldn't go to work
5 talks as if he had known nothing

C 1 I had been more confident
2 seems as if he knew
3 we could ride bicycles outside
4 If you had searched more carefully

D 1 were a famous singer
2 had seen it with you
3 had kept the salad in the fridge
4 would play with my friends

Chapter Test p.144

1 ④ 2 ⑤ 3 ⑤ 4 she could swim well
5 ⑤ 6 ④ 7 would have studied together
8 Tina were kind
9 had the sneakers, Matt could buy them
10 I had seen the shooting star 11 ② 12 ③
13 ③ 14 ② 15 knew 16 had eaten
17 ① 18 ⑤ 19 could have met → could meet
20 would give → would have given 21 ④ 22 ④

1 현재의 사실과 반대되는 일을 가정하고 있으므로 가정법 과거를 쓰고, 가정법 과거에서 if절의 be동사는 주어에 상관없이 were를 쓴다.

2 과거의 사실과 반대되는 일을 가정하고 있으므로 주절에는 「주어 + would, could, might + have p.p.」를 쓴다.

3 • 현재의 사실과 반대되는 일을 가정하고 있으므로 가정법 과거를 쓰고, 가정법 과거에서 if절의 be동사는 주어에 상관없이 were를 쓴다.
• 주절의 시제(현재시제)와 같은 시점의 사실과 반대되는 일을 가정하는 「as if + 가정법 과거」를 써야 하므로 be동사는 were를 쓴다.

4 주절의 시제(현재시제)와 같은 시점의 사실과 반대되는 일을 가정하는 「as if + 가정법 과거」를 쓴다.

5 ⑤ fixed → had fixed

6 ④ would have done → would do

7 '만약 ~했더라면 …했을 텐데'라는 의미로 과거의 사실과 반대되는 일을 가정하는 가정법 과거완료를 써야 하므로 「주어 + would, could, might + have p.p.」를 쓴다.

8 '~하면 좋을 텐데'라는 의미로 현재 이룰 수 없거나 실현 가능성이 거의 없는 일을 소망하는 「I wish + 가정법 과거」를 써야 하므로 「I wish + 주어 + 동사의 과거형」을 쓴다.

9 현재의 사실과 반대되는 일을 가정하는 가정법 과거 「If + 주어 + 동사의 과거형 ~, 주어 + would, could, might + 동사원형 …」을 쓴다.

10 과거에 이루지 못한 일에 대한 아쉬움을 나타내는 「I wish + 가정법 과거완료」를 쓴다.

11 • 현재 이룰 수 없거나 실현 가능성이 거의 없는 일을 소망하는 「I wish + 가정법 과거」를 써야 하므로 had를 쓴다.
• 과거의 사실과 반대되는 일을 가정하는 가정법 과거완료를 써야 하므로 wouldn't have chosen을 쓴다.

12 • 주절의 시제(현재시제)와 같은 시점의 사실과 반대되는 일을 가정하는 「as if + 가정법 과거」를 써야 하므로 were를 쓴다.
• 현재의 사실과 반대되는 일을 가정하는 가정법 과거를 써야 하므로 would stay를 쓴다.

13 '만약 ~한다면 …할 텐데'의 의미로 현재의 사실과 반대되는 일을 가정하는 가정법 과거이므로 「If + 주어 + 동사의 과거형(be동사는 were) ~, 주어 + would, could, might + 동사원형 …」을 쓴다.

14 ① joined → had joined
③ is → were
④ are → were[had been]
⑤ would give → would have given

15 현재 이룰 수 없거나 실현 가능성이 거의 없는 일을 소망하는 「I wish + 가정법 과거」를 써야 하므로 knew를 쓴다.

16 과거의 사실과 반대되는 일을 가정하는 가정법 과거완료를 써야 하므로 had eaten을 쓴다.

17 ① → I wish I had not left the party so soon.

18 과거의 사실과 반대되는 일을 가정하는 가정법 과거완료를 써야 하므로 「If + 주어 + had p.p. ~, 주어 + would, could, might + have p.p. …」를 쓴다.

19 현재의 사실과 반대되는 일을 가정하고 있으므로 주절에는 「주어 + would, could, might + 동사원형」을 쓴다.

20 과거의 사실과 반대되는 일을 가정하고 있으므로 주절에는 「주어 + would, could, might + have p.p.」를 쓴다.

21 현재의 사실에 대한 직설법 문장이므로 '만약 ~한다면 …할 텐데'라는 의미의 가정법 과거 「If + 주어 + 동사의 과거형 ~, 주어 + would, could, might + 동사원형 …」으로 바꿔 쓸 수 있다.

22 ④ → had not told

Chapter 13 일치와 화법

UNIT 01 시제의 일치

Smart Check

p.148

1 ③ 2 ① 3 ②

Practice

p.149

A 1 lost 2 boils 3 had ended
4 would 5 started

B 1 didn't feel 2 would be 3 is
4 makes 5 wanted 6 had stayed

C 1 Mercury is
2 his lecture had been
3 the Vietnam War ended
4 he could finish

UNIT 02 화법

Smart Check

p.150

1 ③ 2 ①

Practice

p.151

A 1 said 2 who had left
3 if 4 I had gotten

B 1 told, my shoes looked
2 said, she wanted
3 asked, when I would, my
4 asked if[whether] I could, her
5 told, she had been, me
6 asked, why he was
7 asked, if[whether] I had

C 1 told, he didn't know
2 asked, if[whether] I was good at
3 asked, what the most popular dish was

Writing Exercise

p.152

A 1 I heard that the new shopping mall would open in July
2 William thought that he had seen someone enter the house
3 They knew that Beethoven died in 1827
4 Lisa said that she might move to another school

5 Ms. Harrison taught us that an elephant lives up to 70 years
6 He told me that he couldn't stay underwater so long

B
1 Daniel asked me why I needed more blankets
2 Mom told me that it was too late for me to play computer games
3 Sandra asked who had drunk all the milk in the fridge
4 He asked me where he could get the information about the contest

C
1 said to me, "I want you to help me."
2 said (that) he had made the strawberry cake by himself
3 said to me, "I will join the soccer team."
4 asked me if[whether] I had been to New York
5 said, "How can they swim so fast in the river?"
6 asked me if[whether] I was familiar with the rules of chess

D
1 she was going to go to the library in 30 minutes
2 where he had bought the blue shirt
3 if[whether] she could borrow his history notes

Chapter Test

p.154

1 ③ 2 ② 3 ③ 4 ⑤ 5 ④ 6 ①
7 asked why my room was
8 his laptop had been broken 9 ⑤
10 ②, ⑤ 11 ⑤ 12 ② 13 your → my
14 is → was 15 ③ 16 could become
17 when I would go to the art museum
18 elephants can't jump 19 ④ 20 ③
21 Mary said, "I will bake cookies for my friends."
22 Thomas said to me, "What do you want for your birthday?"
23 ④ 24 ①, ④

1 주절이 과거시제이므로 종속절에는 과거시제 didn't feel을 쓴다.

2 과학적 사실을 말할 때는 주절의 시제와 상관없이 종속절에 항상 현재시제를 쓰므로 현재시제 freezes를 쓴다.

3 역사적 사실을 말할 때는 주절의 시제와 상관없이 종속절에 항상 과거시제를 쓰므로 과거시제 discovered를 쓴다.

4 의문사가 없는 의문문의 간접 화법은 if나 whether로 주절과 종속절을 연결한다.

5 ④ will → would

6 ① were we → we were

7 의문사가 있는 의문문의 간접 화법은 의문사(why)로 주절과 종속절을 연결하고, 종속절을 「의문사 + 주어 + 동사」의 어순으로 쓴다. 전달동사 say는 ask로 바꾸고, 전달동사가 과거시제이므로 종속절의 현재시제 is를 과거시제 was로 바꾼다. 전달하는 사람의 입장에 맞게 인칭대명사 your를 my로 바꾼다.

8 전달동사 say는 그대로 쓰고, 전달동사가 과거시제이므로 종속절의 과거시제 was broken을 과거완료시제 had been broken으로 바꾼다. 전달하는 사람의 입장에 맞게 인칭대명사 My를 his로 바꾼다.

9 전달동사 say는 그대로 쓰고, 전달동사가 과거시제이므로 종속절의 현재시제 need를 과거시제 needed로 바꾼다. 전달하는 사람의 입장에 맞게 인칭대명사 I를 she로 바꾼다.

10 주절이 과거시제이므로 종속절에는 과거시제 was나 과거완료시제 had been을 쓴다.

11 첫 번째 빈칸: A가 말한 내용을 전달하고 있고 빈칸 뒤에 to 없이 me가 왔으므로 전달동사 told를 쓴다.
두 번째 빈칸: 주절이 과거시제이고 A가 책을 집에 두고 온 것이 말한 시점보다 더 이전에 발생한 일이므로 종속절에는 과거완료시제 had left를 쓴다.

12 첫 번째 빈칸: Kate가 말한 내용을 전달하고 있고 빈칸 뒤에 바로 that이 왔으므로 전달동사 said를 쓴다.
두 번째 빈칸: 주절이 과거시제이므로 종속절에는 can의 과거형 could를 쓴다.

13 전달하는 사람의 입장에 맞게 인칭대명사 your를 my로 바꾼다.

14 전달동사가 과거시제이므로 종속절의 현재시제 am을 과거시제 was로 바꾼다.

15 ③ → They said that they were having fun.

16 주절이 현재시제에서 과거시제로 바뀌었으므로 종속절에는 조동사의 과거형 could를 쓴다.

17 의문사가 있는 의문문의 간접 화법은 의문사(when)로 주절과 종속절을 연결하고, 종속절을 「의문사 + 주어 + 동사」의 어순으로 쓴다. 주절이 과거시제이고, 내가 미술관을 가는 것은 Alice가 나에게 물었던 시점 이후에 발생할 일이므로 will의 과거형 would를 써서 when I would go to the art museum을 쓴다.

18 과학적 사실을 말할 때는 주절의 시제와 상관없이 종속절에 항상 현재시제를 쓰므로 elephants can't jump를 쓴다.

19 • 주절이 과거시제이므로 종속절에는 과거시제 was를 쓴다.
• 주절이 과거시제이므로 종속절에는 과거시제 had를 쓴다.

20 • 역사적 사실을 말할 때는 주절의 시제와 상관없이 종속절에 항상 과거시제를 쓰므로 과거시제 wrote를 쓴다.
• 과학적 사실을 말할 때는 주절의 시제와 상관없이 종속절에 항상 현재시제를 쓰므로 현재시제 is를 쓴다.

21 전달동사 say는 그대로 쓰고, 전달동사가 과거시제라서 종속절에 과거형 would가 쓰였으므로 현재형 will을 쓴다. Mary의 입장에 맞게 인칭대명사 she를 I로 바꾸고 her를 my로 바꾼다.

22 전달동사 ask는 say to로 바꾸고, 의문사가 있는 의문문이므로 「의문사 + 동사 + 주어」의 어순으로 쓴다. 전달동사가 과거시제라서 종속절에 과거시제 wanted가 쓰였으므로 현

재시제 do ~ want를 쓴다. Thomas의 입장에 맞게 인칭대명사 I를 you로 바꾸고 my를 your로 바꾼다.

23 ④ didn't → don't

24 ② had started → started
③ had I → I had
⑤ will → would

Chapter 01 시제

UNIT 01 현재/과거/미래/진행시제

p.2

A 1 lost 2 sleep 3 will teach 4 is melting

B 1 O 2 has 3 spent 4 will[is going to] learn 5 O

C 1 am wearing 2 fed 3 published 4 will complete

D 1 moved to Shanghai yesterday
2 is going to open next month
3 hate Monday mornings
4 is eating lunch with his sister

UNIT 02 현재완료시제

p.3

A 1 for 2 fixed 3 have done 4 O

B 1 went 2 Have you ever been 3 have lived

C 1 have lost my pencil case
2 has taught history for five years
3 has gone abroad to study
4 has taken piano lessons since January

D 1 Have you used this application
2 have just arrived at the airport
3 has donated much money

Chapter Test +

p.4

1 ③ 2 ⑤ 3 has downloaded → downloaded
4 moved → moves 5 ⑤ 6 ④ 7 ②
8 ③ 9 has worn 10 will[am going to] be
11 has lost her umbrella 12 has liked Jessica for
13 ④ 14 ② 15 ⑤ 16 ② 17 ④ 18 ③
19 (1) ⓑ → was (2) ⓓ → know 20 ⑤
21 have gone abroad
22 bought a new soccer ball
23 was taking a bath
24 has never been to the aquarium

1 since는 현재완료시제와 주로 함께 쓰는 표현이다.

2 '나의 엄마가 집에 오셨을 때 나는 나의 고양이와 놀고 있었다.'라는 의미이므로 과거진행시제를 쓴다.

3 an hour ago는 과거시제와 주로 함께 쓰는 표현이다. 현재완료시제는 특정한 과거 시점을 나타내는 표현과 함께 쓸 수 없다.

4 과학적 사실을 나타내고 있으므로 현재시제를 쓴다

5 첫 번째 빈칸: for는 현재완료시제와 주로 함께 쓰는 표현이다.
두 번째 빈칸: tomorrow는 미래시제와 주로 함께 쓰는 표현이다.

6 ④ is liking → likes

7 ② snows → has snowed

8 • last Saturday는 과거시제와 주로 함께 쓰는 표현이다.
• tomorrow는 미래시제와 주로 함께 쓰는 표현이다.

9 since는 현재완료시제와 주로 함께 쓰는 표현이다.

10 in the future는 미래시제와 주로 함께 쓰는 표현이다.

11 Cathy가 우산을 잃어버렸고 그 결과 지금 우산을 가지고 있지 않으므로 현재완료시제를 쓴다.

12 Dave가 Jessica를 2년 전에 좋아했고 여전히 좋아하므로 현재완료시제를 쓴다. two years는 일이 지속된 기간이므로 for(~ 동안)를 쓴다.

13 그녀(Claire)가 미국으로 갔고 그 결과 지금 여기에 없으므로 현재완료시제를 쓴다.

14 yesterday는 과거시제와 주로 함께 쓰는 표현이다.

15 ① is having → has
② takes → has taken
③ has worked → will[is going to] work
④ will make → made

16 ⓐ has sold → sold
ⓓ visited → will[is going to] visit
ⓔ sees → has seen[saw]

17 주어진 문장과 ④: 완료
①②: 경험 ③: 계속 ⑤: 결과

18 주어진 문장과 ③: 결과
①⑤: 계속 ②: 완료 ④: 경험

19 (1) 과거의 상태를 나타내고 있으므로 과거시제를 쓴다.
(2) 인식의 의미를 나타내는 동사 know는 진행형으로 쓸 수 없다.

20 next week(다음 주에)은 미래시제와 주로 함께 쓰는 표현이다. 미래시제는 「will + 동사원형」이나 「be going to + 동사원형」의 형태이다.

21 과거에 일어난 일의 결과가 현재까지 영향을 미치고 있음을 나타내는 현재완료시제 문장이다. 현재완료시제는 「have/has + p.p.」의 형태이다.

22 two days ago(이틀 전에)는 과거시제와 주로 함께 쓰는 표현이다.

23 과거의 특정 시점에 진행되고 있던 동작을 나타내는 과거진행시제 문장이다. 과거진행시제는 「was/were + V-ing」의 형태이다.

24 과거부터 현재까지의 경험을 나타내는 현재완료시제 문장이다. 현재완료시제는 「have/has + p.p.」의 형태이다.

Chapter 02 조동사

UNIT 01 can, may, will

p.7

A 1 go 2 Can[Could/May] 3 get 4 to jump

B 1 ⓑ 2 ⓐ 3 ⓒ 4 ⓒ 5 ⓑ

C 1 wasn't able to find 2 is going to watch 3 Can[Could/May] I look 4 is able to cook

D 1 Fish can breathe 2 Would you tell 3 Gabriel may not like

UNIT 02 must, have to, should

p.8

A 1 water 2 can't 3 must 4 doesn't have to

B 1 should not 2 don't have to 3 must 4 have to

C 1 must be 2 should be 3 don't need to print 4 can't be

D 1 We should eat breakfast 2 You must not watch TV 3 Jake will have to make a decision

UNIT 03 would like to, had better, used to

p.9

A 1 walk 2 to decorate 3 stretching

B 1 used to 2 had better 3 would like to 4 had better not

C 1 had better sleep 2 used to be 3 would like to invite

D 1 They would travel together 2 We had better stay home 3 Would you like to sit 4 Ronald is used to carrying

Chapter Test +

p.10

1 ① 2 ③ 3 ④ 4 ⑤ 5 ③ 6 ③
7 ② 8 ⑤ 9 Clara can bake delicious cookies
10 There used to be an old church in my town
11 must be 12 used to be 13 can't
14 would 15 ④ 16 ⑤ 17 ①, ④
18 ② 19 is going to learn French next month
20 had better not eat fast food 21 ⑤ 22 ③
23 doesn't have to wear glasses[doesn't need to/need not wear glasses]
24 may[might] go to the concert

---

1 충고·의무(~해야 한다)를 나타내는 should를 쓴다.
2 불필요(~할 필요가 없다)를 나타내는 don't have to를 쓴다.
3 would = used to
4 want to = would like to
5 have to(~해야 한다)의 미래형은 will have to를 쓴다.
6 ③: 의무 ①②④⑤: 강한 추측
7 ②: 허가 ①③④⑤: 능력·가능
8 ⑤ is used to taking → used to take
9 조동사 뒤에는 동사원형이 온다.
10 '전에는 나의 마을에 오래된 교회가 있었다.'라는 의미이므로 과거의 반복적인 습관(~하곤 했다)을 나타내는 would는 쓸 수 없다.
11 '그녀는 좋은 사람인 것이 틀림없다.'라는 의미이므로 강한 추측(~임에 틀림없다)을 나타내는 must를 쓴다.
12 '전에는 나의 아파트 건너편에 중학교가 있었다.'라는 의미이므로 과거의 상태(전에는 ~이었다)를 나타내는 used to를 쓴다.
13 • 능력·가능(~할 수 있다)을 나타내는 can의 부정형 can't를 쓴다.
• 강한 부정의 추측(~일 리가 없다)을 나타내는 can't를 쓴다.
• 허가(~해도 된다)를 나타내는 can의 부정형 can't를 쓴다.
14 • '~하고 싶다'라는 의미인 would like to의 would를 쓴다.
• 과거의 반복적인 습관(~하곤 했다)을 나타내는 would를 쓴다.
• 요청(~해주겠니?)을 나타내는 would를 쓴다.
15 ④ affording → afford
16 ⑤ to add → add
17 ② have → to have
③ to rain → rain
⑤ not should → should not[shouldn't]
18 must not '~하면 안 된다'
don't have to '~할 필요가 없다'
19 미래(~할 것이다)를 나타내는 be going to를 쓴다.
20 had better의 부정형은 had better not을 쓴다.
21 첫 번째 빈칸: would like to '~하고 싶다'
두 번째 빈칸: 미래(~할 것이다)를 나타내는 be going to를 쓴다.

22 첫 번째 빈칸: 의무(~해야 한다)를 나타내는 must를 쓴다.
두 번째 빈칸: 허가(~해도 된다)를 나타내는 can의 부정형 cannot을 쓴다.

23 불필요(~할 필요가 없다)를 나타내는 don't have to[don't need to/need not]을 쓴다.

24 약한 추측(~일지도 모른다)을 나타내는 may[might]를 쓴다.

Chapter 03 동사의 종류

UNIT 01 감각동사와 수여동사

p.13

A 1 great 2 sounds 3 O
4 for us

B 1 to 2 of 3 X
4 for

C 1 will buy new shoes for Jacob
2 read his son a book
3 built my little sister a sandcastle
4 passed a camera to the reporter

D 1 get me a towel
2 looks very lonely
3 gave his address to me
4 smells like a rose

UNIT 02 목적격 보어가 필요한 동사

p.14

A 1 dance 2 calm 3 to get
4 know 5 sad

B 1 find[to find] 2 move[moving]
3 laugh 4 to stay

C 1 to bring 2 comfortable
3 a great leader 4 fix

D 1 tell Olivia to be careful
2 named her cat Simba
3 got me to eat vegetables
4 listened to him playing the guitar

Chapter Test +

p.15

1 ③ 2 ① 3 ② 4 ④ 5 ②, ⑤
6 ①, ④ 7 cooked fried chicken for him
8 asked some questions of the citizens 9 ④
10 ⑤ 11 ② 12 ③ 13 fix 14 to drink
15 to wait beside the gate
16 play[playing] Mozart's music 17 ①, ③
18 ④ 19 ③
20 Her mother didn't let her go to the concert
21 Cindy made the photo album for me
22 (1) ⓑ → easy (2) ⓒ → write
23 I helped him decorate the room
24 saw three puppies run in the field

1 「ask + 목적어 + to부정사」

2 「tell + 직접 목적어 + to + 간접 목적어」

3 ② to look → look

4 ④ tell → to tell

5 목적격 보어 자리에 동사원형(read)이 왔으므로 목적격 보어 자리에 to부정사가 오는 get과 tell은 쓸 수 없다.

6 감각동사의 주격 보어 자리에는 형용사가 오거나 「감각동사 + like + 명사」의 형태로 쓰므로 부사 well과 like soft는 쓸 수 없다. 참고로, well이 형용사로 쓰이면 '건강한'이라는 의미이기 때문에 빈칸에 들어가면 어색한 문장이 된다.

7 「cook + 간접 목적어 + 직접 목적어」
= 「cook + 직접 목적어 + for + 간접 목적어」

8 「ask + 간접 목적어 + 직접 목적어」
= 「ask + 직접 목적어 + of + 간접 목적어」

9 ① taking → to take
② finding → (to) find
③ use → to use
⑤ to win → win

10 ① looks like → looks
② expensively → expensive
③ nicely → nice
④ of → for

11 ②의 make는 목적어와 목적격 보어를 필요로 하는 동사이고, ①③④⑤의 make는 간접 목적어와 직접 목적어를 필요로 하는 수여동사이다.

12 • 「expect + 목적어 + to부정사」
• 「hear + 목적어 + 동사원형/V-ing형」

13 「have + 목적어 + 동사원형」

14 「advise + 목적어 + to부정사」

15 「tell + 목적어 + to부정사」

16 「watch + 목적어 + 동사원형/V-ing형」

17 「help + 목적어 + 동사원형/to부정사」

18 ④: 주격 보어 ①②③⑤: 목적격 보어

19 첫 번째 빈칸: 「want + 목적어 + to부정사」
두 번째 빈칸: 「help + 목적어 + 동사원형/to부정사」

20 「let + 목적어 + 동사원형」

21 「make + 직접 목적어 + for + 간접 목적어」

22 (1) 「find + 목적어 + 형용사」

(2) 「make + 목적어 + 동사원형」

23 「help + 목적어 + 동사원형」

24 「saw + 목적어 + 동사원형」

Chapter 04 수동태

UNIT 01 수동태의 쓰임

p.18

A 1 invited 2 was bitten
3 is purchased 4 appeared

B 1 will be served 2 happened
3 is taught 4 was painted

C 1 The tour bus is driven by him
2 The gate was guarded by the soldiers
3 The chicken was heated by Justin
4 The library books will be returned by me

D 1 will be kept
2 was caught by the police officer
3 is used by many people
4 was solved by a young girl

UNIT 02 수동태의 다양한 형태

p.19

A 1 Are, grown 2 must be taken
3 Was, bought 4 weren't discussed

B 1 Was 2 be protected
3 O 4 not selected

C 1 The activities can be planned by him
2 By whom were the plants watered
3 The lecture wasn't attended by most students
4 Was an umbrella brought by Linda

D 1 Where was the event held
2 Homework should not be copied
3 Were these shrimps caught
4 The rules were not explained

UNIT 03 주의해야 할 수동태

p.20

A 1 to 2 to rest
3 for 4 shouting

B 1 with 2 at 3 with 4 to

C 1 was asked a favor, was asked of the police officer
2 was given a cookie, was given to the little girl
3 were allowed to leave early

D 1 This shirt is made of cotton
2 They were made to work together
3 Scott was seen going to the mall
4 Flowers were bought for her mother

Chapter Test +

p.21

1 ④ 2 ⑤ 3 Can the light bulb be replaced
4 ④ 5 ② 6 ③
7 The players were advised to keep calm by the coach
8 The dishes weren't put in the sink by her
9 ① 10 ② 11 ① 12 ② 13 ③, ④
14 speaking[to speak] 15 will be served
16 ③ 17 A nice view was shown to the tourists
18 was built for us by our dad
19 was made to read the book by my friend
20 ④ 21 ① 22 ②
23 (1) ⓒ → will be sent (2) ⓓ → of 24 going, to go

1 도둑이 잡은 것이 아니라 잡힌 것이므로 수동태를 쓴다. yesterday는 과거를 나타내는 표현이므로 과거시제 was caught를 쓴다.

2 주방용 칼이 만지면 안 되는 것이 아니라 만져지면 안 되는 것이므로 수동태를 쓴다. 조동사가 있는 수동태의 부정문은 「주어 + 조동사 + not + be + p.p.」의 형태이므로 not be touched를 쓴다.

3 조동사가 있는 수동태의 의문문: 「조동사 + 주어 + be + p.p. ~?」

4 목적격 보어가 명사인 5형식 수동태 문장에서는 목적격 보어를 「be동사 + p.p.」 뒤에 그대로 쓴다.

5 • be made of '~으로 만들어지다' (재료 성질이 변하지 않음)
• 직접 목적어가 주어진 수동태 문장에서 ask는 간접 목적어 앞에 전치사 of를 쓰는 동사이다.

6 • 지각동사가 쓰인 5형식 수동태 문장에서는 목적격 보어로 V-ing형이나 to부정사를 쓴다.
• be known to '~에게 알려져 있다'

7 목적격 보어가 to부정사인 5형식 문장을 수동태로 바꿀 때는 목적격 보어를 「be동사 + p.p.」 뒤에 그대로 쓴다.

8 수동태의 부정문: 「주어 + be동사 + not + p.p.」

9 행위자인 Ms. Nolan을 능동태 문장의 주어로 쓰고 수동태의 의문문 Was the car accident caused를 Did Ms. Nolan cause the car accident로 바꾼다.

10 ② prepared → be prepared

11 ②③④⑤: 행위자가 일반인이거나 중요하지 않을 때는 「by + 행위자」를 생략할 수 있다.

12 첫 번째 빈칸: be surprised at '~에 놀라다'
두 번째 빈칸: 컵이 깬 것이 아니라 깨진 것이므로 수동태를 쓴다. 수동태의 동사는 「be + p.p.」의 형태이므로 was broken을 쓴다.

13 목적어가 두 개(them, science)인 4형식 문장이므로 두 개의 수동태 문장을 만들 수 있다. 직접 목적어가 주어인 수동태 문장은 간접 목적어 앞에 전치사 to/for/of 중 하나를 쓰며, teach는 to를 쓰는 동사이다.

14 지각동사가 쓰인 5형식 수동태 문장에서는 목적격 보어로 V-ing형이나 to부정사를 쓴다.

15 조동사가 있는 수동태: 「조동사 + be + p.p.」

16 ① → The hero saved many people.
② → My disease was treated by the doctor.
④ → The singer was made to sing one more song by the fans.
⑤ → The fence was broken by the storm last night.

17 '보여졌다'라는 과거의 의미이고 주어 A nice view는 3인칭 단수이므로 was shown을 쓴다. 4형식 문장을 직접 목적어가 주어인 수동태 문장으로 쓸 때 간접 목적어 앞에 전치사 to/for/of 중 하나를 쓰며, show는 to를 쓰는 동사이다.

18 '지어졌다'라는 과거의 의미이고 주어 The house는 3인칭 단수이므로 was built를 쓴다. 4형식 문장을 직접 목적어가 주어인 수동태 문장으로 쓸 때 간접 목적어 앞에 전치사 to/for/of 중 하나를 쓰며, build는 for를 쓰는 동사이다. 행위자는 「by + 행위자」의 형태로 쓴다.

19 '읽게 되었다'라는 과거의 의미이고 주어 I는 1인칭 단수이므로 was made를 쓴다. 사역동사가 쓰인 5형식 수동태 문장에서는 목적격 보어로 to부정사를 쓴다.

20 ① Did → Was
② playing → to play
③ was appeared → appeared
⑤ is using → is used

21 ②⑤: stay와 happen은 목적어를 가지지 않는 동사이므로 수동태로 쓸 수 없다.
③④: have와 fit은 소유나 상태를 나타내는 동사이므로 수동태로 쓸 수 없다.

22 ⓒ kept to warm → kept warm
ⓔ can seen → can be seen

23 (1) 조동사가 있는 수동태: 「조동사 + be + p.p.」
(2) ask는 간접 목적어 앞에 전치사 of를 쓰는 동사이다.

24 목적격 보어가 to부정사인 5형식 문장을 수동태로 바꿀 때는 목적격 보어를 「be동사 + p.p.」 뒤에 그대로 쓴다.

Chapter 05 to부정사

UNIT 01 to부정사의 명사적 용법

p.24

A 1 to ask 2 to win 3 to become

B 1 It is important to protect our environment
2 It was exciting to watch the soccer game
3 It takes a long time to master a language

C 1 where I should visit in Italy
2 what to buy for his birthday
3 how to use the software
4 when she should feed her hamster

D 1 is to finish the homework
2 decided not to quit his job
3 It is impossible to predict the future

UNIT 02 to부정사의 형용사적 용법

p.25

A 1 booked a hotel to visit
2 has the ability to change its color
3 are many benches to sit on
4 take a piece of paper to write on
5 get the dog a ball to play with

B 1 were to achieve 2 are to turn
3 are to buy

C 1 a letter to send his parents
2 a chance to see the musical
3 something sharp to cut the meat
4 No sound was to be heard

UNIT 03 to부정사의 부사적 용법

p.26

A 1 to eat 2 to stay healthy
3 to be a violinist 4 to buy a new laptop
5 to stay awake
6 to tell you the bad news
7 to play alone 8 to catch the plane

B 1 was pleased to receive your invitation
2 must be angry to shout at me
3 was relieved to complete the history project

C 1 to leave my hometown
2 only to damage it again
3 to draw pictures on the wall

UNIT 04 to부정사의 의미상 주어, to부정사 구문

p.27

A 1 for 2 of 3 of 4 for

B 1 too high 2 warm enough
3 O 4 of Joan

C 1 so fast that he could win the race
2 too sick to leave the hospital
3 so expensive that I can't buy them
4 intelligent enough to solve the puzzle

D 1 It is possible for me to get
2 was too boring for kids to watch
3 is clean enough for guests to use

Chapter Test +

p.28

1 ④ 2 ③
3 A motorcycle is dangerous to ride
4 not to lie
5 sensitive enough to hear small noises
6 so scary that we can't watch it 7 ③ 8 for
9 ① 10 ② 11 ② 12 ④ 13 ④ 14 ⑤
15 must be careless to lose her scarf three times
16 was very happy to hear the good news
17 ⑤ 18 ③
19 (1) ⓒ → anything interesting (2) ⓔ → to hang
20 a pen to write with 21 decided not to start
22 grew up to be a police officer
23 The English book was too difficult for us to read
24 Thomas studied hard only to fail the test

1 '배우는 것'이라는 의미의 보어로 쓰이는 명사적 용법의 to부정사를 쓴다.
2 '무엇을 ~할지'라는 의미의 「what + to부정사」를 쓴다.
3 '타기에 위험한'이라는 의미로 형용사 dangerous를 수식하는 부사적 용법의 to부정사를 쓴다.
4 promise는 to부정사를 목적어로 쓰는 동사이고, to부정사의 부정형은 「not to + 동사원형」이다.
5 「so + 형용사/부사 + that + 주어 + can + 동사원형」은 「형용사/부사 + enough + to부정사」로 바꿔 쓸 수 있다.
6 「too + 형용사/부사 + to부정사」는 「so + 형용사/부사 + that + 주어 + can't + 동사원형」으로 바꿔 쓸 수 있다. 문장의 주어(The movie)가 to부정사의 목적어인 경우 that절에 반드시 목적어를 쓴다.
7 ① to going → to go
② to sit → to sit on
④ enough fun → fun enough
⑤ of → for
8 to부정사의 의미상 주어는 「for + 목적격」의 형태로 쓴다.
9 ① to live → to live in
10 ② to wear comfortable → comfortable to wear
11 ②: 부사적 용법 ①③④⑤: 명사적 용법
12 ④: 형용사적 용법 ①②③⑤: 부사적 용법
13 to부정사가 수식하는 명사 toy가 전치사의 목적어이므로 to부정사 뒤에 전치사 with를 쓴다.
14 '…하기에 너무 ~한/하게'라는 의미인 「too + 형용사/부사 + to부정사」를 쓰고, 의미상 주어는 「for + 목적격」의 형태로 쓴다.
15 '스카프를 세 번 잃어버리다니 부주의한 것이 틀림없다'라는 의미로 판단의 근거를 나타내는 부사적 용법의 to부정사를 쓴다.
16 '좋은 소식을 들어서 매우 행복했다'라는 의미로 감정의 원인을 나타내는 부사적 용법의 to부정사를 쓴다.
17 ⑤ → Wood is light enough to float on water.
(「so + 형용사/부사 + that + 주어 + can + 동사원형」은 「형용사/부사 + enough + to부정사」로 바꿔 쓸 수 있다.)
18 ① → to arrive ② → too quiet
④ → to talk to[with] ⑤ → of
19 (1) -thing으로 끝나는 대명사(anything)가 형용사와 to부정사의 수식을 동시에 받을 때는 「-thing + 형용사 + to부정사」의 형태로 쓴다.
(2) '너와 함께 시간을 보내서 신난다'라는 의미로 감정의 원인을 나타내는 부사적 용법의 to부정사를 쓴다.
20 '쓸 펜'이라는 의미로 명사 pen을 수식하는 형용사적 용법의 to부정사를 쓴다. to부정사가 수식하는 명사가 전치사의 목적어이므로 to부정사 뒤에 전치사 with를 쓴다.
21 decide는 to부정사를 목적어로 쓰는 동사이고, to부정사의 부정형은 「not to + 동사원형」이다.
22 '(…해서 결국) ~하다'라는 의미로 결과를 나타내는 부사적 용법의 to부정사를 쓴다.
23 '…하기에 너무 ~한/하게'라는 의미인 「too + 형용사/부사 + to부정사」를 쓰고, 의미상 주어는 「for + 목적격」의 형태로 쓴다.
24 '(…해서 결국) ~하다'라는 의미로 결과를 나타내는 부사적 용법의 to부정사를 쓰고 부정적인 내용의 결과를 말하기 위해 to부정사 앞에 only를 쓴다.

Chapter 06 동명사

UNIT 01 동명사의 쓰임

p.31

A 1 using 2 Finding[To find]
3 cleaning 4 being[to be]

B 1 O 2 being 3 O
4 teaching[to teach] 5 is

C 1 Singing on the stage
2 listening to classical music
3 growing plants in the garden

D 1 couldn't help feeling tired
2 feel like drinking something cold
3 kept talking on the phone

UNIT 02 동명사와 to부정사를 목적어로 쓰는 동사

p.32

A 1 telling 2 to call
3 drawing, to draw 4 to see
5 to buy 6 growing, to grow
7 walking 8 to lock

B 1 to meet 2 closing
3 throwing 4 taking[to take]
5 to go 6 drinking[to drink]
7 to cook 8 talking

C 1 She hates working[to work]
2 My uncle quit smoking
3 Brian wishes to be alone
4 I regret yelling at my younger brother

Chapter Test +

p.33

1 ④ 2 ② 3 ④ 4 ② 5 ⑤
6 bringing → to bring 7 making → to make
8 ④ 9 ⑤ 10 ④ 11 playing with her dog
12 watching the amazing opera
13 try baking bread
14 On finishing her homework
15 is afraid of not passing
16 It is no use complaining about the past
17 ① 18 (1) ⓒ → to find (2) ⓔ → smiling 19 ①
20 ⑤ 21 to save 22 to get 23 ④
24 The restaurant was worth waiting in line

1 「be busy + V-ing」 '~하느라 바쁘다'

2 '문제가 해결되었을 때 우리는 말다툼하는 것을 멈췄다.'라는 의미이므로 동사 stop 뒤에 동명사 arguing을 쓴다. to부정사 to argue를 쓰면 '말다툼하기 위해 멈췄다'라는 어색한 의미가 된다.

3 동명사 taking이 목적어이므로 동명사를 목적어로 쓰는 동사 enjoy를 쓴다. want, plan, wish, promise는 to부정사를 목적어로 쓰는 동사이다.

4 첫 번째 빈칸: love는 동명사와 to부정사를 모두 목적어로 쓰는 동사이므로 helping이나 to help를 쓴다.
두 번째 빈칸: avoid는 동명사를 목적어로 쓰는 동사이므로 thinking을 쓴다.

5 첫 번째 빈칸: deny는 동명사를 목적어로 쓰는 동사이므로 hiding을 쓴다.
두 번째 빈칸: quit은 동명사를 목적어로 쓰는 동사이므로 lying을 쓴다.

6 '(미래에) ~할 것을 기억하다'라는 의미이므로 동사 remember 뒤에 to부정사 to bring을 쓴다.

7 hope는 to부정사를 목적어로 쓰는 동사이므로 to make를 쓴다.

8 「stop + 동명사」는 '~하는 것을 멈추다'라는 의미이고, 「stop + to부정사」는 '~하기 위해 멈추다'라는 의미이다.

9 ⑤ to cry → crying

10 ④ returning → to return

11 'Sandra는 그녀의 개와 노는 것을 즐긴다.'라는 의미이므로 목적어 자리에 동명사 playing을 쓴다.

12 'Jason은 멋진 오페라를 본 것을 결코 잊지 않을 것이다.'라는 의미이므로 동사 forget 뒤에 동명사 watching을 쓴다.

13 '(시험 삼아) ~해보다'라는 의미이므로 동사 try 뒤에 동명사 baking을 쓴다.

14 「on + V-ing」 '~하자마자'

15 전치사의 목적어 자리이므로 동명사 passing을 쓴다. 동명사의 부정형은 동명사 앞에 not을 쓴다.

16 「It is no use + V-ing」 '~해도 소용없다'

17 주어진 문장과 ①: 보어
②⑤: 동사의 목적어 ③: 주어 ④: 전치사의 목적어

18 (1) expect는 to부정사를 목적어로 쓰는 동사이므로 to find를 쓴다.
(2) 「cannot help + V-ing」 '~하지 않을 수 없다'

19 ② to become → becoming
③ eating → to eat
④ to hanging out → hanging[to hang] out
⑤ remember → remembering

20 ① having → to have
② talking → to talk
③ to stay → staying
④ to sitting → sitting

21 '~하려고 노력하다'라는 의미이므로 동사 try 뒤에 to부정사 to save를 쓴다.

22 '~하기 위해 멈추다'라는 의미이므로 동사 stop 뒤에 to부정사 to get을 쓴다.

23 ⓑ: 「stop + 동명사」는 '~하는 것을 멈추다'라는 의미이고, 「stop + to부정사」는 '~하기 위해 멈추다'라는 의미이다.
ⓓ: 「remember + 동명사」는 '(과거에) ~한 것을 기억하다'라는 의미이고, 「remember + to부정사」는 '(미래에) ~할 것을 기억하다'라는 의미이다.

24 「be worth + V-ing」 '~할 가치가 있다'

Chapter 07 분사

UNIT 01 현재분사와 과거분사

p.36

A 1 fixed 2 O
3 disappointing 4 hidden

B 1 excited 2 ringing
3 covered 4 standing

C 1 interesting story 2 torn paper
3 something burning

D 1 playing the violin
2 damaged by the earthquake
3 flying into the forest
4 written in Chinese

UNIT 02 분사구문

p.37

A 1 Waving 2 O
3 Taking 4 Seeing

B 1 Being shy 2 Leaving home
3 Not wanting to waste time

C 1 Because she has homework to do
2 While they lay on the ground
3 If you cut your hair

D 1 Running to the school
2 Drinking too much water
3 Although[Though] trying to catch the thief

Chapter Test +

p.38

1 ④ 2 ③ 3 singing 4 worn
5 ④ 6 ② 7 visiting → visited 8 ①
9 Writing in his diary 10 Not leaving now
11 ③ 12 ④ 13 Sitting on the bench
14 Being ill 15 ② 16 ⑤
17 While[As] he had dinner, Having dinner
18 If you drink too much soda, Drinking too much soda 19 (1) ⓑ → looking (2) ⓔ → Feeling
20 the sun rising over the mountains
21 the dishes washed ten minutes ago
22 The car parked in front of my house 23 ③

1 The famous director's new movie는 감정을 일으키는 원인이므로 현재분사 disappointing을 쓴다.

2 명사 chair를 수식하고 명사와의 관계가 수동이므로 과거분사 made를 쓴다.

3 명사 birds를 수식하고 명사와의 관계가 능동이므로 현재분사 singing을 쓴다.

4 명사 dress를 수식하고 명사와의 관계가 수동이므로 과거분사 worn을 쓴다.

5 • 명사 cookies를 수식하고 명사와의 관계가 수동이므로 과거분사 made를 쓴다.
• 명사 man을 수식하고 명사와의 관계가 능동이므로 현재분사 designing을 쓴다.

6 • 명사 tower를 수식하고 명사와의 관계가 수동이므로 과거분사 built를 쓴다.
• 명사 box를 수식하고 명사와의 관계가 수동이므로 과거분사 filled를 쓴다.

7 명사 town을 수식하고 명사와의 관계가 수동이므로 과거분사 visited를 쓴다.

8 ② interesting → interested
③ shocked → shocking
④ read → reading
⑤ Studied → Studying

9 접속사 As와 주어 he를 생략하고 동사 wrote를 Writing으로 바꾼다.

10 접속사 If와 주어 you를 생략하고 동사 don't leave를 Not leaving으로 바꾼다.

11 ③ covering → covered

12 '나는 코미디 쇼를 보는 동안, 많이 웃었다.'라는 의미이므로 시간을 나타내는 While I watched the comedy show를 쓴다.

13 동시동작을 나타내는 분사구문이므로 Sitting on the bench를 쓴다.

14 이유를 나타내는 분사구문이므로 Being ill을 쓴다.

15 ⓐ played → playing
ⓒ Had → Having
ⓓ using → used

16 ⑤: 현재분사 ①②③④: 동명사

17 첫 번째 문장: '~하면서'라는 의미의 접속사 While[As]를 쓰고, 문장의 시제가 과거이므로 had를 쓴다.
두 번째 문장: 접속사 While[As]와 주어 he를 생략하고 동사 had를 Having으로 바꾼다.

18 첫 번째 문장: '만약 ~한다면'이라는 의미의 접속사 If를 쓰고, 문장의 시제가 미래이므로 drink를 쓴다.
두 번째 문장: 접속사 If와 주어 you를 생략하고 동사 drink를 Drinking으로 바꾼다.

19 (1) 명사 people을 수식하고 명사와의 관계가 능동이므로 현재분사 looking을 쓴다.
(2) '우리는 신이 나서, 우리의 새로운 학교에 대해 이야기하기 시작했다.'라는 의미의 부사절을 분사구문으로 나타낸 것이므로 Feeling을 쓴다.

20 현재분사 rising이 전치사구(over the mountains)와 함께 구를 이루어 쓰였으므로 명사 sun 뒤에서 명사를 수식한다.

21 과거분사 washed가 부사구(ten minutes ago)와 함께 구를 이루어 쓰였으므로 명사 dishes 뒤에서 명사를 수식한다.

22 과거분사 parked가 전치사구(in front of my house)와 함께 구를 이루어 쓰였으므로 명사 car 뒤에서 명사를 수식한다.

23 ③ → Because[As/Since] I am tall

Chapter 08 대명사

UNIT 01 부정대명사 I

p.41

A 1 it 2 ones 3 them

B 1 others 2 any 3 some
4 another 5 Some 6 the others
7 the other

C 1 do any homework 2 cheaper one
3 some students, the others

UNIT 02 부정대명사 II

p.42

A 1 costs 2 want 3 are
4 looks 5 has 6 is
7 like

B 1 all 2 Each 3 one another
4 Every 5 Both

C 1 Both of the cameras were made in Korea
2 Each plate[Each of the plates] in the kitchen has a different pattern
3 All of the crops were destroyed by the storm
4 Every passenger is waiting in line to get on the plane

UNIT 03 재귀대명사

p.43

A 1 X 2 O 3 O 4 X

B 1 seated ourselves 2 cut herself
3 buy yourself
4 disappointed in myself

C 1 Help yourself to 2 for himself
3 beside herself

D 1 believe in myself 2 Between ourselves
3 the house herself 4 used to talk to himself

Chapter Test +

p.44

1 ③ 2 ⑤ 3 ②
4 Each of the rooms has two beds
5 burns himself 6 seated ourselves 7 ③
8 Both of my friends 9 other
10 another 11 others 12 ⑤ 13 ②
14 ④ 15 ② 16 (1) All (2) any (3) every
17 by myself 18 ① 19 ③ 20 ②
21 (1) questions → question (2) problem → problems
22 ② 23 has → have 24 some → any

1 앞에서 언급된 특정한 대상(my bag)을 가리키고 있으므로 it을 쓴다.

2 빈칸 뒤에 단수동사(has)가 왔으므로 단수 취급하는 「each of + 복수명사(the students)」를 쓴다.

3 ②: 재귀 용법(생략 불가능)
①③④⑤: 강조 용법(생략 가능)

4 '각각'이라는 의미의 each를 쓰고, 「each of + 복수명사」는 단수 취급하므로 has를 쓴다.

5 burn oneself '불에 데다'

6 seat oneself '앉다'

7 (A): 「both of + 복수명사」는 복수 취급하므로 are를 쓴다.
(B): 「every + 단수명사」는 단수 취급하므로 has를 쓴다.
(C): 「all (of) + 명사」의 형태로 쓸 때는 all (of) 뒤의 명사(smoke)에 동사를 수일치시키므로 is를 쓴다.

8 「both of + 복수명사」 '둘 다'

9 • Jim과 내가 서로 도왔다고 했으므로 '(둘 사이에) 서로'라는 의미의 each other를 쓴다.
• 「the + other」 '나머지 (전부)'

10 • '하나 더 먹어도 될까요?'라는 의미이므로 another(하나 더)를 쓴다.
• 축구팀 팀원들이 서로를 도왔다고 했으므로 '(셋 이상 사이에) 서로'라는 의미의 one another를 쓴다.

11 • '너는 다른 사람들을 존중해야 한다'라는 의미이므로 others(다른 사람들)를 쓴다. 대명사로 쓰일 때는 주로 복수형인 others로 쓴다.
• 「some ~, the others -」 '(여럿 중) 몇몇은 ~, 나머지 전부는 -'

12 ① boys → boy
② are → is
③ her → herself
④ some → any

13 「one ~, the others -」 '(여럿 중) 하나는 ~, 나머지 전부는 -'

14 첫 번째 빈칸: 「both of + 복수명사」 '둘 다'
두 번째 빈칸: '그는 결국 또 다른 하나를 골라야 했다'라는 의미이므로 another(또 다른 하나)를 쓴다.

15 첫 번째 빈칸: 앞에서 언급된 명사(glasses)와 같은 종류의 불특정한 사물을 가리키고 있으므로 부정대명사 ones를 쓴다.

두 번째 빈칸: 앞에서 언급된 특정한 대상(contact lenses)을 가리키고 있으므로 them을 쓴다.

16 (1) 「all (of) + 명사」 '모든 ~'
(2) 의문문에서는 주로 any를 쓴다.
(3) 「every + 단수명사」 '모든 ~'

17 by oneself '혼자서, 홀로'

18 ①: 강조 용법 밑줄 친 부분과 ②③④⑤: 재귀 용법

19 ③ it → one[another]

20 ② you → yourself

21 (1) every는 「every + 단수명사」의 형태로만 쓰이므로 question을 쓴다.
(2) both 뒤에는 복수명사가 오므로 problems를 쓴다.

22 첫 번째 빈칸: 「both of + 복수명사」는 복수 취급하므로 smell을 쓴다.
두 번째 빈칸: 「the + other」 '나머지 (전부)'

23 「both + 복수명사」는 복수 취급하므로 have를 쓴다.

24 부정문에서는 주로 any를 쓴다.

Chapter 09 관계사

UNIT 01 관계대명사

p.47

A 1 who 2 which 3 O
4 whose

B 1 which 2 whose 3 which
4 who

C 1 whose son is a guitarist
2 which she bought last weekend
3 who(m) I respect
4 which has modern artworks

D 1 The dish which a famous chef made
2 the city which has a beautiful lake
3 her car whose brakes are broken
4 his friend who moved to another school

UNIT 02 관계대명사 that/what, 주의해야 할 관계대명사의 쓰임

p.48

A 1 that 2 that 3 What
4 what 5 that

B 1 O 2 X 3 X 4 O

C 1 who(m)[that] you were speaking to, whom you were speaking
2 which[that] people can sit on, which people can sit
3 who(m)[that] I can depend on, whom I can depend

D 1 The man selling books
2 the same wallet that I bought
3 The girl whom I fell in love with[The girl with whom I fell in love]

UNIT 03 관계부사

p.49

A 1 how 2 when 3 why
4 where

B 1 where 2 when 3 how
4 why

C 1 I remember the day when I introduced myself to my classmates
2 They're looking for the place where they can see the city's view
3 Natalie didn't tell us the reason why she cried yesterday

D 1 why my cookies burned
2 where the couple took their photos
3 when most people go on a vacation

Chapter Test +

p.50

1 ① 2 ③ 3 ⑤ 4 ② 5 ① 6 ⑤
7 ⑤ 8 whose favorite food is sweet potato
9 which[that] a famous director made
10 Do you know the reason why Ted moved to another city
11 (1) who (2) when (3) whom 12 ③
13 What 14 how 15 ④
16 whose players practiced hard
17 where she bought the smartphone 18 ②
19 ③ 20 ④ 21 who → whom
22 the way how → how[the way] 23 have → has

1 선행사(the problem)가 사물이고 빈칸이 관계대명사절 안에서 목적어 역할을 하고 있으므로 사물을 선행사로 하는 목적격 관계대명사 which를 쓴다.

2 선행사가 없으므로 선행사를 포함하는 관계대명사 What을 쓴다.

3 빈칸 뒤에 선행사(the house)가 소유하는 대상인 명사 (walls)가 있으므로 소유격 관계대명사 whose를 쓴다.

4 '그가 과학자가 된 방법'이라고 했으므로 선행사는 the way 이다. 선행사가 방법을 나타내므로 관계부사 how를 쓰지만, the way와 how는 둘 중 하나만 쓸 수 있다.

5 ① that → which 또는 전치사 about을 관계대명사절 끝으로 보낸다.

6 • 선행사(the artist)가 사람이므로 관계대명사 who/whom/that을 쓴다.
• 선행사(the actor)가 사람이고, 빈칸 앞에 전치사가 있으므로 관계대명사 whom을 쓴다. 관계대명사 바로 앞에 전치사가 올 때는 관계대명사 who나 that을 쓸 수 없다.

7 ⑤: 관계대명사 바로 앞에 전치사가 올 때는 목적격 관계대명사를 생략할 수 없다.
①②④: 목적격 관계대명사
③: 「주격 관계대명사 + be동사」

8 두 번째 문장은 첫 번째 문장의 a puppy에 대해 보충 설명하고 있고, 두 번째 문장의 Its가 소유격의 역할을 하고 있으므로 소유격 관계대명사 whose를 쓴다.

9 두 번째 문장은 첫 번째 문장의 The movie에 대해 보충 설명하고 있고, 두 번째 문장의 it이 목적어 역할을 하고 있으므로 사물을 선행사로 하는 목적격 관계대명사 which나 that을 쓴다.

10 두 번째 문장은 첫 번째 문장의 the reason에 대해 보충 설명하고 있고, 선행사(the reason)가 이유를 나타내므로 관계부사 why를 쓴다.

11 (1) 선행사(my classmate)가 사람이므로 관계대명사 who를 쓴다.
(2) 선행사(the day)가 시간을 나타내므로 관계부사 when을 쓴다.
(3) 선행사(a friend)가 사람이고 빈칸 앞에 전치사가 있으므로 관계대명사 whom을 쓴다.

12 ① which → whose
② whom → which[that]
④ which → who[that]
⑤ whose → who(m)[that] 또는 삭제

13 The thing which는 선행사가 없는 관계대명사 What으로 바꿔 쓸 수 있다.

14 선행사(the way)가 방법을 나타내므로 「전치사 + 관계대명사」는 관계부사 how로 바꿔 쓸 수 있지만, the way와 how는 둘 중 하나만 쓸 수 있다.

15 ④: 명사절 접속사　　①②③⑤: 관계대명사

16 선행사(the team)가 소유하는 대상인 명사(players)가 있으므로 소유격 관계대명사 whose를 쓴다.

17 선행사(The store)가 장소를 나타내므로 관계부사 where를 쓴다.

18 • 선행사(an art center)가 사물이고 빈칸 앞에 전치사가 있으므로 관계대명사 which를 쓴다.
• 선행사(the time)가 시간을 나타내므로 관계부사 when을 쓴다.

19 • 선행사(kids and animals)에 사람과 동물이 포함되어 있으므로 관계대명사 that을 쓴다.
• '네가 어떻게 그 산의 정상에 올라갔는지 나에게 알려줄 수 있니?'라는 의미이므로 방법을 나타내는 the way나 how를 쓴다.

20 ④: when　　①②③⑤: which

21 관계대명사 바로 앞에 전치사가 올 때는 관계대명사 who를 쓸 수 없으므로 whom을 쓴다.

22 the way와 how는 둘 중 하나만 쓸 수 있다.

23 선행사(The city)가 단수명사이므로 관계대명사절의 동사는 단수동사 has를 쓴다.

Chapter 10 접속사

UNIT 01 시간/이유/결과를 나타내는 접속사

p.53

A 1 while　2 when　3 Until
4 because of

B 1 so　2 Before　3 Because

C 1 since his best friend moved away
2 because she was thirsty
3 so his classmates like him
4 when she was ten years old

D 1 As soon as the phone rang
2 after I took a short break
3 as he was putting it on the table

UNIT 02 조건/양보를 나타내는 접속사, 접속사 that

p.54

A 1 Though　2 If
3 that　4 Unless

B 1 If you take this medicine, you'll feel better
2 Although the opera itself was great, it was boring to me
3 Unless Sophia keeps her promise, her friends won't trust her

C 1 you don't take a taxi, you will miss the movie
2 Brad was worried about the speech, he tried to be confident
3 Kelly focuses during the class, she will get a poor grade

D 1 Unless you are careful
2 that Jason solved the difficult puzzle
3 although they tried their best

UNIT 03 명령문 + and/or, 상관접속사

p.55

A 1 plays 2 watch 3 work
4 contain

B 1 and 2 O 3 or

C 1 Neither George nor Frank
2 and other people will trust you
3 as well as a pencil
4 or your neighbors will get angry

D 1 Either Joan or Alice will win
2 or the floor will get dirty
3 and I will send you a present
4 Both adults and children can participate

Chapter Test +

p.56

1 ② 2 ⑤ 3 ① 4 ⑤ 5 When
6 after 7 very → so 8 are → is
9 not only cheap but (also) stylish[stylish as well as cheap] 10 that Anne came on time
11 If the test finishes early 12 ② 13 ③
14 ③ 15 Follow the rules, or
16 Before he brushed his teeth 17 ① 18 ④
19 ② 20 (1) as soon as (2) unless (3) because
21 ④ 22 ③ 23 ② 24 ⑤

1 '나는 어린이였던 이후로 스페인어를 공부해왔다.'라는 의미이므로 since(~한 이후로)를 쓴다.

2 '햇빛이 너무 강했기 때문에 Kelly는 선글라스를 샀다.'라는 의미이므로 because(~하기 때문에)를 쓴다.

3 '만약 우리가 예약하지 않는다면, 우리는 그 인기 있는 식당에서 식사를 할 수 없다.'라는 의미이므로 Unless(만약 ~하지 않는다면)를 쓴다.

4 ⑤: '~하고 있을 때, ~하면서' ①②③④: '~하기 때문에'

5 '나는 혼자서 나의 여동생을 돌봤다. 그때, 나는 걱정스러웠다.'라는 의미는 '나는 혼자서 나의 여동생을 돌볼 때 걱정스러웠다.'라는 의미를 나타내므로 '~할 때'라는 의미의 When을 쓴다.

6 'Rosie는 약을 먹었다. 그러고는, 그녀는 잤다.'라는 의미는 'Rosie는 약을 먹은 후에 잤다.'라는 의미를 나타내므로 '~한 후에'라는 의미의 after를 쓴다.

7 「so ~ that …」 '너무 ~해서 …한'

8 either A or B 뒤에 오는 동사는 B(coffee)에 수일치시키므로, 단수동사 is를 쓴다.

9 'A뿐만 아니라 B도'라는 의미의 not only A but (also) B [B as well as A]를 쓴다.

10 '~이라는 것'이라는 의미의 that을 쓰고, that절이 문장 안에서 주어로 쓰일 때는 주로 주어 자리에 가주어 it을 쓰고 진주어 that절을 뒤로 보낸다.

11 '만약 ~한다면'이라는 의미의 if를 쓰며, 조건을 나타내는 부사절에서는 미래시제 대신 현재시제를 쓴다.

12 • '나가기 전에 모든 창문을 닫아주세요.'라는 의미이므로 before(~하기 전에)를 쓴다.
• '미끄러운 바닥을 조심해라, 그렇지 않으면 너는 넘어질 것이다.'라는 의미이므로 「명령문 + or ~」(…해라, 그렇지 않으면 ~)의 or를 쓴다.

13 ① that interesting → interesting that
② or → and
④ like → likes
⑤ will visit → visit

14 ③: 보어 ①②④⑤: 목적어

15 조건을 나타내는 접속사 if가 이끄는 절은 「명령문 + or ~」(…해라, 그렇지 않으면 ~)의 명령문으로 바꿔 쓸 수 있다.

16 '그는 저녁 식사를 한 후에 그의 이를 닦았다.'라는 의미는 '그는 그의 이를 닦기 전에 저녁 식사를 했다.'라는 의미를 나타내므로 '~하기 전에'라는 의미의 Before를 쓴다.

17 ① because of → because

18 ④ If → Unless

19 '비록 ~이지만'이라는 의미의 although를 쓴다.

20 (1) '자명종이 울리자마자 Ron은 잠에서 깼다.'라는 의미이므로 as soon as(~하자마자)를 쓴다.
(2) '만약 내가 다른 약속이 있지 않다면, 나는 너를 토요일에 볼 것이다.'라는 의미이므로 unless(만약 ~하지 않는다면)를 쓴다.
(3) 'Monica가 그녀의 꿈을 이뤘기 때문에 Ben은 그녀를 부러워한다.'라는 의미이므로 because(~하기 때문에)를 쓴다.

21 ④: Unless ①②③⑤: If

22 as/because는 '~하기 때문에'라는 의미로, 이유를 나타내는 부사절을 이끈다.

23 • '이 상자들은 너무 무거워서 Hills씨도 그것들을 들어 올리지 못한다.'라는 의미이므로 「so ~ that …」(너무 ~해서 …한)을 쓴다.
• '나는 너무 졸려서, 수업에 집중할 수 없었다.'라는 의미이므로 so(그래서)를 쓴다.

24 • '나는 촛불을 끄면서 소원을 빌었다.'라는 의미이므로 as(~하고 있을 때, ~하면서)를 쓴다.
• '그는 똑똑하기 때문에 모든 것을 기억한다.'라는 의미이므로 as(~하기 때문에)를 쓴다.

Chapter 11 비교구문

UNIT 01 원급/비교급/최상급 비교

p.59

A 1 tall 2 cheaper 3 O
4 much[even/far/a lot]

B 1 earlier 2 as difficult 3 better
4 the coldest

C 1 as often as 2 faster than
3 the heaviest 4 more, than

D 1 the oldest restaurant
2 far bigger than the old one
3 as intelligent as humans

UNIT 02 비교구문을 이용한 표현

p.60

A 1 as early as 2 emptier, lighter
3 as clearly as 4 more crowded

B 1 three times bigger than
2 as often as she could
3 four times as long as

C 1 The sunnier it got, the more active we felt
2 The more difficult the test is, the more tired students will be
3 The earlier you buy a plane ticket, the cheaper the tickets are

D 1 is getting more and more useful
2 was one of the best singers
3 the more colorful your garden will be

Chapter Test +

p.61

1 ⑤ 2 ④ 3 ③ 4 ① 5 ④ 6 ⑤
7 more expensive than 8 the highest of
9 as[so] high as 10 one of the smartest students
11 The painter became more and more famous
12 ① 13 as early as I could
14 the hotter it gets 15 ② 16 ③, ⑤
17 I studied harder than Jess
18 Russia has the biggest land on earth
19 The more, the more deeply
20 (1) the cheapest (2) as heavy as (3) lighter than
21 ③ 22 ④ 23 ②

1 '이 초콜릿 쿠키는 모든 디저트들 중에서 가장 맛있었다.'라는 의미이므로 최상급 the most delicious를 쓴다.

2 「the + 비교급, the + 비교급」 '~하면 할수록 더 …하다'

3 '새 세탁기는 오래된 것보다 더 잘 작동하고 있다.'라는 의미이므로 비교급 better를 쓴다.

4 빈칸 뒤에 비교급(cuter)이 있으므로 비교급을 강조하는 far를 쓴다.

5 ④ more tasty → tastier

6 ⑤ most → more

7 반지가 팔찌보다 더 비싸므로 비교급 more expensive than을 쓴다.

8 Bill의 시험 점수가 세 명 중에서 가장 높으므로 최상급 the highest를 쓴다. 비교 대상 앞에는 보통 of를 쓴다.

9 '…만큼 ~하지 않은/않게'라는 의미의 「not + as[so] + 원급 + as」를 쓴다.

10 '가장 ~한 것들 중 하나'라는 의미의 「one of the + 최상급 + 복수명사」를 쓴다.

11 '유명해졌다'라는 과거시제이므로 동사는 became을 쓰고, '점점 더 ~한/하게'라는 의미의 「비교급 + and + 비교급」을 쓴다. 비교급이 「more + 원급」의 형태인 경우 「more and more + 원급」으로 쓴다.

12 • '너는 더 많이 울면 울수록 더 슬프다고 느낄 수도 있다.'라는 의미이므로 「the + 비교급, the + 비교급」의 more를 쓴다.
• '튤립이 장미보다 훨씬 더 아름답다'라는 의미의 비교급 비교이므로 more를 쓴다.

13 「as + 원급 + as + possible」은 「as + 원급 + as + 주어 + can[could]」로 바꿔 쓸 수 있다.

14 '지하철은 더 붐비면 붐빌수록 더 더워진다.'라는 의미의 문장이므로 '~하면 할수록 더 …하다'라는 의미의 「the + 비교급, the + 비교급」을 쓴다.

15 • 빈칸 뒤에 비교급(bigger)이 있으므로 비교급을 강조하는 a lot을 쓴다.
• 'Katie의 조언은 너의 것보다 훨씬 더 유용했다.'라는 의미의 비교급 비교이므로 more를 쓴다.

16 ①: Nate가 가장 나이가 많으므로 'Nate는 모두 중에서 가장 어리다.'는 적절하지 않다.
②: Ken이 Josh보다 나이가 더 적으므로 'Ken은 Josh보다 나이가 더 많다.'는 적절하지 않다.
④: Ken이 Josh보다 더 가벼우므로 'Ken은 Josh만큼 가볍지 않다.'는 적절하지 않다.

17 '나는 Jess보다 더 열심히 공부했다.'라는 의미이므로 비교급 harder를 쓴다.

18 '러시아는 지구상에서 가장 큰 영토를 가지고 있다.'라는 의미이므로 최상급 biggest를 쓴다.

19 '그들은 더 많이 이야기를 하면 할수록 서로를 더 깊게 이해했다.'라는 의미의 문장이므로 '~하면 할수록 더 …하다'라는 의미의 「the + 비교급, the + 비교급」을 쓴다.

20 (1) 사과는 가장 싸므로 최상급 the cheapest를 쓴다.
(2) 배는 사과만큼 무거우므로 원급 as heavy as를 쓴다.
(3) 망고는 배보다 가벼우므로 비교급 lighter than을 쓴다.

21 ① fluently → more fluently
② most brightest → brightest
④ than → as
⑤ sweeter → sweet

22 ① → the busiest
② → healthy
③ → better
⑤ → the most attractive

23 ⓑ taller → tallest
ⓒ longest → long
ⓓ the dirtiest → dirtier

Chapter 12 가정법

UNIT 01 가정법 과거, 가정법 과거완료

p.64

A 1 were 2 could call 3 O
4 had exercised

B 1 were in Seoul, could meet you
2 had worn her seat belt, wouldn't have been hurt
3 were tall enough, could ride the roller coaster
4 weren't sick, could go to the party tonight
5 had practiced the piano hard, could have become a good pianist
6 had not forgotten my birthday, would have sent me presents

C 1 had a car, would drive
2 were longer, could travel
3 had been more interesting, wouldn't have left

UNIT 02 I wish 가정법, as if 가정법

p.65

A 1 had been 2 were 3 could go
4 had known

B 1 knew 2 had lived 3 had been

C 1 I could return these shoes
2 she had passed the science test
3 he could swim
4 Joshua had told me the truth

D 1 as if he were a native speaker
2 I had eaten sandwiches for breakfast
3 as if she had been sick
4 the director would make fantasy movies

Chapter Test +

p.66

1 ⑤ 2 ④ 3 ② 4 if
5 you would join our club
6 had not been boring, I wouldn't have fallen asleep
7 had an invitation, they could enter the building
8 as if he owned a sports car
9 I had saved more money 10 ④ 11 ③
12 ⑤ 13 ⑤ 14 he had been 15 ③ 16 ④
17 ② 18 ② 19 had gotten 20 had not been
21 ③ 22 ④ 23 can → could 24 is → were

1 과거의 사실과 반대되는 일을 가정하고 있으므로 주절에는 「주어 + would, could, might + have p.p.」를 쓴다.

2 주절의 시제(현재시제)보다 앞선 시점의 사실과 반대되는 일을 가정하는 「as if + 가정법 과거완료」를 써야 하므로 had walked를 쓴다.

3 현재 이룰 수 없거나 실현 가능성이 거의 없는 일을 소망하는 「I wish + 가정법 과거」를 써야 하므로 could go를 쓴다.

4 • 과거의 사실과 반대되는 일을 가정하는 가정법 과거완료를 써야 하므로 if를 쓴다.
• 주절의 시제(현재시제)와 같은 시점의 사실과 반대되는 일을 가정하는 「as if + 가정법 과거」를 써야 하므로 as if의 if를 쓴다.

5 현재 이룰 수 없거나 실현 가능성이 거의 없는 일을 소망하는 「I wish + 가정법 과거」를 쓴다.

6 과거의 사실과 반대되는 일을 가정하는 가정법 과거완료 「If + 주어 + had p.p. ~, 주어 + would, could, might + have p.p. …」를 쓴다.

7 현재의 사실과 반대되는 일을 가정하는 가정법 과거 「If + 주어 + 동사의 과거형 ~, 주어 + would, could, might + 동사원형 …」를 쓴다.

8 '마치 ~인 것처럼'이라는 의미로 주절의 시제와 같은 시점의 사실과 반대되는 일을 가정하는 「as if + 가정법 과거」를 써야 하므로 「as if + 주어 + 동사의 과거형」을 쓴다.

9 '~했더라면 좋았을 텐데'라는 의미로 과거에 이루지 못한 일에 대한 아쉬움을 나타내는 「I wish + 가정법 과거완료」를 써야 하므로 「I wish + 주어 + had p.p.」를 쓴다.

10 • 주절의 시제(현재시제)보다 앞선 시점의 사실과 반대되는 일을 가정하는 「as if + 가정법 과거완료」를 써야 하므로 had cooked를 쓴다.
• 현재의 사실과 반대되는 일을 가정하는 가정법 과거를 써야 하므로 would watch를 쓴다.

11 • 과거에 이루지 못한 일에 대한 아쉬움을 나타내는 「I wish + 가정법 과거완료」를 써야 하므로 had read를 쓴다.
• 과거의 사실과 반대되는 일을 가정하는 가정법 과거완료를 써야 하므로 had arrived를 쓴다.

12 ⑤ → were

13 첫 번째 빈칸: 과거에 이루지 못한 일에 대한 아쉬움을 나타내는 「I wish + 가정법 과거완료」를 써야 하므로 had come

을 쓴다.
두 번째 빈칸: 과거의 사실과 반대되는 일을 가정하는 가정법 과거완료를 써야 하므로 could have seen을 쓴다.

14 주절의 시제(현재시제)보다 앞선 시점의 사실과 반대되는 일을 가정하는 「as if + 가정법 과거완료」를 쓴다.

15 ③ will eat → would eat

16 ④ have gone → had gone

17 '~하면 좋을 텐데'라는 의미로 현재 이룰 수 없거나 실현 가능성이 거의 없는 일을 소망하는 「I wish + 가정법 과거」이므로 「I wish + 주어 + 동사의 과거형」을 쓴다.

18 ② → If Larry had studied hard, he wouldn't have failed the exam.

19 주절의 시제(현재시제)보다 앞선 시점의 사실과 반대되는 일을 가정하는 「as if + 가정법 과거완료」를 써야 하므로 had gotten을 쓴다.

20 과거의 사실과 반대되는 일을 가정하는 가정법 과거완료를 써야 하므로 had not been을 쓴다.

21 ① were → had been
② had had → had
④ had been → were
⑤ didn't break → had not broken

22 현재의 사실에 대한 직설법 문장이므로 '~하면 좋을 텐데'라는 의미의 「I wish + 주어 + 동사의 과거형」으로 바꿔 쓸 수 있다.

23 현재의 사실과 반대되는 일을 가정하고 있으므로 I wish 뒤에는 조동사의 과거형 could를 쓴다.

24 주절의 시제(현재시제)와 같은 시점의 사실과 반대되는 일을 가정하고 있으므로 as if절에는 동사의 과거형 were를 쓴다. 「as if + 가정법 과거」에서 as if절의 be동사는 주어에 상관없이 were를 쓴다.

Chapter 13 일치와 화법

UNIT 01 시제의 일치

p.69

A 1 made[had made] 2 O 3 would 4 were awarded

B 1 has 2 could 3 opens 4 moves

C 1 Wright brothers invented the airplane
2 I was angry with her
3 his friends would arrive early
4 someone had broken a window of the shop

D 1 the classroom was too small
2 he would be at the library
3 the early bird catches the worm

UNIT 02 화법

p.70

A 1 would 2 told 3 if[whether]

B 1 if[whether] I could get a knife and a fork
2 when I wanted to have lunch
3 (that) he had taken a walk at the park

C 1 You need to drive more slowly
2 Where can I go to fix my laptop
3 Will it rain in the afternoon

D 1 said (that) she enjoyed watching musicals
2 told me (that) he needed my new address
3 asked me how I solved[had solved] the problem

Chapter Test +

p.71

1 ③ 2 ① 3 ② 4 ⑤
5 asked me if[whether] I needed her
6 he could go to the exhibition with me
7 can → could 8 was → had been 9 ③
10 ①, ⑤ 11 ② 12 ④ 13 ② 14 ②
15 ③ 16 would do
17 My father asked if[whether] I could bring the newspaper
18 ④ 19 ②
20 Dennis said to us, "I can speak three languages."
21 She said, "Do you want more soup?"
22 ④ 23 ②, ④

1 주절이 과거시제이므로 종속절에는 조동사의 과거형 would가 포함된 would join을 쓴다.

2 속담·격언을 말할 때는 주절의 시제와 상관없이 종속절에 항상 현재시제를 쓰므로 현재시제 is를 쓴다.

3 과학적 사실을 말할 때는 주절의 시제와 상관없이 종속절에 항상 현재시제를 쓰므로 현재시제 travels를 쓴다.

4 의문사가 없는 의문문의 간접 화법은 if나 whether로 주절과 종속절을 연결한다.

5 의문사가 없는 의문문의 간접 화법은 if나 whether로 주절과 종속절을 연결하고, 종속절을 「if[whether] + 주어 + 동사」의 어순으로 쓴다. 전달동사 say to는 ask로 바꾸고, 전달동사가 과거시제이므로 종속절의 현재시제 Do ~ need를 과거시제 needed로 바꾼다. 전달하는 사람의 입장에 맞게 인칭대명사 you를 I로 바꾸고 my를 her로 바꾼다.

6 전달동사 say는 그대로 쓰고, 전달동사가 과거시제이므로 종속절의 현재형 can을 과거형 could로 바꾼다. 전달하는 사람의 입장에 맞게 인칭대명사 I를 he로 바꾸고 you를 me로 바꾼다.

7 전달동사가 과거시제이므로 종속절의 현재형 can을 과거형 could로 바꾼다.

8 전달동사가 과거시제이므로 종속절의 과거시제 was를 과거완료시제 had been으로 바꾼다.

9 의문사가 없는 의문문의 간접 화법은 if나 whether로 주절과 종속절을 연결하고, 종속절을 「if[whether] + 주어 + 동사」의 어순으로 쓴다. 전달동사 say to는 ask로 바꾸고, 전달동사가 과거시제이므로 종속절의 과거시제 Did ~ watch를 과거완료시제 had watched로 바꾼다. 전달하는 사람의 입장에 맞게 인칭대명사 you를 I로 바꾼다.

10 주절이 과거시제이므로 종속절에는 과거완료시제 had traveled나 과거시제 was를 쓴다.

11 B가 본인이 말한 내용을 전달하고 있고 told는 전치사 to와 함께 쓰여야 하므로 전달동사 said를 쓴다. 주절이 과거시제이므로 종속절에는 will의 과거형 would를 쓴다.

12 그녀가 질문한 내용을 전달하고 있으므로 asked를 쓰고 종속절을 「의문사 + 주어 + 동사」의 어순으로 쓴다.

13 ② that → if[whether]

14 ② were → are

15 ③ → The children said that they could clean the house for their mom.

16 주절이 현재시제에서 과거시제로 바뀌었으므로 종속절에는 조동사의 과거형 would를 쓴다.

17 의문사가 없는 의문문의 간접 화법은 전달동사를 ask를 쓴다. if나 whether로 주절과 종속절을 연결하고, 종속절을 「if[whether] + 주어 + 동사」의 어순으로 쓴다. 주절이 과거시제이므로 조동사의 과거형 could를 써서 if[whether] I could bring the newspaper를 쓴다.

18 • 주절이 과거시제이므로 종속절에는 과거시제 was 또는 과거완료시제 had been을 쓴다.
• 주절이 과거시제이므로 종속절에는 조동사의 과거형 might를 포함한 might come을 쓴다.

19 • 과학적 사실을 말할 때는 주절의 시제와 상관없이 종속절에 항상 현재시제를 쓰므로 현재시제 is를 쓴다.
• 역사적 사실을 말할 때는 주절의 시제와 상관없이 종속절에 항상 과거시제를 쓰므로 과거시제 began을 쓴다.

20 전달동사 tell은 say to로 바꾸고, 전달동사가 과거시제라서 종속절에 과거형 could가 쓰였으므로 현재형 can을 쓴다. Dennis의 입장에 맞게 인칭대명사 he를 I로 바꾼다.

21 전달동사 ask는 say로 바꾸고, 의문사가 없는 의문문이므로 「Do + 주어 + 동사원형」의 어순으로 쓴다. 전달동사가 과거시제라서 종속절에 과거시제 wanted가 쓰였으므로 현재시제 Do ~ want를 쓴다. 그녀의 입장에 맞게 인칭대명사 I를 you로 바꾼다.

22 ④ is invented → was invented

23 ① is → was
③ was the Blue House → the Blue House was
⑤ was → is

MEMO

MEMO

MEMO